# Not a Gap Year
# but a Lifetime

## Katharine Makower

**Apologia Publications**
P.O. Box 3005
Eastbourne
East Sussex
BN21 9BS
UK

Copyright © Katharine Makower  2008

ISBN   978-1-901566-12-3

# Contents

## *Foreword by John Sentamu*
## *the Archbishop of York*

Turn the clock back a hundred years. Hear a visiting preacher challenging Cambridge undergraduates "to evangelize the world in this generation". Dozens of young people were moved to respond to that call by handing over their future to God. Leonard Sharp and Algernon Stanley Smith were two of them, this book is their adventure story.

They both became doctors and served in East Africa, with a shared faith and a burning, Christlike concern for humanity. One of the legacies of these pioneer missionaries was the East African Revival, which had an abiding influence on the Uganda of my childhood and was the catalyst that helped me turn to Christ at the age of ten.

There can be no greater commission than Jesus' call to make disciples of all nations. His family is unconstrained by ties of blood or nationality or culture. His message is holistic: body and soul are intertwined and Christ's healing is both physical and ¡spiritual.

In their travels these two young men encountered hair-raising risks, privations and diseases as well as bureaucratic setbacks, but nothing was going to stop them fulfilling their calling. They gave, not a gap year or two to broaden their minds or satisfy a yearning for travel, but their whole lives. It is my prayer that many young people today will read this book and recognize and respond to Christ's call to them. As they do so, they will experience not a life of ease, but they will discover that inner joy and richness of life which is the Lord's unique gift to those who hand him their future.

† Sentamu Ebor.

# Author's Note

It has been a privilege to be involved in setting down the story of these two determined and humble doctors whose complete faith in God's calling led them to persist against all odds to take medical help and the Gospel to parts of East Africa, breaking new ground. As the title of this book shows, not only did they go there, but they stayed, giving their whole lives to that work. This record of the lives of the pioneers would not have been possible without the enthusiastic support of their children, Miss Mary Sharp, Mrs Joy Gower (née Sharp), Mrs Nora Lyth (née Stanley Smith) widow of Bishop Dick Lyth, Dr Geoffrey Stanley Smith, the Rev Jim Stanley Smith and Mrs Doreen Sharp, widow of Dr John Sharp. Dr H H Osborn gave a great deal of time and effort in collating much of the material and was responsible for its publication. Joy Gower devoted many hours and days in correspondence to ensure as far as possible the accuracy of the accounts recorded in this book of events that occurred many years ago, to avoid misinterpretations of original sources, and to correct some present day misconceptions of the conditions in which Dr Leonard Sharp and Dr Algernon Stanley Smith worked and in which their families lived. She then completed the collation. In reality she did much more work than I did.

None of the work of the *Rwanda Mission* would have been possible without prayerful, interested and faithful church supporters back in England. This link between the pioneer families and their supporters was a close one. The Church Missionary Society was unable to help the missionaries much financially, so it was vital that families and churches in UK gave generously in many ways to enable the work to go forward. Above all the importance of prayer was stressed all the way through. So letters were sent home to a growing number of supporters from the start. These quickly developed into the *Ruanda Notes*, the source of much of the doctors' writings quoted in this book.

In quoting from these letters I have occasionally paraphrased for the sake of conciseness and to keep the narrative moving. Also I have not used the capital H which they always used when referring to God. Customary though that was and largely still is, it is not the usage of the Bible, and because God filled their minds and therefore their writings, I decided that peppering the pages with Hs might make the account less accessible to modern readers. Please forgive me if that decision offends. Similarly, although the doctors of course used the Authorized Version of the Bible, I have given some quotations as from the New International Version, again in pursuit of immediacy.

The world has changed out of all recognition since the time when the pioneer doctors first set out. Travel and communication and the colours on the map are transformed. Far fewer people might now be called to dedicate their lives physically to one needy area; they might not even be needed or wanted there. But I hope that this account will inspire some readers to emulate the spirit of obedience and dedication to God which the two doctors demonstrate, and to follow God's calling whatever it may be.

Katharine Makower.

**Pre-Independence (1962) Map of S W Uganda & Ruanda-Urundi**

# Not a Gap Year but a Lifetime

The lives and work of
Doctor Leonard and Esther Sharp
Dr Algernon and Zöe Stanley Smith
in East Africa

# Prologue
## 1999

It was 1999. Esther Morris, a young medical student on an elective programme from the UK, sat enjoying a welcome drink at the home of a doctor and his wife in Kisiizi, thirty miles north of Kabale in South West Uganda. She had travelled all day by bus from Kampala. Suddenly a midwife came running from the nearby hospital, saying that a woman in obstructed labour needed a caesarian. The doctor hurried over, accompanied by Esther who watched, soon to be relieved by the forceful cry of the emerging baby.

Esther had visited Kisiizi as a child, having been brought up at Kagando Hospital, a similar rural hospital about 120 miles north of Kisiizi where her father Dr Rob Morris was project director, working with TEAR fund. She remembered Kisiizi as a peaceful place with a powerful and beautiful waterfall, an unexpected sight among the rolling hills. She gives her impressions of Kisiizi Hospital:

'My childhood at Kagando had prepared me for the basic conditions in the hospital, the relative disrepair and dirt of the buildings, the smells and severity of the illness of the patients.

The hospital is so different from UK hospitals. In the maternity ward there was a huge hole in the concrete floor. It was ignored by everyone. On the surgery ward there were many people with broken limbs, attached to traction systems using sandbags and pulley systems with weights. Each patient relies on a relative to come and stay at the hospital to provide food cooked on charcoal stoves outside and to help with the nursing. I spent much of my time with a surgeon from UK. He was very skilled, operating on cases rarely seen in UK and others only tackled in specialist centres. Work involved improvisation with equipment and operating from diagrams in textbooks. UK doctors come out to work with Mid Africa Ministries (formerly the Rwanda Mission) but there is a transition now to Ugandan doctors leading the team.

'I was welcomed and enjoyed living in the hospital compound. I joined in with the hospital fellowship meetings, sharing with the members of staff in evening meetings. Each day in the hospital started with drums calling everyone to prayers for the start of the working day. The hospital had expanded since I was there as a child. There were several new wards, built to meet new demands, in particular the emergence of HIV and increasing TB. Kisiizi is a place of training. There is a nursing school producing high standards of care, resulting in the hospital having a good reputation in the region. There is also a constant stream of medical, nursing, dental and physiotherapy students visiting from UK and the developed world.'

Earlier, in 1996, Esther had also had a 'gap year' experience — not in Africa but in South America. Having first worked in the UK to raise the money to travel, 'I went with Latin Link, a missionary organisation that sends groups of young people to go and help local churches in a predominantly practical way. We helped with church building projects in both Bolivia and Argentina. The church in Bolivia was also going to be used as a feeding centre in a remote town; in Argentina it was a church plant to a poor neighbourhood of Buenos Aires. We wanted to share our faith and learn more about God, working alongside people from the local church. We were welcomed amazingly;

people gave up their homes for us to stay, provided feasts of food they could scarcely afford and accepted us. We joined them in their church services and worshipped with them.' Esther saw the gap year as a gift, a time to learn from new experiences and difficulties and from people in very different circumstances to her own. She observed that the gap year is one of the few times in life that adventurous travel is legitimised by society.

Under the title 'Gap Year', in an article in the *Daily Telegraph,* 16th August 2006. students were accused of being charity tourists who do little good. It questioned the value of 'the gap year, [which] has become a rite of passage as young people seek adventure and life-changing experiences in developing nations in Africa, Asia or South America. It is seen as a chance to broaden their minds and learn about other cultures while at the same time making a positive contribution to their host nation.' One young woman who had done one was quoted as saying, 'Gap years are just hedonistic and those who think they do some good really can't.' If they are young and inexperienced, in some cases this may be true, but Esther is a committed Christian and, now qualified as a doctor, hopes to use her paediatric training to contribute to health care for needy children in some part of the developing world — probably in Africa. Whatever the pros and cons of the flying visits of young westerners, her motive was serious, and she intends to follow it up with long-term commitment.

This book is an account of the life and work of Esther's great-grandfather Dr Algernon Stanley Smith and of his friend, colleague and brother-in-law Dr Leonard Sharp, pioneering Christian missionaries who founded the Rwanda Mission and between them established many churches, schools and hospitals in East Africa, including Kisiizi. At a time when travel and communications were very different from now, they gave, not a year or two, but their whole lives to this work.

# Chapter 1

# Foundations
## 1890-1908

It was October 1908. Gap years had not been invented. The two world wars had not begun. Students — the majority at that time young men from comfortable backgrounds — went straight from school to university. Some would already have a sense of privilege, and of responsibility for distant parts of the world where some of them might have parents slogging it out in the heat as civil servants or missionaries; for many of these distant countries were part of the British Empire, coloured red in the atlases they had pored over at school. At a meeting for new students arranged by the Christian Union at Trinity College, Cambridge, that autumn, two medical students were introduced and became firm friends: Leonard Sharp and Algernon Stanley Smith.

Len's background was partly associated with Cambridge, and included among his paternal ancestors a butler to Queen's College and gown-makers in Silver Street. His parents, Ernest and Mary (née Ballance) were first cousins of Huguenot ancestry. Their

great-great-great-grandfather Samuel Heudebourk, a prosperous
silk merchant in mid 17th century France, had fled with his family to England, hidden in an apple barrel, to escape persecution.[1]
The family prospered, remaining true to their deeply committed
Christian faith. Ernest Sharp fell in love with his beautiful little
cousin Mary Ballance, aged 7, when he was 18 years old. They
eventually married in 1886 when she was 28 and he 39. Ernest,
a civil engineer, worked at the Public Record Office and was
promoted to Senior Assistant Keeper. A man with a strong public
spirit and sense of responsibility, he organised working men's
clubs, cricket matches and a private savings bank with interest,
to encourage thrift. Wherever he lived, he always took up the
duties of church warden, and when retired on the Isle of Wight
refused to flee his cliff top house to escape the threatened D-day
aerial bombardment, saying it was not quite the thing for a man
of his seniority to quit at a time of danger, and moreover he had
not yet completed the church accounts, so that was that! Ernest
celebrated his 90th birthday with a flight over the Isle of Wight;
he bathed in the sea at 91 and played his last game of golf at 96.
He died aged 103, alert to the last.

Mary and Ernest had 8 children, of whom the third, Leonard Ernest Steigenberger Sharp, was born on 29th June 1890.
Mary longed that her children would grow up to be Christians
and her Bible contained many prayers for them, prayers which
were answered. [2] They knew and loved the stories of the great
explorers in Africa and elsewhere, especially the life of David
Livingstone. Their childhood was happy, with a good mix of
affection, freedom and discipline. From their London homes first
at Harrow on the Hill and later in Wimbledon, summer holidays
were often spent by the sea, usually on the Isle of Wight where
Ernest would take his family, their nurses and governesses. He
taught his children to swim and to sail and took them on long
walks over the downs or along the shore, walks enlivened by
stories or observations from nature: woods, clouds, open grass-
lands, birds and animals. He had a wide interest in astronomy,
geology, politics and wild life.

Leonard grew up sharing similar interests to his father, with practical and engineering skills, a sense of responsibility and determination, and a great admiration for his Huguenot ancestry. He enjoyed sporting activities, walking, camping, shooting, fishing, photography, swimming, and had a great love of the sea and of boats. Leonard built his first boat while at Harrow School, and he and his brother Guy took their friends out in it for trips on the Thames. Len was quiet by nature, thoughtful and kindly, and to please his mother agreed to go to a Christian camp for young people after leaving school in the summer of 1908, and there he committed his life to Jesus Christ.

Algie's background could have catapulted him into a gap year adventure, had such things existed. His father was Stanley Smith, son of a surgeon, who along with six other Cambridge students, outstanding athletes and with promising careers ahead of them hit the headlines in the 1880s by giving everything up to go to China as missionaries — the 'Cambridge Seven'. Stanley was a rowing Blue, having rowed as stroke for Cambridge in the Boat Race of 1882. Their departure on the Boat Train from Victoria Station in London on 5th February 1885 was widely publicized, and they arrived in Shanghai on 18th March to work with the China Inland Mission. Stanley and another of the seven, the brilliant young cricketer C T Studd, were located to the Shan-Si province in North China. Stanley mastered the Chinese language and proved to be as fluent a preacher in Chinese as he was in English. Later, helping with a men's opium refuge being set up in the city of Ho-Chai, he met a Norwegian girl, Sophie Reuter, who with her friend Anna Jakobsen was working to open a similar refuge for women. If Stanley Smith was well known in Britain, Sophie Reuter and Anna Jakobsen were even more so in Norway. They have been acclaimed as the first Norwegian missionaries to China and hold an honoured place in Norwegian history. Stanley Smith and Sophie Reuter were married on 16th September 1888 by Pastor Shi, with a civil wedding in Shanghai on November 10th.[3] Entries in his diary reflect the deep love Stanley shared with his beloved 'Feah'. In January1889 they set up home in Lucheng and it was there that Algernon Stanley Smith was born, on 14th February 1890. Stanley wrote in his diary, 'God has given us a fine little boy. Such a sweet child and so well developed — Hallelujah! We asked God to accept him for the Chinese.'

In February of the following year, Sophie was taken seriously ill with typhus. After much prayer she recovered, only to suffer a miscarriage in March. From this she did not recover and died on March 1891 only two and a half years after their marriage. Stanley was heartbroken but married again, two years later, another CIM missionary, Anna Grace Lang. In 1894, Stanley wrote in his diary, 'In the morning went to Feah's grave with little Algie and all placed the cross from Norway on Feah's grave and all prayed.' That occasion engraved itself upon Algie's mind. Although he was only four at the time, he remembered it for the rest of his life. Despite the love and care of his father and step-mother, Algie's early childhood was not entirely happy. Stanley and Grace had further children and he found it hard being the only stepbrother. This made him sometimes difficult and his father had to discipline him severely. For three years from the age of six he went to the boarding school for missionaries' children at Chefoo, where a different regime and a wide circle of friends — understanding teachers and friendly fellow 'mish-kids' seem to have had a healing effect. His behaviour and his relationship with his father improved from that time.

In November 1899 the Stanley Smith family sailed from China. They anchored in Plymouth Harbour at midnight on 16th December, so they were not in China for the Boxer Risings, when many missionaries were killed and Lucheng was totally destroyed. The next two years were probably the happiest that Algie experienced with Stanley and Gracie. A close bond appears to have been woven between them. Bicycles often featured in the family travels between Croydon and London, but they also travelled more widely as Stanley was often invited to different places to preach and talk about his work in China. Missionary work attracted great interest and support in Britain at that time.

After two years, Stanley and Gracie sailed for China again, having arranged for the Misses Alice and Emily Watney whom Stanley had come to know previously, to be Algie's guardians. The sisters were kindly, friendly and very sincere Christians who had used their inherited fortune to build Emmanuel Church and a mission hall in Croydon where they lived. As he grew up, Algie appreciated the humour of his being educated from funds which had their origin in the brewing industry. He was educated at Winchester College.

After a further seven years of service in China, Stanley and Gracie Smith, with their other children, boarded the Trans-Siberian Railway to Moscow and Warsaw. They crossed the English Channel and reached London on 27th May 1908. Ten days later, as Stanley recorded in his diary, 'In the morning left by 11.40 for Winchester. Got there about twenty past one. Had the intense joy of seeing dear Algie, grown to about 5ft 10in. A dear, frank, amiable boy'. Algie had committed his life to Jesus Christ at the age of thirteen in response to gospel preaching at the Croydon mission hall, so now Stanley found not only a dear son, but also a brother in Christ. This was the year that Algie left Winchester and went up to Trinity College, Cambridge.

From the moment they were introduced to each other as new students, Len and Algie hit it off. 'In a few moments we were shaking hands, and in a day or two we had paired off in the laboratories, in the 'meat shops' and in the lecture rooms', remembered Algie. 'From that day on we were inseparable in work, in play and above all in the Christian life as it was lived out in the thrilling and challenging fellowship of the CICCU' [4]. Both Len and Algie added sport to their studies. Both joined the rowing club and both played hockey — Algie for the 1st team and Len for the 2nd. Although Len in particular had not until then considered missionary work and was rather planning to be a GP in the south of England, he responded to a talk by a visiting preacher John Mott, who appealed for students to 'evangelise the world in this generation'. In December 1908, as the two recalled later, 'at the close of our first term, we definitely decided that

God should have the disposal of our lives, and we knew that that spelled the mission field'.

Before returning to China, Stanley visited Algie at Cambridge, and he noted in his diary for Wednesday 9th December, 'Breakfast with Algie — his friend Sharp was there who studies medicine with him. Asked Algie what country he had a predeliction for; he said China and so did his friend. I told him of my dedication of him for that country. Went to lunch with Algie ... in afternoon to the laboratories to see where Algie works.' Stanley Smith returned to China to continue his missionary service. He did not see Algie again for eleven years, but he then visited him when on leave, and wrote regular letters to him until he died in China in 1931.

Note  1. *For fuller genealogical account, see appendix p285*
      2. *See appendix p285*
      3. *See p 240*
      4. *The Cambridge Inter Collegiate Christian Union was founded in 1877. From the start it was known by its initials, and pronounced CICCU.*

# Chapter 2

# Preparation
## 1908 - 1919

Algie and Len were not alone in taking up the challenge to consecrate their lives to God's service. As Len Sharp recorded many years later, 'We were drawn into fellowship with a great band of students whose hearts the Lord had touched, and whose lives were dedicated to missionary endeavour. Their friendship has been a precious encouragement to us through all the years.' On 8th June 1911 forty-two young men united to form the Cambridge Missionary Band, pledging to pray for each other every Sunday, wherever God would send them. A circular letter kept them in touch with each other and their work throughout their lives. The collected letters give a fascinating overview of what they all did. Although very different in many ways, they shared great unity of faith in God and a determination to spend their lives in his service whatever that might involve. Later on, Dr Algie was secretary of the CMB for many years. In addition, a network of small prayer groups sprang up in many churches around the country in support of those members of the Band who served overseas in pioneering situations. It is important to realize how much Len and Algie relied on the prayer support of others. This reliance is emphasized again and again in their letters and in reports of their work.

At Cambridge, as at Oxford and indeed throughout the country, the challenge of the unexplored parts of the world was presented through the national as well as the Christian press. The exploits of Dr. David Livingstone were well known. His book *Missionary Travels and Researches in South Africa*, ran to 70,000 copies. Fifty years before the two young students were undertaking their medical studies, Dr Livingstone had visited their university and the record of his parting message gripped their imagination. 'I direct your attention to Africa,' he had said, 'I know that in a few years I shall be cut off in that country which is now open. Do not let it be shut again. I go back to Africa to try to make an open path for commerce and Christianity. Do you carry out the work I have begun. I leave it with you.'

Within living memory, the explorations of Henry Stanley had provided another source of inspiration. In a much publicized dispatch which appeared in the *Daily Telegraph* of 15 November 1875, Stanley had written, appealing for missionaries, and with particularly Uganda in mind, 'The Bishops of Great Britain collected, with all the classic youth of Oxford and Cambridge, would effect nothing by mere talk with the intelligent people of Uganda. It is the practical Christian tutor, who will teach people how to become Christians, cure their diseases, and turn his hand to anything, like a sailor — this is the man who is wanted. ... He must be tied to no church or sect but profess God and his Son and the moral law, and live a blameless Christian life, inspired by liberal principles and charity to all men, and devout faith in Heaven.' The work of the Church Missionary Society (CMS) began in Uganda in 1877 in response to that call.

Charles T Studd, one of the Cambridge Seven and colleague of Stanley Smith, Algie's father, was another inspirational role model. When explaining why he gave up cricket, the sport in which he had gained national fame, he said, 'How could I spend the best years of my life in living for the honours of this world, when thousands of souls are perishing every day?'

A man who made a deep impression on the Christian student world of that time was Dr Karl Kumm, a German who became a naturalized British citizen. He later became the founder of the Sudan United Mission, now Action Partners. Many years later both Len and Algie paid tribute to the influence of Dr Kumm in challenging them to missionary service in Africa, and also in proposing a process of missionary activity in unevangelized areas with the aim of establishing Christians who were secure in their faith, and in the formation of a truly biblical church. Among his most notable contributions to missionary strategy was his urging of the Christian world to establish missionary centres stretching from East to West Africa, south of the Sahara desert, to withstand the growing Islamic pressures from the north.

Dr Kumm's strategy for missionary activity began with a first stage — the faithful teaching of the biblical truths of the Gospel and applying them to the needs of the people in the power of the Holy Spirit, so that converts put their trust in Jesus Christ and not in a church or other organisation. The second stage was to teach people to read and write, and to make God's word, the Bible, available in the language of the people so that they could read it for themselves. In this way biblical truth would not be solely dependent on the missionary nor on the interpretation of others. The third stage was establishing schools. The most successful missionaries in Africa, Dr Kumm stressed, in line with Henry Stanley's analysis, would be men of character, integrity and practical abilities — medical, engineering, industrial.

Among the missionary pioneers whom Len and Algie met in their student days, two in particular were to prove a strong influence as they faced the future. They were Dr (later Sir) Albert and Dr Jack Cook. These doctors had set up Mengo Hospital in Kampala, Uganda, as part of the work of the Church Missionary Society. The two students shared the combined spiritual and medical aims of the Cooks and looked to them as examples as they faced the prospect of similar pioneering work to which they were sure God was calling them.

Len and Algie, as medical students and members of the CICCU, joined the student camps at the Keswick Convention[1] for at least three years. The most memorable of these for the two students was that of 1910, where there was a powerful call for missionary outreach to the world. There, both young men faced and accepted the challenge of God to missionary service overseas. Len, in particular, looked back to that convention as the time when God anointed him with the Holy Spirit for further service.

On completing their studies at Trinity College, Cambridge, the two graduates moved to London for further medical training; Algie Stanley Smith to St George's Hospital, and Len Sharp to St Thomas's. Len's choice was influenced by the fact that one of four of his uncles, all doctors, was Sir Charles Ballance, consultant at St Thomas's Hospital and with rooms in Harley Street. On qualifying in 1913, Dr Len was house physician for a year.

Both men were convinced that God was leading them to use their medical skills to spearhead pioneer work in an area unreached by the Gospel. They studied maps to locate such places. In 1912 C T Studd set out with four other CMB members, under the auspices of the Africa Inland Mission, for a visit to the north eastern corner of what was then Belgian Congo. Since Len and Algie also felt the call to pioneer work, the visit of their friends to north east Congo suggested that God was directing them elsewhere, and they gladly accepted an invitation from Dr Albert Cook to work at Mengo Hospital for a year as the next step.

In 1914 Algie also qualified, but his plan to go with Len to Uganda was interrupted by the onset of war, when he and the entire medical staff of St George's Hospital volunteered for military service. He was posted to the front line in France, where he served as a Medical Officer to a battalion which suffered very much in fighting around Ypres in the middle of 1915. Dr Algie was twice mentioned in dispatches and awarded the Military Cross for bravery in looking for wounded soldiers — on more than one occasion his horse was shot under him. A letter from Edward Cuthbertson, the Colonel of the Battalion in which Dr Algie served while in France, from the Headquarters in Chester and dated 16.5.16, bore testimony to his bravery.

My dear Algie,
    I cannot tell you how pleased I was to get
your letter, and how glad I was to see you had
got the Military Cross. I would have written
had I known your address. That you deserved
the M.C. goes without saying, and I would like
to put on record that your services to my  Battalion were invaluable.
    You showed us all an example of magnificent
self sacrifice and unflinching courage, and I
cannot tell you how much I admired your quiet
unostentatious heroism.
    You were and are one of the best friends I
have ever had, and I am proud to call you  com-
rade.
    In another fashion you helped the Battalion.
Your manly Christianity free from cant in all
ways helped to raise the tone of all of us and
I can tell you honestly that there is not an
officer or man who did not admire you.
    Write to me again. I am glad you are taking a
wife and I hope you will be very happy. My leg has
given me much pain and bother, and is far from
well, but I expect to go out again in about 10
days.
    God bless you dear boy,
    Yours ever,
            Edward Cuthbertson

So Dr Len continued with the plan and sailed alone for East Africa in October 1914.

'The train to Uganda', he wrote in 1934, 'crosses the source of the Nile at the Ripon falls which were discovered by Speke. We crossed this fine bridge for the first time when we came home this year. But 20 years ago it meant crossing Lake Victoria by boat. In 1914, I sat on that boat, a young fellow seeing Africa for the first time. As we drew near to the source of the Nile, Central Africa stretched out before me with its hills and impenetrable forests, the repeated prayer came again from my heart: "Lord if it is your will, send me to the unevangelized." And he said to me, " Would you be willing, if it meant illness?" And I said "Yes". And he said again, "Would you be willing, if it means a shortened life? An early grave?" And after a good long time I said, "Yes" to that too. So that was the covenant we made together. He has given me these 20 years in Central Africa, 14 of which have been among the unevangelized. I have had my share of illness, but I have had the unspeakable privilege of preaching Christ where he was not known.'[2]

On arrival in Uganda, Dr Sharp lived on Makindiye Hill with Dr and Mrs Albert Cook and worked at Mengo Hospital, Kampala. Although Europe was the scene of the most severe fighting, hostilities extended to German colonies overseas including German East Africa, and Mengo Hospital became a base hospital during the East African Campaign against the Germans. In April 1915, Dr Len received a commission as Medical Officer with the 4th King's African Rifles and continued to work at Mengo.

The increasing number of military casualties made things very difficult there. An article, published in 1914, explained: 'The very important position of Uganda, particularly of Mengo Hospital, renders it rightly desirable that this centre should be adequately maintained. Owing to the great extension of the work it has become increasingly difficult for two doctors (Drs Albert and Jack Cook) to do all that is required, and it is almost impossible for either of these to get away either for holiday or for purposes of itineration. Seeing then that Dr Ernest Cook [their nephew] is home on furlough, Dr A R Cook and Dr J H Cook are left alone, and as the latter is due home shortly on furlough, it is imperative that some help should be given.'

Given this situation, Dr Albert Cook needed two military doctors to help him in his responsibilities for the armed forces in the area. At his request Dr Algie Stanley Smith was released from the war zone in France and drafted to Mengo Hospital. He sailed for Uganda with his friend Wallace Hillbrook under wartime maritime conditions in October 1915. So, at the end of 1915, war service brought the two young doctors together at the very hospital to which they had been invited two years previously. God's guidance was clear.

Dr Algie served as a military doctor at Mengo Hospital throughout 1916, but Dr Len was posted, with Dr Wallace Hillbrook, to the advance base hospital at Mbarara in January 1916. There they were able to stay with a CMB friend, Rev Myres Grace, who was headmaster of a school there. Later in the year

Dr Len and Wallace Hillbrook were ordered to leave Mbarara, first for Simba, where they were stationed for a short time, before embarking on a ship at Sango Bay for Mwanza in Tanganyika, where the invasion of German East Africa was taking place. When they arrived, the Germans had just been driven from the town and Dr Len occupied a German doctor's quarters and inherited his pet baboon. The baboon died soon afterwards from sampling too many medicines in the dispensary!

Dr Len worked with four other doctors in the German hospital with 500 beds. During the time in Mwanza, a very serious epidemic of cerebro-spinal meningitis broke out among the troops, in the course of which Wallace Hillbrook became ill and died. He was buried in Nairobi with the following tribute at his funeral, 'The missionary cause has lost a promising young doctor and the Army, a fine Christian officer'. (It was a double blow to his parents whose other son had just been interned in Holland). An isolation camp was set up for the large number of victims and many died.  On Dr Len's daily visits to the camp, he treated a patient named Mutiaba, whom he led to Christ. On his recovery, Erisa Mutiaba returned to Buganda and later volunteered to help Dr Len at Kabale as a medical dresser, where he gave invaluable service for 20 years. Dr Len caught dysentery and was invalided back to Mengo early in December.

By the end of December 1916 hostilities had ceased in Western Tanganyika. Mengo Hospital regained its civilian status and Drs Len and Algie were decommissioned. They stayed on at Mengo, reasoning as follows: 'At the close of the Victorian era, and before the first World War had begun the break-up of the old established order, the doors were wide open for evangelization in almost every part of the world, and the question to us was, where was the greatest need? For many reasons Africa seemed to be the place laid on our hearts, and it seemed to us in our total lack of experience both as doctors and as missionaries, that it would prove of the utmost value to us to begin by working in a mission hospital under an experienced missionary. Here I think my acquaintance with Dr. Albert Cook and my admiration for him was the guiding factor in our choice. This great man, great in every way, both as a man of God and a brilliant physician, had pioneered medical work in Uganda and founded Mengo Hospital, renowned all over Africa. Where better could we go to get experience, and at the same time keep our eyes open to see among the surrounding countries where the needs and opportunities seemed greatest? The time spent there was thrilling, as we worked first under Dr. Albert Cook, and then under his brother Jack, as we learnt missionary methods in action from men and women who had come out in the nineties, as we learnt to know and love the Africans, and to pick up their language.'

Of their medical experience Dr Algie wrote: 'During those years at Mengo we found a rich variety of the main tropical diseases, in which we had had no previous training. In 1916-7 in addition to the work of a crowded general hospital of 300 beds, we passed through four serious epidemics — one of smallpox, then among the troops an epidemic of bacillary dysentery, many of the fatal cases of a choleraic type against which we had no remedy except heavy doses of sodium sulphate and worst of all, bubonic plague which broke out in the bazaar in Nakasero. Day after day we would be called out by Indians living there, and enter their houses in rubber boots thigh high in a vain attempt to help the dying. Dr Cook reported a mortality of over 95% in the early stages of the epidemic.'

In 1916, a book came to the notice of the two doctors, *In the Heart of Africa* by the Duke of Mecklenburg. This is a record of a trek across Africa from west to east by a group of German explorers. In the course of that exploration the team passed through Ruanda-Urundi,[3] then a German colonial territory, the Duke describing Ruanda as 'a land flowing with milk and honey, where the breeding of cattle and bee-culture flourish, and the cultivated land bears rich crops of fruit … a hilly country, thickly populated, full of beautiful scenery, and possessing a climate incomparably fresh and healthy' (p 44). His description of the country caught the imagination of the two doctors and they wondered if this was where God might want them to work.

In December 1916, they obtained permission to visit Ruanda-Urundi during a three weeks' leave from military service. Due to an error, this permission was granted by the British authorities in Uganda without approval or knowledge of the Belgians, now in charge.[4] The CMS missionary, the Rev. Harold Lewin, who was working at Mbarara, accompanied them. The party also included Yoweri Bunirgwire, from Ankole, who spoke the language of Ruanda and could interpret for them. Their own knowledge of Luganda and Lutoro were of limited value. The two doctors had bicycles and Lewin rode on a mule.

The group crossed into Ruanda some fifteen miles west of the present frontier post of Kakitumba. The roughness of the bush country resulted in the doctors having to repair about 15 punctures a day until they reached Rubare where they left the cycles and continued on foot. Eventually they reached Kigali, which had been a German fort. The Belgians were now in occupation with a Major in charge. He said he had not heard of permission being given for them to come and he sent to enquire of his General further south. No reply came, so after five days the doctors' party started north again. Two days later they were approaching along a ridge when they saw ahead a small Belgian military post, with an earth fort. (Dr Len and Rev Lewin were in uniform). Great activity was going on there. Drums were beaten and Belgian soldiers lined up with their officer, and the party was given a red carpet reception. Too late, the officer, who had been posted there 'to get him out of the way', realized that they were not his senior officers coming on an inspection! Dr Len always laughed whenever he remembered the incident.

'We were tremendously impressed by the country', wrote Dr Algie after the visit, 'the density of the population, the almost entire lack of medical services, and the wide open door for preaching the Gospel', and as they surveyed the country stretched out before them, God's word to Moses came into their minds: 'The land you are crossing the Jordan to take possession of .. a land of mountains and valleys that drinks rain from heaven .. a land the Lord your God cares for.' (Deut 11: 10-12). They came back assured that this was their 'Promised land'.

Further support was given to them by the young Church of Uganda, which, at a meeting of the Synod in January 1918, urged that moves be made to evangelize Ruanda. Reading a small booklet, written by Bishop John Jamieson Willis, the Bishop of Uganda, entitled *Uganda 1919*, increased the certainty of the two doctors that God was guiding them to Ruanda-Urundi. In a brief but comprehensive survey of missionary activity in Ugand — pastoral, educational, medical and industrial, Bishop Willis indicated the kind of men and women needed to start work in new areas. Referring to one of the areas he had in mind, the Bishop wrote: 'Ruanda, one of the largest native kingdoms in Africa, with some 2,000,000 people, can best be entered by a medical mission. There is, therefore, a pressing demand for four new doctors.'

In his heavily underlined copy of this booklet, Dr Len added to the 2,000,000 in Ruanda, 'Urundi 3,000,000'. He also underlined the type of man Bishop Willis reckoned was needed for this work: 'Physically strong and wiry, capable of roughing it, fond of travel; clear thinking, capable of learning a language without books or teachers, quick to make friends; strong enough to stand alone, a man who knows his own mind, forms his plans and will carry them through in the face of discouragement; a living example, a man of prayer.' Could it be that the two doctors reading the booklet in Kampala in 1919, were two of the 'new doctors' needed for this missionary challenge?

In early 1917, the first medical training course for dressers was opened at Mengo Hospital with nine students under the direction and tuition of Drs Len and Algie, but after making a good start , all nine caught smallpox during an epidemic which swept Kampala that year and three of them died. Surviving a severe epidemic for the second time, one of the survivors who completed his training was Erisa Mutiaba who was to join the doctors in Kigezi in February 1921. 'This was a valuable experience,' wrote Dr Algie, 'and later we in our turn, first at Kabale and later at Buye in Burundi, carried on the same task of training.' Many of the young men they trained then became invaluable medical evangelists later on.

While at Mengo Hospital, the doctors made friends with men with wide experience in the practical problems of planning and carrying out the construction of various kinds of buildings. 'Outstanding among them,' recorded Dr Algie, 'were Harry Bowers, the founder of the C.M.S. Masindi Technical School, and Leslie Lea-Wilson, the farmer of Namutamba tea-plantation. Over and over again in the days to come we were able to turn to them for advice.'

In 1918, when the war was nearly over, some of the missionaries in Uganda who had not been able to go to the UK for leave were anxious to travel home. Dr Algie had a special reason for this. Since 1915 he had been engaged to marry Len's sister Zöe. Algie first met her in 1908, when Len invited him to his home in Wimbledon. There he met Len's mother who, as he wrote many years later, 'had brought up her eight children in the fear of God with a charming mixture of tender affection and discipline, and this characteristic of affection brushed off remarkably in the whole family. One of her daughters, who most resembled her, and who was Len's special sister, Zöe, captivated my heart and we became engaged in September 1915 ... so the ties that bound us to each other were doubly strengthened.'

As Leonard inherited from his father Ernest a determined, practical, vigorous, adventurous approach to life, so Zöe showed many of the gracious characteristics of her mother, Mary. One childhood incident when she was eight had left a lasting mark on her. Len and Zöe, always 'special brother and sister' to each other, made 'various hair-raising contraptions' through the trees of their spacious garden, including a swing. One day Zöe slipped off it and seriously fractured her left elbow. Although her uncle, the Harley Street specialist, performed several operations on her arm, the fracture affected parts of the elbow which were still growing, and her arm never fully developed and remained crippled all her life. Zöe finished her education in Switzerland, and then during the war she helped her mother run a meeting for girls in the East End of London. She kept up a regular correspondence with some of them when in Africa, and it was one of these girls who later, as Matron, was in charge of the nursing home which cared for Zöe in the weakness of her old age.

In the absence of passenger ships after the war, Algie, with two other missionaries, set off, first on motorcycles, then by foot and boat, through the Sudan to reach the Nile. There he embarked on a steamer to the UK for a joyful reunion with Zöe. Troubled by the weakness in her crippled arm, she confided her concerns to Algie, who replied, 'I will be your left arm!' It was something she often quoted to women in her ministry in Africa. Dr Algie and Zöe were happily married on 7th January 1919.

Len stayed on in Uganda during most of 1919, working at the CMS hospital, Toro, but was able to accompany Dr Algie on his journey as far as Masindi from where he set off for Toro by way of Lake Albert. He had arranged to be met by porters when he disembarked from the steamer at Nkoreko but at first there was no sign of them. The boat left and he found himself alone on a crocodile-infested shore. He was very relieved to hear a shout, and found the porters ready for him on a nearby hill.

Dr Len stayed at Toro until his furlough in 1919. Because he had a gun, he was often asked for help, which led him into one or two dangerous situations. Once, travelling back to Toro from a distant village where the District Commissioner wanted him to investigate an epidemic, his porters asked him to shoot a buffalo for them, as they seldom had meat and the very thick hide was valuable to them for making sandals which did not wear out. So he agreed. There were two buffalo fairly near, which had come out of the forest to graze on the hillside. 'I shot at one, but it ran into a very thick bush in a gorge where there was water. I didn't like the look of the place but the men said it was dead, and that they would cut it up next morning.

'Next day they came back, "It's still alive but it's nearly dead"! So I went with them to put it down. Buffaloes weigh about a ton and have huge horns for fighting, they are so strong and can push their way through the thickest bush and have the habit of making a tunnel through the bushes to get to water, and it is very dangerous to follow them, but I was young and inexperienced, and I trusted the hunters who were with me. The buffalo had gone into a gorge and I could not see it. "It's just down there", they said as they led me to the tunnel, so I went down and came out in a little glade of grass with a band of elephant grass in the middle. The buffalo was behind the grass so I fired at it. The next moment it leapt to its feet and came straight for me. I fired again, I was in a bad place, there was only this little tunnel and there was no time to go back down it. I was in a very dangerous position. It came through the grass at me. I fired again and it still came on, I fired once more and the buffalo fell dead at my feet. I sat down just a bit shaky at the knees and looked round for my faithful hunters with their spears but they were nowhere in sight! Then, after a few minutes. "Oh well done Bwana," "Good shot," "So happy," but I was not happy with that particular hunter, who should not have taken me there. It is very dangerous hunting buffalo and he had led me into a very bad place. How important it is in life to choose true friends, otherwise we can be led into all kinds of temptations and dangers. I was thankful that I was still alive as that was the closest shave I have had — or nearly. So they had their buffalo, and after eating what they could, they carried it home in great chunks for their families.'

Another time, when Len was asked for help when a leopard had repeatedly taken a neighbour's chickens, he fixed his shot-gun over the chicken-house door so that the leopard would shoot itself during the night. The gun went off in the night and next day a blood trail ended in long grass near the Mukama (King) of Toro's palace. The Mukama had the hunting drums beaten, men gathered with their spears, and suddenly as the patch of elephant grass where the leopard was hiding was beaten down, 'I saw the leopard spring into the air over their heads. They all threw their spears and it was transfixed and killed at once. So the chickens were avenged.'

Dr Len could see that this time in Toro was planned by God, for the trust and friendships formed then, meant that it was to Toro that he could often turn for helpers, and from there many volunteers, nurses, teachers and clergy were to come to help in Kigezi later on. While there he caught flu which brought heart complications. Eventually, at the end of 1919, accompanied by his CMB friend the Rev Arthur Pitt Pitts, he travelled to Mombasa and from there by boat to the UK.

Ernest and Mary Sharp, Len's parents, with whom he stayed during his leave, combined their wide interests with a love of entertaining. Their home was often alive with young people. They arranged garden and tennis parties, and weekends to which they invited the family's friends. Among those invited was a girl called Esther Macdonald, 'a fine, live-wire of a girl whose practical common sense and strength of character well fitted her for a pioneer experience' [5].

Esther was three years younger than Leonard. Her parents were Robert Graham Macdonald, 'of the Isles', and Beatrice nee Bliss, daughter of Sir Henry Bliss, Governor of Madras. Sir Henry traced his ancestry to Thomas Bolyne, brother of Anne Bolyne, second wife of Henry VIII. Sir Henry married three times. By his first wife he had four children, of whom Beatrice was his only daughter, and three sons by his second wife. Robert was an Accountant General in the Indian Civil Service and Esther was born in Simla. The family returned to England when Esther was a small child, but her later childhood was not very happy, largely because her father died when she was twelve years old. A beautiful, friendly, outgoing girl, she trained as a Froebel teacher, and Leonard first saw her at Emmanuel Church, Wimbledon in 1914. He did not speak to her then, but she was one of those invited to his home in 1919. God was in this 'arranged meeting' as Len and Esther in their separate ways were searching for God's will for their future, and found themselves attracted to each other. They were married in Wimbledon, on 14th April 1920, by the vicar of Emmanuel Church. At first the Bliss family were not very pleased with the match as missionaries were looked down on by Indian civil service officialdom. 'Esther is only marrying a missionary, so give her plate, not silver'! However, Len soon became a greatly admired and much loved member of the family.

On their honeymoon at Southbourne in Dorset, they were cut off by the tide and were forced to spend part of the night high up on the cliffs until their landlady raised the alarm and a search party was sent out. They were hauled to the top of the cliff by ropes which Len saw afterwards were rotten and considerably more dangerous than a night spent on the rock face. A good introduction to their future life in Africa!

1. *Keswick Convention: Annual gathering for evangelical Christians held in Keswick, where the Bible was expounded, missionaries reported on their work, and new recruits often heard their call to God's service*
2. *Rest of text on p.164 and in appendix.*
3. *Pre-Independence spelling. Now Rwanda and Burundi.*
4. *See Appendix*
5. *Patricia St John, Breath of Life*

# Chapter 3

# Into the unknown
## 1919-1921

Together again in England, Dr Len and Dr Algie approached the Church Missionary Society in November 1919, confident of gaining the support of the Africa Committee. But there were problems — the increased cost of maintaining existing work throughout the world due to the war, and the shortage of manpower. The committee was aware that once begun, a new mission would have to be maintained, so doubts were expressed over whether permission should be given. Moreover there were political complications. The recently captured German East African territory of Ruanda-Urundi was allocated by the League of Nations as a mandate to the Belgians, so any new work would be under a foreign power. But the Africa Secretary of CMS, the Rev G T Manley, was convinced that it was a call by God and the matter was discussed at length over a period of time in CMS committees and sub-committees. The matter was reinforced by the arrival on leave of Bishop Willis who begged them not to let the opportunity be missed, and the Uganda Synod passed a resolution urging advance into Ruanda. The Colonial Office agreed.

Finally, on February 10th 1920, the General Committee of CMS approved the opening of pioneer work by the Ruanda Medical Mission. They were willing to pay the doctors' salaries for four years, but all other expenses in opening and sustaining a medical mission would have to be raised by the doctors themselves. This Dr Len had already offered to do. But the doctors would also need sanction for the Mission from the Belgian Government. 'You will have the whole strength of the Committee behind you,' assured G T Manley. The doctors accepted this as a challenge of faith and gathered their friends to pray.

Within days, they received great encouragement. The Rev. Canon Stather-Hunt, Vicar of Holy Trinity Church, Tunbridge Wells, was a sympathetic member of the CMS committee. On the Sunday, after the decision by the CMS to accept the doctors in principle but to limit their financial responsibility, Canon Stather-Hunt mentioned this new move by the CMS in a Sunday sermon, and went on to emphasize the need of the countries of Ruanda and Urundi to hear the Gospel. An officer of the Coldstream Guards named Smith, later to become General Sir Arthur Smith, was passing the church and came in late, but in time to hear the sermon. He gave £500 to the two doctors. This was doubled by the gift of another £500 from the parents of Wallace Hillbrook.

In the CMS journal *The Gleaner* for June 1920, commenting on their decisions Rev G T Manley wrote, 'we believe the thing which weighed most heavily was the feeling that the strong sense of compulsion in the two doctors was a call of God, to them and to us.' And in an article in the same *Gleaner*, Dr Len wrote, 'Subject to the consent of the Belgian authorities... it is hoped to make a start for Ruanda in early autumn this year...Our hope is to open a medical mission and hospital near Nyansa, the King's capital. The privilege is as great as the opportunity. Without God we can do nothing. We need prayer most of all.'

At first the prospect of gaining Belgian permission seemed likely. The doctors contacted Monsieur Anet, of the Belgian Protestant Mission which had been asked by the Government to take over work started by the German Lutheran Church in west

Ruanda. M. Anet welcomed the possibility of CMS cooperation in Ruanda as they had few resources themselves, but eventually after long and patient negotiations, although he obtained the hearty consent of his own society and the Belgian Colonial Office to their starting work in Urundi, permission for Ruanda was refused. Urundi was a part of the mandate immediately south of Ruanda. In November the doctors visited Belgium, and had encouraging interviews with the Belgian Resident of Urundi who recommended that they should start work at a place called Kokabami, in a large and densely populated district where no Roman Catholic work had been established.

Writing to supporters on 23rd November, a few days before sailing, Dr Algie explained developments and continued, 'While still in Africa, Dr Sharp and I felt greatly drawn to the people of the Ruanda Province, as being the greatest need and opportunity in that part of Central Africa. A people of one language, numbering at least threee and a half million with no Protestant Mission is not to be found anywhere in Central Africa as far as we know. ...On our arrival home some of you banded yourselves with us in prayer, that, if it were God's will, this opportunity might be seized — and I am convinced that you who gave yourselves to this work prayed the Ruanda Mission into existence.

'One more of God's mercies to us has been the supply of a nurse. Miss C Watney, MBE, CMB, who has for many years worked at Mengo Hospital, has offered to come with us and has been gladly welcomed by us as well as by the Society. A Belgian decoration and a knowledge of French, as well as her great experience in medical missionary work makes her a worker who will be invaluable to us in Ruanda-Urundi. We will have to build two houses and possibly a third for our nurse; these will be at first of the most primitive kind. We will also build some sort of hospital. Our policy of medical mission work as far as we can tell will be to have some central established work, and have one of us touring through the country and so extending our influence as widely as possible. We are fortunate in the possession of a Christian... trained at Mengo Hospital... Erisa Mutiaba... an efficient worker and also a real spiritual force. Also Yusitasi, one of Dr Sharp's workers from Toro Hospital. We feel greatly the necessity of establishing some sort of school, and for that purpose it would be an immense help if God would choose out for us some Mugandan school teacher full of the Holy Spirit and missionary zeal.'

Dr Len and Dr Algie had many interested and praying friends, and to keep them in touch with the work a small Ruanda committee was formed. Mrs Beatrice Macdonald acted as secretary, duplicating and forwarding letters, named *Ruanda Notes*, to supporters. Mrs Mary Sharp was responsible for distributing photographs, and Norman Sharp, Dr Len's brother, agreed to be the first treasurer. He did this until 1924, after which Mrs Macdonald took over the work of both treasurer and secretary until 1926, when she retired from ill health.

Final preparations were going ahead for starting work in Urundi, though they were certain that somehow God would open a way into Ruanda. But in a letter written from the boat on 27th November 1920, Dr Algie wrote: 'On the day before sailing, a letter came from Monsieur Anet, with news of the most serious setback we have yet experienced. Just at the time of our visit to Belgium, political difficulties arose in their Foreign Office, and colonial circles connected it with a frontier question, which produced an atmosphere of mistrust of the British influence and intentions. As a result the verbal permission which we had definitely received, has not yet been confirmed, and Monsieur Anet feels that he has come to an end of what he can do to help us in these negotiations. This sudden slamming of the door prevented our sending the letter as it stands and we ask your earnest prayers that we may be guided aright.'

He continued, 'We do not feel that there is sufficient reason to give up all hope of getting to Ruanda, for the CMS has had no direct communication with the Belgian government and no definite refusal has been given. ... It is difficult to see on what grounds they can give a direct refusal as there is no mission society in a position to undertake this great work. We pray earnestly for these fresh negotiations that "he who openeth and no man shutteth" may show his power on behalf of this needy people.' With some anxiety but with great faith, the two families — Dr and Mrs Leonard Sharp, and Dr and Mrs Algernon Stanley Smith with baby Nora (born 1st February 1920), set sail for Africa in the SS Garth Castle. Dr Olive Sharp, Leonard and Zöe's sister, had hoped to travel out with the doctors for work at Mengo Hospital, but the post of honorary house surgeon had already been filled. Sadly, she accepted this as God's plan and later pursued a medical career in the south of England.

It came as a great blow to the little party when they arrived at Marseilles to receive a letter from Mr Manley, the Africa Secretary of CMS, confirming the refusal for them to start work in Urundi. With this great disappointment and the future uncertain the doctors were determined to go on and in this Mr Manley encouraged them. 'It is quite impossible to think adequately of the year lying ahead' Dr Algie wrote in his diary, 'but this God is our God for ever and ever. He will be our guide even unto death. (Psa 48:14).' The two families disembarked at Mombasa and travelled from there by train up-country. On arrival at Nairobi their hopes were temporarily raised by rumours that part of Ruanda might be transferred to Britain. They boarded a lake steamer at Kisumu and arrived in Kampala. On the 3rd January 1921 the doctors were in Mengo again and they resumed medical duties in the hospital, bringing back many happy memories of the years they worked there.

Three days after their arrival the doctors discussed their future with Bishop Willis and Dr Cook. Various places were discussed and it became increasingly clear that they should go to Kigezi in the south west of Uganda. Kigezi district comprised four counties, Ruzumbira on the east bordering on Ankole, Kinkizi to the north, British Ruanda (also named Bufumbira) to the west and Rukiga in the centre. The main population was composed of the Bakiga, a sturdy mountain tribe who had proved difficult to control and who had been under the sway of a witch doctor who had stirred up a rebellion some years earlier. The Provincial

Commissioner made an appeal to the Uganda Mission to send a medical missionary to the area as in his opinion that was the best agency to quieten the fears of the people and bring peace. Moreover British Ruanda was attractive to the doctors, being on the border of Ruanda-Urundi itself. It was finally decided that they should go to Kigezi, to the capital Kabale, and open a mission there.

In 1912, the border between Uganda and German East Africa had been set along the crest of the Mufumbira Mountains (now called Virunga), known world wide today for the gorilla sanctuary on its slopes. As in other parts of Africa, boundaries between countries were set by colonial powers, based on geographical and political factors. Often this did not take full account of ethnic groupings. The border between Uganda and Ruanda-Urundi, running along the peaks of the Mufumbira Mountains severed about 40,000 Ruandans from their country of Ruanda (see map p.39).

Missionaries of the Church Missionary Society had been working in Uganda since 1877 and established work in many areas. The Rev. Harold and Mrs Lewin had developed the church centre at Mbarara, Ankole, from where trained evangelists had been sent out to teach in the district and a few had reached Ruzumbura in Kigezi. Elsewhere the district of Kigezi was almost untouched by the Gospel. According to the Ugandan historian, Paul Ngologoza, writing of the Kigezi district, 'The first African evangelist was Zakaria Balaba, a Mugandan. He built the first church at Rukungiri, Ruzumbura, in 1912, but after the matter was discussed with the District Commissioner, this place was later abandoned, and he moved to Kabira Hill, Rugarama, where he built a church,' leaving behind a small group of Christians. Zakaria then tried to take the Gospel to Bufumbira, (British Ruanda) but met resistance and was speared to death.

'The blood of the martyrs is the seed of the Church.' Zakaria Balaba was the first martyr in Kigezi. No other attempts were then made in Bufumbira, until the doctors arrived, when Dr Len said 'We must try again.' 'It has been a great delight to us to arrive in Africa' wrote Dr Algie. 'Mrs Sharp and my wife have settled most happily into the country. Our little baby Nora, who is just a year old, took to the people at once and they all love her. As soon as they see the little one with her smiling face and her hands outstretched to them, they make friends. And I believe that, by the grace of God, she will prove one of his most effective instruments in winning the hearts of this highland race.' (A generation earlier, Algie himself had been a similarly effective ambassador, travelling with his missionary father who wrote, 'Algie greatly amused the people with his little ways'.)

The doctors were concerned whether the change of plan would disappoint some of their supporters, and Dr Algie wrote, 'Those of you who have contributed towards the Ruanda mission will we believe, feel happy in the fact that this work is being started on the borders of Ruanda itself, the country that is still our first love. But if any of you feel that this new venture is not in accordance with your intentions, please let us know and we will of course be prepared to return the money you have given. In as much as the Mission is a direct offshoot of the Uganda Mission, it is being arranged that our houses at any rate will be built out of Uganda Mission funds. The cost of transport, of equipment as well as of personal effects is tremendous, and you will I am sure not forget this aspect of the work in your prayers.'

Relying on this support and on God's leading, in the days that followed the doctors continued their surgical and other medical care at Mengo as they prepared for the move to Kigezi, confident that they were on the threshold of their promised land.

# RUANDA MEDICAL MISSION
## before 1927

Dr & Mrs Len, Erisa Mutiaba & Yonisani leave Kampala for Kabale  pg48

Leonard Sharp

Esther Sharp

Algernon Stanley  Smith

Zöe Stanley  Smith

Dr & Mrs Len with Robin  pg66

Three blocks of hospital ready pg67

Dr Len with patients

Group with
Nora at tent door pg74

Kigezi High School boys pg66

'Sunday  September 24th a memorable day for Ruanda'
The first baptisms at Kisoro  pg68

Kisoro High School 1922  pg58

Dr Algie and family
go on holiday January 1923

Hutu Chief

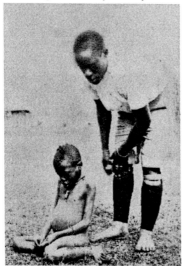

The beginnings of the
Girls' School  pg75

Erisa Mutiaba with a sick boy  pg51

The first Urundi patient: 'A small chief
trudged with us 200 miles' pg73

Rev. Jack Warren  pg82

Captain Geoffrey Holmes pg83

A dangerous moment! pg107

Musinga, King of Ruanda,
beating the royal drums  pg96

Safari in Kigezi pg123

St Peter's Church & the re-roofed hospital
at Kabale Nov 1926 pg 107

Food supplies arrive by head porterage for
feeding centre Gahini 1928 pg122

The Royal Kraal 1925  pg96

Zöe feeding starving children  pg122

# Chapter 4

# The verge of
# the Promised Land
## 1921 - 1922

Dawn rose over Kampala on Friday 4th February 1921 like any other morning, but for the two families, Dr Leonard and Mrs Esther Sharp and Dr Algernon and Mrs Zöe Stanley Smith with their baby daughter Nora, it was particularly significant. They stood on the threshold of the first step towards the achievement of the mission to which they were convinced God was calling them. Things had not worked out as they had planned, for their way to Ruanda and Urundi was blocked, but the thought of giving up did not occur to them. Rather, there was a certainty and earnest expectation that although they could not see clearly the farther steps ahead, the nearest one was clear and they could go forward in the confidence that God was in control. One of the doctors wrote home later: 'We were under sealed orders known only to our Guide.' The border of the country of Ruanda was over 300 miles away but this, south west Uganda, which included 40,000 Ugandan Ruandans, was the first step into the 'promised land' — the land of God's promise to them 'to take the Gospel to those who have never heard it'.

So on 4th February, waved off by the Stanley Smiths, Dr and Mrs Len Sharp left Kampala on a motorcycle — Mrs Sharp ('quite terrified of going into the unknown' as she remembered later) riding pillion, with their baggage and some medical equipment following them separately in a van. The road to Mbarara was familiar to Len, and after the journey of 170 miles on rough murram roads, they were welcomed by the Rev and Mrs Harold Lewin, the missionaries in charge of the CMS centre at Mbarara. The next two weeks were spent in recruiting about 100 porters to carry their belongings, since vehicles could go no further at that time, and making arrangements for the next stage of their journey. Then, after seeing the porters, with Erisa and Yusitasi, on their way, Dr and Mrs Len followed on the motorbike on 21st February, reaching Kabale on the afternoon of 24th. Esther always afterwards remembered the night-time campfires and Dr Len telling the people for the first time about the God who loved them. 'What a back-breaking ride it was for her, over 300 miles pillion on rough roads and tracks' commented Dr Algie later. In fact she suffered several falls on the way and was badly grazed and bruised when they eventually arrived.

Esther described the moment they climbed the Government hill to ask directions: 'When my husband and I arrived at the Government centre of Kabale on 24th February, we found a very primitive little place. Our mission hill was pointed out to us across the valley and very bare it looked too. It was raining and the motor bike on which we had travelled had to be left at the bottom of the hill as we toiled up the slippery path, often literally on our knees.' So they arrived soaking wet, with a puppy, and very little else, and were offered welcome swamp water and tiny potatoes by the small group of baptized boys and a teacher who met them, till the porters arrived hours later with their possessions. There were two small buildings on the hill, a little mud and daub thatched church and a two-roomed Government mud and wattle rest house without door or windows.

Meanwhile in Kampala, Dr Algie acquired a motorcycle and sidecar. He continued working in Mengo Hospital. Three weeks later, on Thursday 24th February, he and Zöe, with baby Nora, set off on their motorcycle and sidecar from Kampala on their way to Mbarara. A van transported their baggage. Their first stop was Masaka, about halfway between Kampala and Mbarara. Dr Algie's diary noted: 'We arrived at Masaka at about 5.15 pm. Road from Lweza to Kako very poor. ... Kindly welcome from Mr Warren D.C. Beautiful site for his house. Keeps a tame eland and a baby buffalo.' They stayed there for the night, then on to Mbarara.

Four days later, on Monday, 28th February, Dr Algie with Bishop John Willis and Rev. Harold Lewin set off from Mbarara for Kabale. It was a great occasion when Dr Algie Stanley Smith joined up with Dr and Mrs Len Sharp at Kabale. They were amazed to see, on arrival, that the future positions for the hospital and church had already been chosen and the sites for their houses were being levelled. The state of things at Kabale, with no house, made it unwise to take a baby there so Mrs Algie remained at Mbarara until their home was built. After three days at Kabale, on Wednesday, 2nd March, Dr Algie, with Bishop Willis and Rev. Harold Lewin returned to Mbarara leaving Dr and Mrs Sharp at Kabale while Algie returned to Zöe.

For the next several months, Dr Len and Esther lived in the small two-room rest house. Dr Len broke up packing cases to make a door, shutters and shelves. This was necessary to protect them not only from bad weather but also from leopards, which frequently prowled around at night. Dr Len urgently set about building, first Dr Algie's house then his own, from mud and wattle roofed with grass, and Dr Algie joined him as soon as he was able. Then came the momentous day, Monday 6th June, when their house was almost finished, that Dr Algie, with Zöe and Nora set off for Kabale on a motorcycle and sidecar.

Dr Algie's diary gives details: 'Very poor going up Lutobo hill. Arrived at top at 12.45. Had lunch, left at 2. Soon found that the road was being remade and was nothing but a ploughed field ... stuck time after time. Decided to stop at Bukinda. Arrived there at 4.0. Chief Stefano very good in providing us with heaps of milk, eggs, chicken etc. Sent runner off to Len.' The family spent the night in a Government rest house by the roadside.

On the following day the situation was made worse. 'On overhauling bike,' wrote Dr Algie in his diary, 'soon saw that the original crack in frame was serious and increasing. And sidecar frame was cracked almost in half in one place. Decided to send Zöe in sidecar body with baby and to walk with them. Went short cut over the hills — terrifically steep ascents and descents. Zöe walked a good deal and had many nerve-racking jolts and twists. It was well on in the afternoon as we were getting down to the Soko road that we met Len, who had been hunting for us for two days. Len took Zöe in on motorbike and came back for baby and me. Baby often very frightened at the sudden heaves of the carriers. Very glad to be in. Poor Zöe very tired and I took baby and she only stirred once.' It is not surprising to read in Dr Algie's diary for the following day: 'Zöe very weak and suffering strain.' The two families were now together on Rugarama hill. Dr Algie, Zöe and baby Nora lived in a tent until the house was ready, and three weeks later Dr Algie wrote, 'Very delightful sleeping in our own house and home for the first time.'

Then began the real test of their missionary call. Dr Len began a sun-dried bricks industry with a view to the construction of the hospital (a quarter of a million bricks required initially), and collection of papyrus from the valley below, for its roofing. Papyrus was more durable, less inflammable than grass and a widely used roofing material. The two doctors shared their vision for the future, but in the practical planning and executing of their joint plans, particularly those which involved buildings and equipment of every kind, Dr Len excelled. There was no skilled labour to call on and bricklaying and carpentry had to be taught. Timber was cut and carried in from forests many miles away. The District Commissioner, Mr Adams, gave invaluable help. For three months Mrs Sharp and Mrs Adams were the only white women in the area.

It was hard work, but it was God's work and that made the difference. Slowly they saw the visible results of their labours, bricks piled up, windows and doors prepared under their firm but kindly supervision. In this way the doctors set about their carefully thought-out course of action: first the necessary houses for themselves, their staff and a nurse; then the building of a hospital, and then after some central work was established, to have one of them touring through the country in order to extend their influence as widely as possible.

Three months after their arrival at Kabale, the doctors were able to begin medical work thanks to the unexpected but welcome use of two small dilapidated buildings on Government Hill, one and a half miles away, with Erisa Mutiaba in charge. The twelve beds were soon full to overflowing. Morning and evening the staff and patients gathered for prayers, and the doctors took turns in visiting the centre. Erisa Mutiaba was a pioneer missionary in the same sense as were the two doctors and their families, learning another language and longing to lead men and women to Christ. He had been one of the medical students at Mengo Hospital, Kampala, when the doctors had served there during World War I. Twice Dr Len had saved his life — once in Tanganyika during World War 1, and again in Uganda. Hence there was a special relationship between them. He came to Kabale with his young wife in February 1921. He told his remarkable story:

'When I look back to the time when I met Dr. Sharp during the Great War, it would have been difficult for me to think that I could remain among the workers for the sick when the war ended. But my enlistment in the Uganda Native Medical Corps was like the making of bricks (i.e. the first preparations), for the work of nursing was one which I despised above all others. But when I was taken ill with cerebrospinal meningitis, Dr. Sharp's visits to me were the voice of Jesus, calling even me to be his workman, even as I am still. For thus it was, that when Dr. Sharp gave up his time for strolling in the streets of Mwanza at 5 pm. to visit me every day, I was filled with joy, and I forgot my pain. His conversation with me was as the very word of our Lord when he asked me "Are you afraid to die? (Whoever lives and believes in Me (Jesus) will never die. John 11.26.)" But, my friends, although the billows of this world were beating on me, I cannot forget his word, which was to me as gold, and filled me with joy whenever he came to me.

'When I recovered, I did not fail to write to him to tell him how happy I was. He also rejoiced and answered me thus, "When the war is ended, would you like to work with us in Ruanda?" My answer was full of gladness, when I thought on his care of me, and how it all came from the grace which is in Jesus; so I consented to his request. for it was not his voice only that called me, but our Lord Jesus also. So when I came back from my holiday in November 1916 my heart was knit to the messengers of Ruanda.

'In 1917, we started to read (study) in the Mengo Medical School, and did not return to the war in East Africa. But in August, in the midst of our reading we were taken ill with smallpox, and two of our friends died. And here it fails me to praise the courage of Dr. Sharp, which he showed in visiting us: these things are worthy to be remembered even today. Our two friends who died had hearts which thought upon Ruanda in our converse together; and so we were left only two, namely Yusufu Mukasa and I. In February 1919, our reading started again under Dr A R Cook, and in January 1920 we were examined and were victorious in the Government examination.

'But although I ought to have remained among my own nation, and nursed my own people, my spirit pained me for those people in Ruanda who did not know the Saviour of the world. Therefore I asked Dr. Cook if I might go to Ruanda at the end of the year. And he gladly agreed when he saw that I wanted to go to a nation not my own. In January 1921 the Messengers of Ruanda arrived, having decided to start work in the Kigezi District, as Ruanda was closed owing to political difficulties. But what Yusufu Mukasa and I thought was this: we saw that if we both left Mengo Hospital, it would be like a child trying to beat its mother. So Yusufu stayed behind.

'On February 24th we arrived at Kabale, and we had nowhere to sleep. My friends, you know that for a Muganda to eat potatoes and feel the cold is a terrible thing for him. However, I bore it for the word's sake.'

In 1921 Dr Len was appointed District Medical Officer for Kigezi, a post he held for nine years. This greatly helped in the enforcement of public health measures and opened many opportunities for outreach into the district, along with the authority to carry out health surveys into typhus, sleeping sickness, yaws and leprosy and to initiate health remedies with full Government support. The salary for this appointment was used entirely on the hospital.

The cause of sleeping sickness had been identified by Dr Albert Cook and others in 1902. It was found that the trypanosome parasite was transmitted through the bite of the tsetse fly. Bishop Tucker, then Bishop of Uganda, and Sir Geoffrey Archer, the Governor of Uganda, had been seriously concerned by the large numbers of deaths from the disease. In 1908 a long term sleeping sickness eradication programme was set up to separate the population who lived near the great Lakes and on the islands from the tsetse fly areas. A strip of land approximately 25 miles wide along the shores was depopulated and left to the wild animals that roamed there in huge numbers. In Kinkizi, a few fishing villages on the shores of Lake Edward were permitted to remain, but these could only be reached by passing through the wild area. These villagers had to have their blood examined twice a year for signs of the disease, the duty of the DMO. Yaws was responsible for huge and terrible ulcers, and typhus was transmitted by the lice in the skins that people wore at that time.

'Kigezi affords remarkable contrasts as regards both the variety of its scenery and the diversity of its people', wrote Dr Len. 'To the north on the shores of Lake Edward, the Bahundi, a tribe of fisherfolk, eke out a precarious existence in hot, jungle country infested with lions, buffaloes and elephants. Further south the country rises 2,000 feet to the rolling pasture lands inhabited by the Bahororo, a tribe whose whole life is bound up in their cattle. The wealthy among them own enormous herds, and yet so devoted are their herdsmen to every cow that each is known by its own personal name and answers to it when called. When the cattle are attacked by wild beasts, great courage is often shown by these herdsmen, who, regardless of personal danger, rush to the rescue, and drive off the lions, even if armed only with sticks. A climb of another thousand feet takes us into central Kigezi, where ranges of great hills rise precipitously a further two thousand feet above the valleys between them. Kabale, a small township and the administrative headquarters of Kigezi lies among these hills. It was here, in this strategic position, that the mission station was opened which has become the centre of Christian activity for the whole of Kigezi, with over a quarter of a million people.

'A great ridge of wild country separates the Bakiga from their neighbours in Ruanda and the Congo. Much of this region is trackless forest, the only home of the gorilla to be found in British territory. Part of it is covered with dense bamboo forest, where herds of elephants and buffaloes roam, and here are still to be found small groups of the Batwa, a tribe of pygmies similar to those living in the Congo. Although few in number, these little people were much dreaded by the Bakiga, for on moonlight nights they would descend from their mountains to set fire to the grass huts of their larger enemies and carry off sheep, goats, cows or even girls.

'Westwards of this ridge, the whole plain below is marked with numerous circular craters, like those seen on the moon's surface through a telescope. Beyond these rise nine mighty volcanoes towering to 15,000 feet. The two furthest, away to the west, show white plumes of vapour above them and, at night, a rosy glow, for they are still very active volcanoes and have recently erupted. All this region is called by the Africans "Bufumbira", meaning "the Place of Cooking", a singularly appropriate name. Eastwards from this, far below, shimmering in the sunlight lie the calm waters of Lake Bunyonyi, meaning "Lake of little birds".'

'We are set on the very summit of Africa,' wrote Dr Algie as he surveyed the scene from their centre at Kabale. 'I wish I could draw you an adequate pen picture of the beauty of this place. In coming here one toils up a great hill 1000 ft or more and finds oneself transported away from the hot steamy plains of Ankole up into a spacious upland country of piled-up hills and deep-cut valleys, and everywhere the signs of cultivation. These industrious people, who live mostly down in the depths of the valleys, carry their cultivation away up to the mountain tops, sometimes 1500 ft above, and here at Kabale, through a gap in the hills we can see the great extinct volcano, Muhavura, one of the finest peaks of the Mufumbiro range.'

In contrast to this natural beauty was the spiritual darkness which the doctors saw all round them. 'The 200,000 inhabitants of Kigezi are heathen almost to a man. There are, however, scattered points of light in the surrounding darkness, for some 20 teachers are distributed throughout the land, consisting largely of the first converts of the Bakiga themselves, and they greatly need your prayers. But otherwise, drunkenness, witchcraft and the grossest heathenism are the chains that bind these people in Satan's thrall. Our first aspiration is thus fulfilled — we are in a pioneer district, for, except at the centre here at Kabale, the converts are almost non-existent.

'A closer inspection of the people's homes revealed a most miserable condition of dirt and squalor. The healthy wives usually departed early in the morning to cultivate their crops or to fetch firewood, and the men disappeared to drink beer at a neighbour's hut, leaving the rest of the family in a parlous state. In one typical homestead we found the old people, half-naked and ill-nourished, propped up against the side of a hut, seeking to gather a little heat from the sun. A woman, too ill to go to the fields with the other wives, was sitting in the shade of a spirit-hut, trying in vain to keep the flies from an enormous ulcer on her leg, while she prepared a mixture of leaves and cow dung with which to cover it. The children were wandering aimlessly and painfully about, walking on the flat of their feet, their toes turned up and in a terrible state of infestation with boring jiggers and subsequent infection. If there had been a beer-drink the night before, even the children would have been lying about drunk in the dusty courtyard among the goats and chickens. Conditions such as these were universal; they compelled us to take urgent public health measures without delay and press forward the building of the hospital with all the speed that primitive conditions allowed.' [1]

Even at this early stage, there were grounds for hope that God would eventually lead the doctors into the Belgian mandated territory of Ruanda-Urundi. 'Almost from the start we have come into contact with the Ruanda people,' wrote Dr Algie in the first issue of *Ruanda Notes* in May 1921. 'We have made friends with the ruling chief of British Ruanda and several of his Batutsi retainers. One of the Batutsi, Zekeriya, who was taught at Mbarara, is one of our headmen, and he has proved very helpful with the language. With his help we are compiling a First Reader in their language. We have started a weekly meeting which we hope may be of great benefit to the work; a devotional meeting for the teachers and senior Christians here.' A further encouragement was the arrival in May 1921, of the nurse, Constance Watney, with fifteen years experience at Mengo Hospital.

Work was progressing well at Kabale but the hearts and minds of the doctors were looking further afield in Kigezi and beyond. Only four months after their arrival at Kabale Dr Len went on the first of many exploratory and medical safaris. The modern concept of a safari is either of hunting for big game for sport, sometimes with the additional object of obtaining specimens of African game, or of a comfortable lodge surrounded by a secure fence, well appointed rooms, electric light, all 'mod cons', 3-4 course meals and drinks, even a swimming pool, with escorted land-rover game-drives with up-market, safe tented accommodation with all facilities. This was not what was meant by safari for the doctors. To quote J Bikangaga, who later became the first person from Kigezi to get a university degree:

'Those safaris were not full of fun because life was difficult, they had to walk, there were no roads. They had to cover hundreds of miles, all over the country.' [2] A missionary safari was planned for different reasons.

Sometimes missionaries would take some time out to do some shooting, if opportunity arose, and in doing so provided food for his party, or as gifts to otherwise unapproachable chiefs and to make friends by giving presents of meat. But the primary object in planning a safari was to carry the good news of Jesus Christ to the many scattered villages far away from the Mission centre and to treat people who would otherwise have no access to medical treatment. It was the opportunity to plant churches and village schools, encourage existing evangelists and teachers and question their readers. Crowds of sick and suffering people received help and at every stop, the Gospel was preached to the inquisitive crowds who gathered, so that many could hear for the first time the Good News of God's love.

Planning a safari lasting several weeks, as Dr Len did in Kigezi and later in Ruanda, meant taking the whole family and everything required for that period. Tents, bedding, towels, clothing, food and utensils, tables, chairs, a tin bath, hurricane lamps, paraffin, requirements for staff and porters, medical supplies, instruments, anaesthetics, water containers, microscope and slides especially when travelling to Lake Edward for the sleeping sickness surveys twice a year. Safari days started at daybreak and marches lasted about seven hours. Tents were erected in early afternoon, after which contacts were made with the local chief and his people. Then patients were seen and treated, teaching given. The duration of a stay in camp depended on circumstances. Then they would move on to the next destination.

'Towards the end of June when our house was nearing completion,' wrote Dr Len, 'my wife and I took a three weeks' journey through the counties of Ruzumbura, Kinkizi and British Ruanda, partly as a medical itineration, but chiefly to find out what opportunities would be found and what reception the Gospel would receive from the chiefs and people.

'The work in Ruzumbura was started about six years ago by active Christian teachers from Ankole. There has been some fruit of their labours and there is now a little group of Christians there. Kinkizi we found to be entirely heathen, though a Christian from

Ruzumbura has been working there for a few months ... he had quite a number coming daily to be taught. Kinkizi... is thinly populated and much of it is impenetrable forest which is inhabited only by Pigmies. ... They are a bright and intelligent little people, held in considerable awe by their larger brethren and as capable as you or I, under the influence of the Holy Spirit of God of becoming sons of God and inheritors of all the riches of Christ. There are now four evangelists in Kinkizi, one of whom is where the Pigmies live. From Kinkizi we travelled south through 30 miles of virgin forest never traversed by a white woman before and arrived in British Ruanda. To give you an idea of what it was like, from one hilltop we saw six of the Mufumbiro Peaks and from the camping ground at 8000ft above sea level we were surrounded by five lakes. I feel evangelism of this part is supremely important, not only for its own sake but because from it, it may be possible to reach other parts of Ruanda. We have heard that another slice of Ruanda is to be handed over to the British in January 1922 and we must do something for them too.'

The first boys' boarding school in Bufumbura was started on the outskirts of Kisoro at Seseme in June 1921. It aimed to concentrate on the sons of chiefs in order to set an example to the rest and to contribute to a later generation of chiefs and sub-chiefs as well as other leaders in their society. The school proved to be particularly encouraging despite the difficulties which the two teachers there — Silas and Zechariah — had experienced in finding food during the drought. Three months later there were 20 boys from 8 to 16 years old. 'They were keen and obedient,' recorded Dr Len, 'and if they only had some boy scout shirts and shorts they would make quite a smart little school. The chiefs have promised to send more boys of the best type and their own sons, so I hope before long to have 50 or 60, and I am returning here this month to arrange for the erection of proper buildings. I feel that in this school as much as in the work of the village teachers lies the hope of evangelizing Ruanda.' Some antagonistic local chiefs later burned down the first school building but it was soon rebuilt. Also in September, building was started on a boys' school at Kabale , which was ready to open in February 1922.

It was on one such a medical safari to Kinkizi that Dr Len's party were held up by a river in flood. It was too deep for any to ford except Dr Len and one porter who were taller than the rest and who could swim. After testing a route, Dr Len took each one across the river one by one, family members, staff and porters, with water up to his chin. The tallest porter carried each load across on his head and so all arrived safely on the other side to continue their journey.

From May to August of that first year at Kabale, Kigezi suffered a drought. Although Dr Len's advice as Government Medical Officer was acted on, it could not prevent a widespread epidemic of dysentery resulting in many deaths. The lives of a number of children were saved and this contributed to the confidence of the local people in the medical services offered to them. In fact, the care of the doctors for children proved to be a very rewarding part of their testimony to the love of Christ for all and certainly including children.

Adding to their problems was the difficulty of obtaining essential supplies, such as flour, sugar, salt, paraffin. Periodically, a number of men were hired to push a cart the 260 miles to Kampala, load it with supplies bought in bulk and then push it back to Kabale, taking about six weeks. A small Post Office was run by an Indian on the Government hill. Telegrams could be sent and received there provided the miles of telephone wire needed were intact. Apart from breakdowns due to storms, telephone wires sometimes disappeared mysteriously to reappear woven into women's bracelets! Letters arrived irregularly from Kampala by 'runners' — men who walked over 500 miles there and back. On a number of occasions the letters, when collected, bore an apology from the Postmaster with the note 'Damaged by lions'. Lions' teeth marks on the letters proved the accuracy of the note, but no mention was ever made of the fate of the runner concerned.

Dr Len built their own house between April and August 1921. During this time Esther laid out their garden with lawns, flowers, vegetables and fruit. Fruit was unobtainable in Kabale but Esther planted strawberries, strasberries, cape gooseberries, oranges, lemons, mulberries, figs and custard apples for the benefit of all those working on the hill. The road to the mission centre was planted with trees and the centre laid out with flowering shrubs, while the sides of Rugarama hill were forested for timber. The bare hill was transformed.

After a few months the doctors reviewed their activities. After prayer and considerable thought it was decided that British Ruanda, Ruzumbura and Kinkizi should be the special responsibility of Dr Len, while Dr Algie would concentrate on the county of Rukiga. The doctors recognized that, while they shared medical skills, Dr Len's other strength lay with planning, building and engineering and Dr Algie's with the development of education — schools, teacher-training and literature.

In September, Dr Algie and Zöe visited the area of Rukiga to the east of Kabale. 'We found an apparent readiness to receive teachers and to hear the Gospel. I was particularly struck by the numbers of young men of splendid physique in nearly every place. ... Most of the way we were hugging the Belgian border, and it was a pleasing comment on British administration to see the well made road running itself to a stop on the boundary line, to see that to the very last village, Britain's rule was effective. One chief said to me, "They are killing one another over the border and murderers go unpunished, but here we are at rest." In one such village we found a young fellow who had just learned his alphabet and, as both chiefs and people showed a real keenness to read, I gave him our little first reading booklet. I have heard since that with that as his only book, and the alphabet and syllables as his entire stock of education, he has collected over 30 to come together to worship and to learn. There is many a privileged Christian at home who will have to take a lower place on the Great Day, than this simple lad who had learned the secret of giving.'

Everywhere Dr Algie and Zöe travelled they found friendliness but also clear evidence of the bondage in which many lived through fear of the powers of the witchdoctor. Although there were some good aspects of the witchdoctors' use of some plants for medicinal purposes, the overwhelming impression was of a dark world of evil powers, which held its victims in a powerful grip from which only the Gospel could free them.

One Sunday after their return to Kabale, 'an excited little crowd gathered at our house, and we found the cause of it to be two wild-looking men, tied together by a rope round their necks, who had been captured in the performance of witchcraft. This is the bedrock principle of the religious life of these people — the cult of Nyabingi. It is the worship of the personal devil, and in every heathen home you will see the little grass huts where her offerings are laid. From time to time there arises a man or a woman possessed by Nyabingi and all who are discontented and tired of making the white man's roads and paying the white man's taxes, resort to that person. Nyabingi is the cause of all the rebellions and all the reactions against progress. The people credit him [the possessed person] with causing sickness and death. Cattle, sheep and goats are offered to appease his malice. A devotee of Nyabingi will sometimes build a whole kraal for his occupation. He will order cattle and sheep to be brought to him, girls will be offered to him and married for a big dowry. Such a wife marries her man, but never leaves the home of Nyabingi all her days. They are called the "handmaidens of Satan"'.

When Dr and Mrs Len Sharp remained at Kabale to super-vise the work there, Dr and Mrs Algie toured through the north and west of Rukiga. 'It was more than ever a journey through tremendous hills, and this time through belts of forest.' Dr Al-gie wrote, 'We passed a boiling spring and along fern-covered paths ... On one morning of exceptional clearness, we saw away over the plains of Lake Edward to where, a hundred miles away, towered the snow fields of Ruwenzori. In this part of the country we found that the Roman Catholic teachers had got some hold, though even they only touched a fringe of the population; our work too, is in a very small way. We saw many sick — in one place well over a hundred. There was one boy among them who showed me his arm. The upper left arm was much shortened though fully developed, and was set at a wrong angle so that his arm projected back towards his shoulder. When asked the cause, he said that Satan seized his arm in his youth and twisted it round. One cannot help believing in a personal devil but on this occasion it was probably an onslaught by an angry parent.' Such experiences made the doctors acutely aware of the spiritual enemies they faced in proclaiming the Gospel and leading men and women to faith in Jesus Christ. Becoming a Christian for the people among whom they were working, meant a revolution in almost every aspect of their lives.

The last months of 1921 were marked by joy, anxiety and grief. There was joy at the birth of a baby boy to Dr Len and Mrs Esther Sharp. He was named Robert Leonard but more often called Robin. Soon afterwards first Mrs Sharp and then Mrs Adams, the wife of the District Commissioner, were taken seriously ill. After eight days illness, Mrs Adams died, leaving a grieving husband and a small baby. As Dr Algie described, she was 'a true Christian woman and one eminently suited for the life out here.' Mrs Sharp slowly recovered, emerging from a time of great anxiety and much prayer to look after Robin, 'a fine little man of the most perfect manners', together with the motherless baby, until a relative of Mr Adams took charge.

At Kabale, building of the hospital and school progressed rapidly. Buildings were thatched and walls plastered, all under the constant supervision of the doctors, particularly Dr Len. His skill in planning and supervising the construction of buildings was matched by his wisdom and patience in handling workers who were often desperately unskilled until taught. He also applied his skills in very down-to-earth ways. 'Our water supply came from the neighbouring swamp,' recorded Dr Algie, 'and was most unsavoury. We made two attempts to dig a well, the second of which has proved successful. Dr Sharp has built it round with homemade brick, and a fairly pure water supply is the result and an inestimable boon.' Dr Algie also commented on Dr Len's interest in wild life. 'One of the features of our hill here is Dr Sharp's menagerie. His collection of animals is, or has been, three dogs, two puppies, a cat, three baby leopards, swamp otters and a civet cat, locally known as Mondo. It resembles the traditional cat in its extreme tenacity to life, for it has had three miraculous escapes already from an untimely end.' Some of these were young orphan animals brought to Mrs Len by Africans.

In January 1922, Dr and Mrs Len, with Robin, embarked on a safari to Bufumbura, British Ruanda, on the southern border of Uganda with the Belgian territory of Ruanda-Urundi. 'Visiting the little village schools started by our teachers has been most interesting, and questioning the children on what they know of Jesus Christ.' wrote Dr Len, 'Sometimes we are disappointed, sometimes encouraged, but I want you to remember that our teachers themselves need to be taught of God, for they are still very unlearned and ignorant; but we feel that for the present half a loaf is better than no bread for the starving children of Ruanda.' On this safari to British Ruanda, Dr Len noted another link with Belgian Ruanda. 'We were able to become really friendly with the chiefs and, I think, win their trust and confidence, especially Nyirimbirima, the paramount chief of British Ruanda, who is a cousin of Musinga, King of (Belgian) Ruanda. We stayed with him for some days and also made friends with his wife who is a native princess and seemed a wonderfully refined woman.' There were strong family links between the ruling chiefs of British and Belgian Ruanda, which were an advantage to the doctors on occasions. Most chiefs were Tutsi, but some areas had Hutu chiefs in those days.

In January 1922, a political event was to have far-reaching effects in the fulfilment of the vision of taking the Gospel to what was then Ruanda-Urundi. After the First World War, through the Treaty of Versailles, German East Africa was divided between the British and the Belgian colonial powers. Tanganyika came under British rule while Ruanda-Urundi became a Belgian Mandated Territory, next to Belgian Congo. However, in 1922 the British Government, hoping to fulfil long-standing plans to build a railway on British governed territory from Cape Town to Cairo, negotiated with Belgium for a band of territory along the eastern border of Ruanda-Urundi on which to construct this railway. As soon as the transfer of power had taken place, British administrators were located to the eastern part of Ruanda, which had become British. The two doctors saw this opportunity as God-given and Dr Len wrote to the British Provincial Commissioner of western Tanganyika asking permission to work in the newly acquired territory in east Ruanda. He received a very favourable reply and arrangements were made for the District Commissioner to meet him at the border.

In June 1922, Dr Algie accompanied Dr Len as far as the ridge over looking Bufumbira. The present scenic road from Kabale to Kisoro with its summit at the Kanaba Gap did not exist then, and the doctors had to cross Lake Bunyoni, then climb the high mountain paths that led to the steep slopes which formed the border of the valley separating Bufumbura from the Mufumbira range of mountains and extinct volcanoes of north Ruanda.

'As my brother-in-law and I stood on the edge of the Rukiga rampart of hills and gazed over the rolling country of Ruanda where in this part alone there are 250,000 heathen without any missionary of the gospel,' remembered Dr Len, 'we wondered if the land ...we had spied out six years ago, and not been able to enter in, was at last to be given to us for an inheritance, and we prayed that we might possess it for Christ.'

1. *Island of Miracles by Leonard Sharp and Janet Metcalf, pp.13-16*
2. *Canon John Bikangaga,BA. Mukiga, Protectorate Executive Council,*
   *Elected Constitutional head of Kigezi,Lutakirwa Ngabo*

# Chapter 5

# The door flung wide open
## 1922-1923

Their hopes were further strengthened as Dr and Mrs Len went on to meet the British District Commissioner. 'I found from the first and all through this journey that God had prepared the way, and that all the hundreds of past prayers were being answered', he wrote. In the first place the Administrator was a man I had met in the war. He was a Christian and was most anxious to help me in every way. He tried to persuade me to come and settle at Rukira, the capital, and start a mission station there as soon as possible. He offered any site I liked to choose and attended the simple preaching of the Gospel to the chiefs and people, which it was my joy to give.

'The country which is about 100 miles by 30 has been provisionally divided into eight large chieftainships, each subdivided into numerous lesser chieftainships. I was able to make friends with seven of these chiefs. In fact all that I met, and many of the lesser chiefs were most friendly. One chief chose the site for building his church before I left him, and you will rejoice to hear that the first evangelist to offer is now daily preaching the gospel there and teaching them to read God's word. His name

is Joel. I am very anxious to start a good school for chiefs' sons
in this district. In the meantime I have four fine youngsters to
come into the High School in British Ruanda as a start. The first
seeds are sown now and I feel sure that the opportunity is ripe to
enter in and possess this land for Christ with native evangelists.
There has been so much prayer in the past that a great harvest is
a glorious certainty.'

On his return to Kabale, Dr Len wrote to Bishop Willis, the
Bishop of Uganda, telling him of this opportunity for work in
Ruanda itself, and explaining the need for an ordained missionary
to come to Kabale and so release the doctors to pioneer the new
country that was now open to them. He was back in Kabale in
time for the opening of Kigezi High School by the Provincial
Commissioner, Mr Cooper, who declared the school open in a
short speech in Luganda. The boys, clad no longer in skins, but
smart in red fezes, white sashes and khaki uniform mostly provided by mission supporters, sang *God Save the King* in English,
recited Scripture, and performed drill and exercises. After a tea
for Europeans and chiefs, Mr Montgomery, the veterinary officer,
gained great popularity by giving the smaller boys rides in his car.
With sons of most of the big chiefs in the school, the potential was
promising. The devil was at work though, and eager to destroy.
The schoolmaster had to be sacked for 'evil living'.

An added joy for Dr and Mrs Algie was the birth of a second
daughter, Eve on 5th July. But for Dr and Mrs Len, so soon returned with the good news on Ruanda, their lives were suddenly
plunged into grief. Five days later, their little son Robin, aged
nine months, became infected with dysentery and despite every
effort was taken from them on July 12th. Dr Len also became
infected, 'I was very bad' he said later, and Mrs Len feared for
his life. To Ruanda friends he wrote, 'A few days after my return
from Eastern Ruanda my wife and I were called to give up what
was most precious to us, our little son, and both of us were also
taken ill. In this great sorrow we were comforted by the presence of our Saviour, and upheld by the everlasting arms of him
whom we can love and trust even in the darkest hours; but those

who have known the same suffering can understand. Pray with us that this trial of our faith may be to the glory of God and the extension of his Kingdom, and that even in this it will prove to have been more blessed to give than to receive.' It was a difficult time for both families. The delight of the birth of a new baby to one family was clouded by the bereavement for the loss of an only child by the other. Referring to baby Eve, Dr Algie commented later, 'She is a happy little maiden of two months now, but you will realize how much greater our joy would have been if her little cousin had still been here.'

Although unfinished, the hospital began to admit patients in July 1922. While the women patients occupied their own ward, the men were treated in part of the dispensary. 'It is a great delight,' wrote Dr Algie, 'to see the sick starting to come to us. They already have some faith in our medicines, though they fear our knife. We believe it will not be long before our 50 beds are filled and the hospital becomes, as our prayers would have it, a centre of healing and salvation to all the country around.'

But just when Dr Len had hardly recovered and when she was so needed, Constance Watney, the hospital Matron and the only English nurse, became seriously ill and had to leave. She was much loved, both at Mengo hospital where she had worked for many years, and already in Rukiga. This was another trial to overcome, but 'through the generosity of Toro Hospital, additions to the hospital staff included an assistant medical orderly to support Erisa Mutiaba, three native nurses and two Bakiga girls, one of whom was the first baptized Christian among the women of Rukiga, to tend the sick women and children who constantly filled the wards.' Some of these additions to the staff were pygmies.

Esther Sharp, although trained as a teacher, contributed greatly to the hospital. She acted as Matron when there was no missionary nurse. She cared for both European and African patients including the dying. Esther was also Dr Len's secretary for mission and personal correspondence, acknowledging gifts like the beds and equipment for the women's ward from ladies in Harrogate. An anonymous donor provided a sterilizer. These and other gifts covering the costs of building the hospital 'with nothing over' as well as uniforms for the boarding schools, were gratefully acknowledged. Her lively and informative letters, giving donors an understanding of how their gifts were being used, were a major reason for the sustained level of giving and prayer support experienced by the mission. It was the practice of CMS to indicate a missionary's marital status in their records by the use of an 'm' after their name. Esther Sharp objected to this since she and many others like her, were not only devoted wives and mothers but also fully engaged in the missionary enterprise with their husbands.

Esther always accompanied Dr Len on his medical safaris, which Zöe was not always able to do. These sometimes lasted several weeks. Esther found walking long distances very tiring and sometimes resorted to a 'carrying chair'. From babyhood, the Sharps' children always went with them. On arrival at a village, while Dr Len and staff set about examining patients and teaching all who came to listen, Esther supervised the setting up of tents and cooking of meals, helping where she could, and in the free moments, would be writing letters to supporters in the UK. It was the details she gave in these letters together with frank details of their difficulties as well as joys, which ensured a praying and giving 'band of helpers' in the UK. In the last four months of 1922, Dr and Mrs Sharp travelled 2000 miles, of which 500 were on foot, driving over rough tracks and walking where it was impossible even for a motorcycle to pass. Half a mile of level track is rare in this mountainous area.

In September they travelled south to Bufumbira. 'Sunday September 24th was a memorable day for Ruanda, for the first twenty five Christians, led by their chief, his wife and two sons, were baptized by the Bishop in the new church at Kisoro. And so was born the beginnings of the Ruanda Church.' After the baptism service, the chief and his wife (now with Christian names George and Esther) were married in a Christian service. It was the first step to the later addition of Ruanda-Urundi to the

Anglican Diocese and to what was to be many years later still, the Anglican Province of Uganda, Rwanda and Burundi.

Here a geographical feature was to influence church practice. Before baptizing the new converts, Bishop Willis had raised the question as to whether the baptisms should be by immersion or by sprinkling. In that situation, he favoured the former but there was a problem. Most of the water which fell on the mountains of the Mufumbira range soaked away into the porous lava soil and ran underground, emerging in lakes ten to twenty miles away. Water, even for cooking, had to be carried many miles so was a very precious commodity, therefore sprinkling was chosen. This became the customary way to the extent that, when many years later, missionaries of the Baptist denomination arrived, their seemingly new ideas of baptism by immersion were treated with a considerable amount of suspicion!

Following the service, the first church teacher, Yoeri, a volunteer from Toro, was sent to Eastern Ruanda. He was the first African missionary from Uganda to Ruanda. Many more were to follow in the years to come.

Two major concerns threatened to cloud the horizon for the doctors. The first was financial. The prospect of maintaining the level of progress, with hospital and schools at Kabale, 50 village and two high schools in the Rukiga district and in British Ruanda (Bufumbira) and now Eastern Ruanda to evangelize, until their ideal of a fully self-supporting work was achieved, was daunting. However, they were so convinced of God's directing hand that they did not doubt that he would provide all that was needed.

The second concern related to reports which the doctors were receiving from the UK. The Church Missionary Society, their parent Society, was passing through a crisis, as its theological basis was being challenged. The issue centred on the authority and trustworthiness of the Bible. From its beginnings the CMS had been strongly 'conservative evangelical' in its acceptance of the Bible as God's inspired word, not only as the supreme authority in all matters of faith and doctrine, but also as the inerrant record of the words of Jesus, particularly in Jesus' use of the Old Testament scriptures.

In the early part of the 20th century, modernist and liberal views of the Bible placed reason above revelation, that is, the revealed word of God was to be subject to reason in order to gain a valid interpretation. Over a period of time, some senior men who held these views or supported those who did, were found among members of CMS committees. It followed that some officers of the CMS appeared either to support these views themselves or were sufficiently tolerant of them that offers for service overseas were being accepted from candidates who held them. As this situation came to light, meetings were arranged to review the standing of the CMS relative to these issues. The final conference, held in 1922, reiterated the unwavering acceptance of the 'supreme authority of Holy Scripture in all matters of faith and doctrine' but recognized that there were differences of opinion within the Society.

The final report omitted to affirm the supreme authority and trustworthiness of Scripture as God's written word in all matters, and not only in 'all matters of faith and doctrine', and the absolute truth of the words and teaching of Jesus, despite these being the central issues. Consequently, this opened the door to the Society sending out missionaries who held views with which many conservative evangelical committee members and supporters totally disagreed. One group broke away from the CMS over this issue to form the Bible Churchman's Missionary Society.

News of this crisis greatly concerned both Dr Sharp and Dr Stanley Smith. As they were part of CMS, they could see the possibility of missionaries being sent to the area in which they were working who were not in agreement with their strong stand on the authority of the Bible. Their concern was expressed by Dr Algie: 'We have as yet only heard rumours, but enough definite news has come through to confirm our fears. In this matter we have no hesitation as to the course we must pursue. Heart and soul we stand up with those who hold to the whole Bible, the impregnable rock of Scripture. We, out here, cannot conceive what the outcome of this will be, but we pray that under God, the Society, which has for so long stood for the faith once delivered

to the saints, may be purified by this trial and brought out into...
unequivocal witness to the whole truth of God.'

In October, after the loss of their son and their own sickness,
Dr Len and Esther were invited by the Rev H Bowers to Toro for a
much needed rest. This included ten days near Lake Albert, where
'Nearly every night we heard the lions growling and prowling
round our tent and always the moaning hyenas, but our porters
were not content. Although they had their food, they wanted meat,
so on our way back I shot two buffaloes for them. It was getting
towards evening and all the porters came dashing up to get their
meat for supper and to take what they could back to their families,
dried by the fire as a sort of biltong. They were going to collect
the rest of the meat next morning. All night we were woken by
the howls and laughing of the hyenas but we heard no sounds of
lions. Next morning Esther and I went with a few porters to see
what had happened to the carcasses. I took my 22 rifle in case a
hyena was still around. There was an animal there, not a hyena
but a lion! It didn't like the look of me and I didn't like the look
of it, so I fired, and it ran off. It was a dangerous situation with
only a 22, so I sent a porter to camp for a larger rifle and waited.
It started to rain, but when the sun came out — there into the
sunlight stepped suddenly another lion. I fired again and it too
bounded away. I was about to follow it when there were snarls
in some bushes and then silence. On investigation we found
the first lion dead. My little bullet must have found a vital spot.
There were very many lions in Toro, more than anywhere else,
and everyone was thankful for each one that was killed. They
killed a lot of people, breaking into their houses. The lions of
Toro were as notorious as the lions of Tsavo in Kenya, when the
railway was built.'

From the mission centre in Toro Dr Len was able to enlist two
trained evangelists — Israel and Samson — to work in Eastern
Ruanda, and three hospital workers — Rosette, a certificated
midwife and Vashti and Janie, nurses. This was a missionary call
for them to leave their homes and work in another language area
and, for Israel and Samson, in another country.

In November 1922, after Dr Len had returned to Kabale, Dr Algie went on safari to Kinkizi and Ruzumbura by motorbike. 'There were a large number of sick at Kinkizi', he reported, 'and a couple of incisions for abscesses reduced a large audience to gasping astonishment and helped to remove the great wall of prejudice and fear, which keeps serious cases from coming forward for treatment. At the capital of Ruzumbura, where the Government has built a branch dispensary under our control, there were nearly 200 sick, and everywhere one saw an increasing spirit of friendliness. The ruling chief of that District — Kalyegesa-after years of indifference, now comes regularly to church and is daily being instructed in his home in the word of God. I fear his motives are not of the highest but we pray that a man of his influence may be truly converted. One longs to see signs of real heart repentance for sin and a hunger and thirst after righteousness and one sees it so rarely in our African Christians.'

In December Dr and Mrs Sharp returned to Eastern Ruanda, covering 400 miles. 'Most of the important centres were seen, and acquaintances made six months before were changed into friendships. As my wife went with me everywhere, we were able to visit them in their homes and were introduced to their wives and families. After my first visit I had sent two more evangelists, Joel and Jeremiah, and I found that they had made quite encouraging starts. One influential Mututsi chief, quite 6ft 8in in height, who had heard me speak several times of Jesus, like Nicodemus came to me at dusk and drawing me aside that no one might hear, explained that he wanted to be taught the words of Jesus, but it must be in secret. No one must know. Could he not have a teacher in hiding in his hut, for if they heard he was being taught, the other chiefs would despise him. The entry of Christianity into one of Satan's stronghold is not accomplished without opposition and also sacrifice.

'Israel was placed at Rukira to hold the fort until the white missionary so necessary appears. Samson, we left in the distant kingdom of Bugufi, originally part of Urundi. He has 50,000 heathen to himself, but all things are possible to faith and prayer.

The young King will look after him.  On our return journey on arriving at a hill where we intended to camp, we were suddenly charged by a herd of buffalo.  Surprising the speed with which our apparently exhausted porters shinned up trees or vanished into the distance!  A small chief from Bugufi trudged back with us 200 miles in the hope of being relieved of suffering.  I had to remove his lower jaw, but I trust he will return to his distant land and friends possessed of lasting wealth and happiness.' He was their first Burundi patient.  Despite discouragements, the doctors saw evidence of the value of their work, both medically and spiritually.  'We have had a real encouragement in evidences that the Lord is working with us.  A young man was to all appearances dying of obscure internal haemorrhage.  An operation had failed to relieve him.  So we knelt by his bedside, told him of his almost certain end and prayed for his recovery, if it were God's will.  He was a Roman Catholic and seemed to be really trusting in Jesus.  From that moment he never looked back, and went out cured.

'Our first in-patient, a Mohammedan, left us an avowed believer in Jesus.  When he was asked what had led him to change he said, "When I fell sick, and had no power to help myself, my friends the Mohammedans came round me.  They sacrificed all my goats and when that availed nothing, they left me to die.  Then the Roman Catholics came and they said, 'Let us baptize you, that you may die in peace,' but this One (Jesus) took me in and healed me.  How can I serve another?"'

In the medical work in the hospital at Kabale, the Doctors paid tribute to the head hospital assistant, Erisa Mutiaba.  'He gave the anaesthetic at all operations, dispensed drugs, gave out food for the nearly 60 patients, and applied all the more important dressings.  In the absence of Mrs Esther Sharp, he acted as Matron.  A most trustworthy fellow worker.'  In March 1923, two additions to the staff encouraged the doctors. The first was Beatrice Martin, a very much needed and welcome replacement of Constance Watney. Beatrice took over the nursing work in the hospital. And the second was Constance Hornby, who had worked as a teacher for five years in Uganda and a further two years helping as a midwife at the Lady Corydon Maternity Training School, Mengo Hospital. The work among women and girls was greatly strengthened by her arrival and a start was then made on building a girls' boarding school.

In March 1923, Dr and Mrs Algie with Nora went on a safari through Rukiga. Almost everywhere they saw signs of encouragement. The 'light of the knowledge of Jesus Christ' was illuminating the 'gloom of heathen darkness'. 'My wife and Nora,' reported Dr Algie, 'proved a lodestar of attraction to the women and girls. In nearly every centre they number less than 10% of the adherents, and it needs the presence of a lady and winsomeness of a little child to break down the walls of prejudice and fear that keeps them from coming to Jesus. Nora played her part nobly as she went along the road in her carrying basket, shouting out greetings to them, and as she sat in her tent with her simple toys around her, they responded to her innocence and once again "a little child did lead them."'

As the work progressed, the Doctors saw the need to stimulate the regular reading of the Bible. The Scripture Union had already begun work in Uganda and its daily Bible Reading notes were available in Luganda. After much thought and prayer, a covenant was drawn up for each member to sign. They saw in this move the promise of forming an inner circle of believers who would be 'a vital force in our Christian community'. Members would covenant with God to read the Bible daily, to pray regularly, to yield themselves entirely to God, to give up all that causes another brother or sister to stumble, and to seek to bring others to Christ. This initiative for both missionaries and Africans was made a special prayer request to supporters in the UK.

In May 1923, Dr and Mrs Len went on a three weeks safari in the Bufumbira region, accompanied by Constance Hornby. Of this Dr Len wrote, 'I think that this region is one of the least known in Central Africa, and yet in many ways it is one of the most interesting. There are eight great volcanic cones, the highest being almost 15,000 feet, and one of them is in constant activity. These mountains are never climbed by the natives and are, therefore, practically unexplored regions. ... there alone, in British territory, the mighty gorilla dwells. Another feature of interest is the subterranean rivers and unexplored caves that are found in this region. Some of them we explored for 250 paces into the bowels of the earth, others even larger I have yet to explore.' As Len observed the powerful action of water on the rock, his mind turned to the even more wonderful action of God's Holy Spirit on people's hard hearts. It was on this safari too that a problem for African Christians came to the attention of Dr Len. 'It has been the custom in the Uganda Mission for a man who has several wives to be persuaded to drive away all but one on his becoming a believer.' While accepting the eventual decision of the church on this matter, Len's initial reaction was of concern for the human pain and the barrier between the people and God which could result: 'It is open to grave doubt whether this custom is in line with Christ's own teaching on the subject, but in any case, God grant that to no man or woman may the grace of God and the free gifts through Christ be made of none effect through our tradition, or anything prevent the Saviour's free salvation being offered to all. This is one of the problems which came prominently before me on this itineration. ...

'There are now eleven teachers at good centres of popula-tion, and perhaps 700, mostly children, regularly attending. In questioning these we rejoiced to find how many understood the essentials of the Gospel. A number of chiefs asked for teachers and seven new places were chosen. ... Miss Hornby also returned richer than she went, for she was given four girls to form the nucleus of her future boarding school.' On their way back, all four girls ran off home in the night with Miss Hornby in pursuit next day. Their fathers, angry at being defied, sent them back weeping with Constance, accompanied by their mothers. As soon as the first classroom was ready, Constance gathered together those and the other girls whose parents she had persuaded to let their daughters attend school.

By November she wrote, 'I am writing now in the new school-
room.  There are 20 girls all sitting on the floor.  It is the time
for sewing class and they are learning on an odd bit of cloth as
happy as can be.  All are here with the full consent of their parents.
Our wants, simple as they are, are supplied daily.  We have no
store, but we live from day to day.  One of my boxes holds all
our worldly wealth.  Each girl has a blanket, a mat, a dress and
a cloth for digging in ... no fees or help come from these people
as yet, for they are poor, they have just nothing.'

In her practical, down to earth assessment of the situation of
women in their culture, Constance was able to understand their
situations, sympathize with them, but never despise them, always
seeking their best in Christ's name.  'What a life these women
and girls live, work, work, nothing else.  Often with a baby on
their back, a basket on their heads, a huge hoe in one hand, a
wee piece of fire (a small piece of glowing wood in grass) in the
other hand, they are off to their food patch away on the top of
some hill where they stay until nightfall when they return and
cook for the men.  Such is their life, and yet in spite of this fact
they won't try to save their girls from the same fate. "It is good
enough for me, and was for my grandparents, why do you want
to teach our girls?  Let them alone!"  Sometimes I feel that if
only I could get the older women away, the girls would come.
However, as I tell the teachers when, to cheer me up, they say,
"Oh, you'll never get girls to come and learn", I say to them and
to myself, "God is able, and they are his people when all is said
and done", even if they have been left in darkness so long.  And
he has done wonderful things.'

Soon after their return to Kabale, the hospital was completed.
It was a great occasion for praise to God who had made it possible and for thanks to all the local artisans who had made the
bricks, prepared the wood and thatched it with papyrus.  'It is a
great satisfaction to us,' wrote Dr Len, 'to find how the suffering,
afflicted and destitute are appreciating the hospital as a refuge
in their distress.  We now have accommodation for 45 women
patients, of whom 5 may be lepers, and 80 men, of whom 7 may

be lepers. The hospital keeps practically full, and as the majority have to be fed we are feeding nearly 100 persons a day. But over and above the joy of ministering to this multitude, we are seeing one and another being lifted out of their heathenism into the glorious liberty of the children of God.' Feeding so many people including the staff, especially in times of drought was a big problem, even when some patients had food brought by relatives. Among those who were changed in heart as well as healed in body, Dr Len mentioned 'Kinuka' [1] (meaning 'it stinks'), a very appropriate name, for when he came in, the poor fellow was full of disease and had many sores and ulcers. He came to us months ago, and to him the word was like seed sown in good ground springing up into everlasting life. There seems no doubt that he has accepted Christ and understands the meaning of salvation. When ready to be discharged cured, he asked to stay with us and be a hospital assistant, so now he is one of the staff.'

In July, 1923, Dr Algie joined Mr Elliot, the Acting District Commissioner, to visit the area near Lake Edward which had suffered from the scourge of sleeping sickness, where they found two small villages inhabited by the Bahundi, lake-dwellers who lived by fishing. They left a teacher there, as 'a flickering point of light in that waste of desert and darkness'. Travelling was made somewhat easier when, in the autumn of 1923, both the doctors were able to obtain cars. The existence and state of roads limited their usefulness, but they proved to be of increasing value.

The church work was expanding so rapidly that in September 1923, Dr and Mrs Sharp visited the regions of Buganda and Bunyoro in Uganda to appeal for workers for both Bufumbira and Eastern Ruanda. 'God abundantly answered prayer with the result that seven trained evangelists and one schoolmaster are coming from the Kingdom of Bunyoro and three schoolmasters from Buganda. I have also heard that two evangelists are coming from the Kingdom of Toro. This response to the     missionary call by native Christians is an example which, God grant, many may follow in the home land, when the open door into Ruanda has been made known.'

The Africans gave the missionaries perceptive nicknames, Dr Algie was known as 'Onwonyi' meaning 'Salt' a rare and precious commodity in those days, and Dr Len either 'Eyebrows' or more usually 'Mwami' meaning 'King'. Esther Sharp became known as 'Kirungi' 'which stood for all the attributes of charity, kindness, joy, tenderness and love', recalled Eli Bisamunyu.[2] 'In calling her Kirungi, the Bakiga had recognized what she brought to their region. They had not known many Europeans even at a distance, so her personal manner disarmed any tendency to be unwelcoming. Previous contact with Europeans, while not bad, had been tentative and largely with British military men on surveying and administrative missions. Getting to know the doctors' families was an important first contact for the region because it helped to pre-empt any tendencies towards racism or xenophobia in Kigezi. Kirungi's constant smile was a blessing to us all at Rugarama.'

In November 1923 another visit to Ruanda was undertaken, this time by Dr Algie, since Dr and Mrs Len were due for UK leave in December. 'I did the northern half alone,' he wrote, 'but to my great joy my wife was able to join me for the most important half.' They had heard rumours that the eastern district of Ruanda was to be handed back to Belgium and it was essential to know the situation before Dr Len left. 'We had friendly welcomes everywhere, and the women were especially delighted to see my wife, but only when she was alone.' On reaching Rukira, the rumours were confirmed and Dr and Mrs Algie felt 'the clearest possible guidance to go to the Belgian headquarters and seek an interview with the Belgian Resident. It was not the least of our encouragements on the way that words and phrases in French, long since forgotten, came flooding back into our memories, so that by the time we reached Kigali, we were able to make ourselves understood.

'The night before we reached Kigali, we read in *Daily Light*[3], "Fear not, little flock, for it is your Father's good pleasure to give you the Kingdom". So we went to Kigali with the conviction that at last, seven years after we first entered there, the door was to be opened to the Gospel of Jesus Christ. We were kindly received by the Vice-Resident and the district Administrator, and the upshot of our conversation with them was that our work in Eastern Ruanda was to be recognized and respected, and that if we could raise men and means, there was nothing to hinder us spreading through Ruanda and Urundi. The door has been flung wide open.

'Three million people of one language, who have till now practically never heard of the truth as it is in Jesus, except for the error as it is in Rome, are waiting for the good news of salvation. Those of you who have followed our fortunes till now and wrought for us in prayer, will bow your heads in worship at this exhibition of God's overruling power. Why did God hand over Eastern Ruanda to England for those two years, but to open the door for our teachers to get established and so prepare the way for the fuller occupation that was to come? All this too, just as Dr Sharp is going home on furlough and just as news has come to us of possibilities of larger support. It invests his visit to England with extreme importance for all who are truly the friends of Ruanda.'

Again God's timing of events, experienced by the doctors on so many other occasions, was a great encouragement. It had been decided that Dr and Mrs Len should take leave first because they had both experienced life-threatening illnesses during the past three years and Dr Len was far from well. More important to them was the pressing need for new missionary workers, especially an ordained man for Kigezi and now a worker for Ruanda. Financial support was urgently required and it was essential to obtain the backing and support for expansion from CMS headquarters. 'It was decided that Esther and I should go and make known the great need and wonderful opportunity.' They left before Christmas and arrived in England in January 1924.

'Christmas was a time of great rejoicing', wrote Dr Algie, and a crowd of some 800 must have been present at the service, which was held in the big ward of the hospital with an overflow in the little church. Then followed the Christmas feast: four oxen were slain, and the meat was divided up between the sick, the schools and the readers. Huge pots of 'barley water' (the national teetotal beverage) were distributed and quantities of peas, beans and potatoes. The readers sat in groups on the grass, by their churches, in the courts of the hospital, and considering they numbered about 600 they fed reasonably well.'

The Christmas festivities were hardly over when preparations were made for a most notable occasion, the official opening of Kigezi Hospital by His Excellency Sir Geoffrey Archer, the Governor of Uganda. Dr Algie wrote to supporters in the UK: 'Under Miss Martin's supervision, the hospital was looking as clean as a new pin, and the archway before the central block was wreathed with flowers and papyrus. A large European party arrived with His Excellency, including the Principal Medical Officer of the Protectorate, Dr Redford, and the Provincial Commissioner, Mr Cooper. The five big chiefs of the country were seated facing the central arch where the Governor was placed. Behind them stood their under-chiefs and a great crowd of people, who spread themselves out along the 120 yard frontage of the hospital. On either side nearest the Governor stood the hospital staff. And next to them the boys of the Kabale and Kisoro high schools.

'In a few words of praise and prayer, the hospital was dedicated to the glory of God and for the sake of these sin-sick and suffering people. The Governor then made a speech in Swahili, interpreted by an ex-schoolmaster, in which he praised the work of the Medical Mission, and urged the natives to take advantage of the opportunities of healing thus brought to their doors. His Excellency then inspected the hospital, and showed the greatest individual interest in the cases which were in the ward. He and the ladies in his party were particularly impressed with the beautiful equipment sent by the friends from Harrogate, and they promised to send 50 lengths of cloth for the dressing of the women patients.' This was a momentous occasion. Kigezi Hospital was the only one in the large district of Kigezi.

Statistics can be misleading, but there was much to praise God for as the doctors recorded the numbers known to have been reached within the first three years of their arrival: In Rukiga: 40 small churches; 2,000 readers (those attending church services); about 180 baptized Christians; and over 300 women and girls 'hearing the words of Jesus'. In Bufumbira: over 1000 readers; 25 baptised Christians and 70 under instruction; nearly 200 women and girls readers. Kinkizi: 1 church; 400 readers. Ruzumbura: the work at a low ebb but opposition breaking down. Eastern Ruanda: 1 teacher; about 200 readers.

1  *Yosiya Kinunka  A leader of the Ruanda Revival*

2  *Eli N Bisamunyu BA London, Mukiga, MP and Deputy Speaker, Director General  East African Harbours Corporation*

3  *Daily Light, a collection of themed Bible readings for each day, selected and published by Samuel Bagster, very popular at the time and often a source of God's guidance.*

## Chapter 6

# Horizon aglow with hope
## 1924

Dr and Mrs Sharp arrived in England in January, and Dr Len immediately presented CMS with a report on progress, first in Kigezi and now in Ruanda; on the new opportunities in both areas and on the need for more workers. He asked whether CMS were prepared to grasp this opportunity, and their reply put on record their 'intention to maintain the work which has been started, and to advance as men and means permit'. They regarded the need for new workers as urgent and encouraged him to find them.

There were many requests for Dr and Mrs Len to speak at meetings and by March, three new workers had been found. The first was the Rev Jack Warren, who had won an MC during the war, to work in Kigezi. A lung condition contributed to his being selected for work in a climate which it was hoped would suit him. On being told that a new permanent brick church needed to be

built at Kabale, he had responded at once, undertaking to raise
the finance for its construction, and before he left for Africa he
had attracted a large group of supporters, many of them children,
to help him achieve his goal. His brief, as well as the building
of the church, included the teaching of African evangelists and
the training of village schoolmasters, the rebuilding of the boys'
school at Kabale, and the laying out of an adequate compound
for the women's and girls' work.

The longed for missionary to pioneer the work in Ruanda
was Captain Geoffrey Holmes, MC Royal Artillery. He would
be starting virtually from scratch, for as Dr Len recognized, persecution and famine and human frailty had seriously hampered
any fragile beginnings there. He had been called out of the
'Gunners' to missionary service abroad, and at the Missionary
Training Colony at Norwood, had heard the call to Ruanda. He
was an ideal person to pioneer work in Belgian Ruanda, where
his knowledge of French would be invaluable in his relations
with the officials, and his athletic prowess would appeal to the
sport loving Batutsi. (He was a member of the British Olympic
and captain of the Army Ice-hockey teams.) The third offer of
service came from Miss Margaret Davis who came out at her own
expense to be the dispenser to the hospital. The plan was for all
three to sail with Dr and Mrs Len in October 1924.

Dr and Mrs Sharp spent their leave visiting supporters and in
getting necessary medical treatment. On 26th March a daughter,
Mary Rosalind was born to them in Wimbledon. In July Len and
Esther were in the Lake District for the Keswick Convention.
Here Mary was baptized in Crosthwaite Church, Keswick, and
dedicated in the Convention tent the following day with the
words, 'You were publicly dedicated to the foreign field, should
God call you to it.'

'Our whole horizon is aglow with hope and encouragement
at the thought of the reinforcements coming to our aid', wrote Dr
Algie, in one of the many letters the doctors wrote at this time.
'I was very struck by a short verse quoted in *Spiritual Life* from
the advertisement of a firm of engineers at Panama:

"Got any rivers you think uncrossable,
    Got any mountains you can't tunnel through,
We specialize in the frankly impossible,
    Doing the things which no man can do."
'Now the God of the impossible, the master Engineer of the universe, wants to hearten us with such a message. The door into Ruanda which is slowly opening inch by inch, has always been frankly impossible to open except to the faith that believes God. Now he calls us to co-operate with him by prayer and work to achieve the evangelization of Ruanda, which still to many is impossible.'

It was not only in England that the mission was gaining new helpers. At Kabale, the new headmaster of the High School was a young man who was to become a remarkable leader, Kosiya Shalita. Kosiya, a Mututsi, was born a few miles from Gahini, but at the age of five he was taken by his parents to live in Ankole, Uganda. There he did exceptionally well at the mission school run by a CMB friend of the doctors, the Rev Myres Grace, and went on to King's School, Budo, the premier college of the Uganda Mission. He left Budo just when he was needed for the work in Ruanda, working first for a year at Kabale and then going back to his place of origin, equipped with the best education Uganda could afford, with a sound knowledge of English, and with a heart steadily fixed on the goal of being a missionary to his own people.

In April, the head teacher of the school at Rukira in Eastern Ruanda, Ezekiel Kaheru, a man recently arrived from Toro, agreed to go to visit Musinga, the Mwami (King) of Ruanda to ask for his permission for the work begun in Eastern Ruanda to continue. Clearly, as the doctors recognized, to the Ruandan people such sanction would bear more weight than the dictates of European rulers. Meanwhile, Dr Algie sent out urgent appeals to Buganda, Toro and Bunyoro, all parts of Uganda where there were relatively strong groups of Christians, and where he and Dr Len already had links and good will, for teachers to come and help with this new work.

Among four members to join the staff at Kabale in the second half of 1924, the first to come, in August, was the Rev. Azaliya Mutazindwa, from Toro. 'He at once took over the pastoral care of the churches, and the personal supervision of 150 teachers, whose needs demanded the whole-time work of one man, and the understanding of a native pastor to enter into their temptations, trials, and failures. He came as a very gift from God, a man full of zeal and real spiritual power.' He was to serve at Kabale for two years before returning to Toro.

In Eastern Ruanda confusion in the attitude of the Belgian authorities led to some discouragement among the African workers. Early in 1924, Dr Algie made a brief visit to that area which had so recently changed back from British to Belgian administration. He reported that, 'with the change of administration, the position of a Protestant and English mission had become, in the eyes of the natives, dubious; so I found that in nearly every place the work had gone back, and our teachers were no longer being supported by the chiefs. But our worst enemies were the Roman Catholics. For 20 years they had been content to sit down at Nyanza, their only station in the district, and not stir a hand to evangelize the thousands at their doors; but as soon as they heard that the "accursed Protestants" had asked for new stations, they immediately sent out and built churches on the very sites where we had asked for concessions. Four out of the five asked for, they had captured in this way.

'In one place the chief who was under their influence had forbidden all our 80 readers to come to us, and had ordered them to read with the Roman Catholics; and he even went so far as to send threatening messages to our teacher, if he did not pack up and clear out. Of these 80, only 15 could be persuaded to read with the RCs and the rest were waiting for the clouds to pass by.' On arriving at Rukira, Dr Algie found the Belgian officer in charge ill with influenza and was able to help him. He proved very friendly and sympathetic, and did what he could to help.

The situation in Eastern Ruanda did have its encouragements. Fifteen boys in the school at Rukira were making good progress.

Five of them had asked for baptism and two expressed their determination to be missionaries to their own people. One chief, a Mututsi, with his wife, had started to attend church. However the danger of a nominal acceptance of the Christian faith and a mere observance of its outward rituals was recognized very early in the life of the Mission. At Kabale, there was disappointment as a newly baptized Mukiga girl, trained as a hospital dresser, and two others had to be dismissed for immoral behaviour, and Dr Algie called upon home supporters for sustained, heartfelt prayer. 'We wrestle not against flesh and blood, but against ... the powers of this world's darkness,' (Eph 6.12). 'One is increasingly convicted of the sin of prayerlessness. We house our people, feed them, pay them wages, and teach them, but how much time do we spend in praying for them?'

In the present political atmosphere, where past missionary work is often equated with colonial expansion, it is important to realize that many missionaries were not conscious of the politics of the situation. They primarily regarded the people they were serving as those to whom God had sent them, to demonstrate God's love in action and to bring them the Gospel which would save them spiritually and give them a new perspective in every aspect of life.

A letter written by Constance Hornby in March 1924 illustrates this relationship. After describing recent developments, the addition of one teacher, 28 girls in the school, the planning of reading classes for those who could not read, sewing and basket work, and digging and cooking their food, Constance wrote: 'As for the young ones, they are just my babies, and just like English little ones, only their brown skins make them more beautiful... The girls all seem so happy, and when one realizes what homes they have come from, one can but thank God.'

Dr Algie added to this letter: 'Miss Hornby does not mention here the number of times she has gone off for week-ends to visit and stimulate the village churches. It is impossible to exaggerate the importance of this work. These village churches, which now number some 90 or more in the whole district, I could not possibly visit more than once or perhaps twice a year, and the teachers are for the most part far too young and untaught to be left unsupervised. So you can see what a help it is to them, and what a great burden it lifts off me, when Miss Hornby goes out all over the district, shepherding these "other sheep"'.

In September 1924, Dr Algie went on a medical safari to Kinkizi and Ruzumbura, passing through the sleeping sickness area. 'The work, which I had often thought so dead, seems now really reviving. Any possible monotony in the sleeping sickness area safari was relieved by a journey of some three hours by punt canoes along the shores of the Lake Edward to Nyalubwiga, surely one of the most desolate of the outposts of our wide-flung Empire. As we were going down the Ntungwe River to the lake, we found our narrow stream perhaps 18 feet wide completely blocked by a school of about 8 hippos. We very politely stopped till they had moved on. Our return journey was made thrilling by a sudden storm. The canoes had been beached for a year, so all their seams were starting to come apart and they leaked like a sieve. As the waves literally washed over us, it was a full time job for one man to bale out the water. I am sure our land-lubberly Bakiga boys, who had never seen more water at a time than a three-foot stream in a swamp, never expected to see their home or friends again. And in fact our position might have been precarious, if it had not been that, had our baling failed to keep us afloat, we need only have stepped out of the boats and waded ashore, so shallow is the water there. However small our actual danger, I can assure you our discomfort was acute. But it was well worth it, for there at Nyalubwiga, where East and West are divided by a little muddy stream, quite one-third of the little fishing villages are being instructed in the Word of Life.'

Dr and Mrs Len were due to sail with the new reinforcements on 23rd October but shortly before sailing the medical board of CMS decided to delay Len's return by three months. 'It was a disappointment' he wrote, 'and beyond the medical reasons which made it necessary, one wondered what God's purpose in it might be. Then soon after we had said good-bye to our friends on their journey to Kigezi, while I was resting by the sea, I came across a man who was at Cambridge with me 15 years ago. He and his wife became interested in Ruanda. God called them very unmistakably, and they felt compelled to offer to go out in an honorary capacity for a few years for the special purpose of translating the Scriptures into the Ruanda language. The Rev Harold E Guillebaud, for that is his name, has been endowed by God with very special mental gifts, most eminently suited for the literary linguistic work which he is longing to do.' The great contribution which Harold Guillebaud and, later his children, played in translating the Bible and in providing other literature in the Ruandan language over the succeeding years shows yet again God's amazing timing and guidance.

The doctors knew that for a people who had never heard of Christ and whose lives were dominated by fear of evil spirits, disease, unrelieved pain and squalor, the message of a Creator God more powerful than evil spirits, who loved and cared for them, and which was demonstrated practically, was one to which people initially responded. Such a response could develop into real faith as they were taught about Jesus in the hospital, schools and little village churches, but it was essential to translate the Bible into the language of the people as soon as possible, because it is only through the written word of God that the Spirit of God brings understanding of his ways and purposes to the human heart. Literacy was also clearly a priority so that men and women could read it for themselves. (Romans 10.17)

News of the visit of Ezekiel Kaheru to Musinga, the Mwami (King) of Ruanda reached Dr Sharp while on leave in England. He wrote: 'I have had a number of interesting letters from Africa ... one of these tells how Ezekiel Kaheru, the head teacher in East Ruanda, and a friend set out to visit the King of Ruanda, Musinga. These two took every opportunity of preaching the Gospel on this journey, which was not an altogether easy one, as you will agree, when I tell you that at one place they could not sleep all night as there was a lion outside, and at another they were attacked by men with spears. Ezekiel had two interviews with Musinga, and in his letter seemed greatly impressed by two things; first, the enormous multitudes of people in Ruanda, and secondly by the wickedness of their heathenism. I am sure that these people will not be easily wrested from the power of Satan. We have experienced difficulties, hindrances and discouragements at every attempt to go forward, but we have found that these can be overcome by prayer, and we believe that a great harvesting lies ahead.'

In Kigezi, Dr Algie reported a conversation with a man in the hospital who was 'riddled with disease and inevitably dying'.

'Do you trust in Jesus?' Dr Algie asked him.

'Haven't we come here to your hand, we sick folk, to be healed by you, and to become your people?' he replied.

'Oh,' I said, 'I don't want you to be my people, but Jesus' people.'

'Yes,' he said, 'when I came, I came to you. But when I heard you telling about Jesus your Lord, I turned to trust him.'

'But,' Dr Algie asked, 'What is your heart's attitude towards Jesus?'

'My heart is good,' he replied; 'don't we sing every day "Trust him, Trust him, and he will give you rest"?'

'Has he given you rest?'

'Yes, he has.'

Dr Algie went on to comment: 'Poor broken body of corruption, there is enshrined in it some fragment of the eternal, and before long, he will be delivered from the body of corruption, and be clothed in the glory of immortality.'

The culminating event of 1924 and early 1925 was the arrival in Africa of Miss Davis, the Rev Jack Warren and Captain Geoffrey Holmes. 'It was an unspeakable joy,' wrote Dr Algie, 'to go into Kampala to meet our recruits. As one views the future, one is quite overwhelmed with an irrepressible optimism....'

A letter from Jack Warren gave a picture of a not-so-straightforward arrival. 'Patience is a virtue and one that Africa is specially suited to teach one! Geoffrey Holmes and I have now been a month in Africa and a wonderfully interesting month it has been. After waiting a fortnight here at Kampala where we are most happily housed with the Bishop and Mrs. Willis, our motorbikes arrived from the coast after lying there for six weeks. Geoffrey's was slightly damaged but mine was almost a complete wreck. This, I hope, will be fully met by insurance, but meanwhile I have had to buy a new bike. On this and with Geoffrey on his Sunbeam and Dr Algie Stanley Smith and Miss Davis in the former's car, the cavalcade started off for Kabale a week ago. Twenty miles out, however, through his brakes failing to work, Geoffrey was thrown off on a steep hill and dislocated his shoulder. So, very sadly the cavalcade retraced their steps to Kampala, where the injured shoulder was put right. The following day, Dr Algie Stanley Smith and Miss Davis went on and arrived without incident at Kabale. My new bike, however, developed trouble and after examination it was found to have been wrongly assembled and so instead of starting on Tuesday morning the 15th, I am still indefinitely held up. However, who knows but that a young menagerie of man-eating lions (which abound in a part of the country one passes through en route to Kabale), were not lined up waiting for me had I gone through this week! Anyhow, one knows that all things must be working together for good'. (Rom 8.28).

The year 1924 had been an eventful one, with the official opening of the hospital and the arrival, or near arrival, of new workers. Despite the discouragements of moral lapses in some workers, there had also been a steady breaking down of barriers among women and girls as well as progress among men and boys in the school and hospital at Kabale. As the year closed, their statistics revealed considerable increase in the work done. The in-patients were considerably over 1,100 and the operation cases performed over 200. There were also new church centres and church teachers in the more distant regions of Kigezi, notably British Ruanda (Bufumbira) and Belgian Eastern Ruanda.

The year ended with a special event for Dr and Mrs Algie. On December 27th a baby boy, named Geoffrey, was born, a brother to Nora and Eva. Dr Len's health improved and he and his wife sailed for Africa on 21st January 1925.

# Chapter 7

# Fiery trial
**1925-1927**

Dr Len returned with the prospect of another big building programme ahead: a big new church, worthy of God's name and adequate for the increasing numbers of people, three missionary houses and new boarding school houses for boys and girls.

The joy of the arrival of the recruits was checked by the sudden alarming illness of Jack Warren. He had gone on a short safari in Bufumbira with Dr Algie and Geoff Holmes, but the exertion of climbing the steep hills proved too much for him and he had a severe lung haemorrhage. 'It seemed as though at one blow God was going to take from us this most valued gift, just as we had received it', wrote Dr Algie, 'but if ever prayer was answered, it was in his case; and as I write now, he is entering into the work of the school and the church almost as though he had never been ill. And yet six short weeks ago all the fair visions we had planned for the extension of the work bid fair to tumble about us in ruins and despair.'

Jack himself commented, 'God has wonderfully restored me, in answer to so many prayers at home and out here, and I am now back again at full work, but I am not allowed to go itinerating for a year, and then I will have to be carried up the hills, most humiliating thought! The language, or more accurately the first of three languages to be mastered, is at present one's greatest mountain of difficulty.'

After three months in Kigezi, Geoff Holmes set off for Ruanda. He would be travelling for two months, meeting the people, learning the language, encouraging the evangelists, and looking for a site for a mission centre in Ruanda. For any other man new to Africa, with primitive living conditions, unknown African customs and terrain, this would be a daunting prospect, but not for Geoffrey. His army experience, resourcefulness and stamina were invaluable assets. Kosiya Shalita was the ideal companion.

Although the Gospel, planted in Ruanda in 1922, had begun to take firm root, so that by the end of 1923 there were fourteen evangelists in the district and a boys' high school at Rukira, once Eastern Ruanda reverted to Belgian rule the work rapidly declined. The withdrawal of the British Government inevitably gave local people the impression that the British mission would also have to leave. Although Belgian government officials were friendly, others were keen to see the end of the protestant mission, so much so that many people were afraid to show the friendliness they felt. Under threats and persecution the teachers, without a resident missionary to guide and encourage them, began to lose heart, and the occasional visits of the missionaries could not really counteract the desolating sense of isolation and the discouragement of dwindling congregations.

The coming of Captain Holmes early in 1925 literally saved the work from at least temporary extinction. Heartened by the prospect of his coming, a few faithful African workers held on; and he went down in the spring of that year with Kosiya Shalita to relieve the beleaguered garrison. After one year in the Kabale boys' high school as head master, Kosiya was set free to accompany Geoff Holmes, and found himself stationed a few miles from where he was born. Only God could have planned things so perfectly, preparing Kosiya and bringing him into the work at the very moment he was needed. As the doctors recognized, he was of as much value to the Mission as a European missionary.

Personal contact with the Belgian officials soon led to friendly relations, and Captain Holmes was able to visit the Belgian protestants working in Western Ruanda, and to become acquainted with Musinga and the great Ruanda chiefs. With his survey of the district, a site was chosen at Gahini to be the first permanent mission station in Belgian Ruanda. As the doctors reported, 'Gahini stands at the eastern end of Lake Mohazi, which runs for twenty-five miles among hills crowded with villages, and the shores of which form the favourite pasture land for the king's cattle. Gahini is ideally situated as the centre for the whole of the district which we can at present reach. It stands at the crossing of all the main lines of communication running between the administrative centres. And the lake forms an additional means of communicating with the otherwise inaccessible villages along its shores.'

By the end of 1925 Geoff had brick-making underway, and soon had a small school started, a two-roomed dispensary with five beds staffed by a Kigezi-trained dresser, and a house nearly built, as well as evangelists established in important places in the district. He also saw the potential advantages of a motorboat on the lake to save at least 80 miles of walking. It was his Officer Christian Union friends who supplied this. *The King's Own* arrived and was launched in November 1927. Very soon afterwards, in 1928, this boat was to prove invaluable, bringing food from the other end of the lake to the feeding centre at Gahini during a severe famine, bringing the starving to get food and taking food to those too weak to fetch it.

At this time, the young Ruandan Church faced the problem of its attitude to polygamy. As the doctors were well aware, it was a sensitive and difficult issue, and as noted earlier, the last thing they wanted to see was human barriers being erected which made it harder for people to come to Christ. In the older Church in Uganda, where African Christians and missionaries shared in decision making, the Synod had imposed the rule of one man one wife before baptism could take place and a man or woman be accepted into the Church. This ruling had led to difficulties. Some Christians were reluctant to send away other wives whom they loved and who had been faithful to them for years. For some it led to deceit and hypocrisy. Now a ruling was needed for the young Church in Ruanda, and the hope was to avoid the problems of the Uganda Church. In consultation with their African clergy, who at this stage were in fact from Buganda and had been trained at Mukono Theological College, and after much prayer, Dr Algie wrote, 'we are now dealing with each case one by one; and we are making it the rule that those who fall into this sin, and who refuse to repent after prayerful pleading will (a) be publicly mentioned before the whole Church as backsliders from the faith; (b) their voluntary help in gifts or kind will not be solicited or accepted; and (c) that they will be cut off from the fellowship of the Church until they repent. This sounds tough, but in the long run no doubt it was wise. Dr Len told of a paramount chief in Bufumbura who had 40 wives. He pointed out to him in conversation that this was very hard on 39 men who would also like one wife each, to receive the reply that as he was 40 times better than they, it was quite proper that he should have that number!

As Dr and Mrs Stanley Smith travelled to Mombasa on their way to the UK on leave in April 1925, 'At one place where a goods train had been derailed in a cutting, we waited from 4 in the afternoon till 2 in the morning while we changed from one train to another. The actual change was effected in inky darkness, and we staggered along with the children in the uncertain light of flares, and walked out on a plank on a high trestle bridge by the side of the new train in which all the lights had gone out. We arrived at Mombasa to be told that we had just half an hour in which to get on board our boat.' All was well, and they reached England safely.

Happy to meet many 'Friends of Ruanda' back in Britain, Dr Algie also found that the CMS was experiencing financial difficulties, which meant they could not ask for the support of new workers from headquarters. Certainly new workers were needed. By now, for example, more patients were coming for treatment in Kigezi Hospital, including some coming over the border from Ruanda. A second nurse could make the difference between life and death for some of them.

In June Geoffrey Holmes returned to Kabale from Ruanda. The need for more workers was so great that he then went by motorbike to Toro, a distance there and back of about 1,000 miles, where he enlisted four new African workers, then on to the Bishop Tucker Memorial College at Mukono, where three students offered to work in Ruanda.

On the 13th July, 1925, Dr Len and Geoffrey Holmes, joined by Mr Roome, a much travelled representative of the British Bible Society, set off for Ruanda. One of their objectives was to see the site for the new mission station proposed by Geoff Holmes. A further important aim of this exploratory visit to Ruanda was to confer with the missionaries of the Belgian Protestant mission, who were working in the south west of the country. A large tract of Ruanda to the north of Kigali was without any Christian witness. Beautiful though the country was, with its round grassy hillsides on which thousands of cattle grazed, the visitors were saddened by the spiritual poverty of the people, seemingly with no one to care for their bodies or their souls. Even the small group of evangelists recently based there had been fighting a losing battle.

As Dr Len described the position in Belgian Ruanda, 'The eastern and northern part of this country contains probably a million heathen. No missionaries of the Gospel are there except Capt. Holmes and his little band of evangelists. The opportunities round him are limitless, but his ability to meet these opportunities depends upon reinforcements in missionaries and evangelists. One mission station can only meet the need if it is reasonably staffed. I consider that a second missionary, preferably ordained, to work with Captain Holmes, and a doctor and nurse to start a medical mission there, is needed. There is no doubt that the Lord's commission is incomplete unless it includes the healing of the sick. I believe that a hospital planted down in Ruanda would exert such an influence that success in other branches of the work would be assured.'

While in Nyanza, where the Mwami (King of Ruanda) had his court, Captain Holmes and Mr Roome were visited by the King himself. 'Musinga and his staff called on us yesterday afternoon with his two sons,' reported Captain Holmes. 'He was very nice and sociable, and Mr Roome took two photos of him and his two sons, who are great lads, one about 12, but he looks 16, and the other about 15 but looks 20. After a chat in the rest house I asked Musinga if he had any good runners, and said I'd like to try one out. So he picked out two and we ran 100 yards. One of them beat me by about a foot; and I beat the other about the same! Musinga was very bucked, so I asked him to show me some jumping, and we went down to the football field, and he put a few men over the tape. The chap who beat me running did about 6ft. 2in. I did not compete! The next morning I think that Musinga got the wind up that we were coming to see him. So he sent his headman here to say that we were not to come round, but to wait for him to send for us. I think he had some big witch doctor business on! Nothing further happened till 4 pm, when his head boy came along and commanded us to go. I went, taking along an alarm clock, which pleased him very much.'
In their book, *Ruanda's Redemption*, Dr Len and Dr Algie also described King Musinga holding court at Nyanza, surrounded by a retinue of tall and handsome chiefs; the war dances performed by his pygmy bodyguard and the superb high jumps of the tall athletic Tutsis, who could take off from an ant-hill nine inches high and with a graceful twist of the body reach a height of eight feet. Recognizing the influence of the aristocratic and often arrogant Batutsi, they commented presciently, 'We need to remember, however, that the Lord Jesus delights to choose the weak things of the world to confound the mighty.' Had this

truth been absorbed at a deep level among the different social strata in the nation, might the conflagration of seventy years later have been avoided?

The arrival in August of the Rev Harold and Mrs Margaret Guillebaud and their family was a major step forward for the emerging church. The story of their journey is recounted by their grand-daughter, the Rev Margaret (Meg) Guillebaud: 'So, Combe Royal (their home) having been sold and their affairs put in order as best they could, on Thursday 25th June 1925, at their own expense, they boarded ship en route for Uganda, with their three elder daughters and governess. They took a vast amount of luggage with them, including a piano, all of which was conveyed by train from Mombasa to Kampala in Uganda, and then carried to Kabale by lorry over very rough roads.'[1]

Harold Guillebaud described their arrival in a letter dated August 30th 1925: 'Here we are at last after our long journey, safe and sound. Dr Sharp met us on the landing stage at Entebbe on August 10th after our thrilling train journey, in which we saw not only the usual game, zebra, ostriches, etc., but giraffes as well, to the children's great joy. We did not spend much time at Kampala (though we managed to get to Mukono to see the wonderful Bishop Tucker Memorial College), but started at dawn on Wednesday, the 12th, for our 275 mile motor drive, arriving in time for tea on Thursday. It is a most wonderful road, but exceedingly difficult driving in places, an absolute scenic railway in its corners and gradients. Our house was ready for us when we arrived, and we have been living in it for over a fortnight.'

Realizing that Harold would need a competent Ruandan to help in both learning and then translating the Bible and other literature into the language of Ruanda, Dr Len had gone to Bufumbira, British Ruanda, to find a man named Samsoni Inyarubuga who was chief of a small area in that region. Samsoni was a cousin of the King, Mwami Musinga, and grandson of Mwami Rutarindwa, who had been defeated by Mwami Musinga. The defeated King had fled to Bufumbira. Samsoni had gone to school in Mbarara and was baptized there but he had reverted to his old animistic habits and had almost renounced any Christian faith. Dr Len found him and talked to him. 'Samsoni repented and renewed his Christian vows, but insisted that he could no longer continue as a chief, because his duties involved immersing himself in ancestor worship and the temptations were too great. Dr Sharp suggested he might like to help the new missionary who was coming to translate the Bible, and so began a long and fruitful partnership.' Harold Guillebaud was enthusiastic, 'Dr Sharp has secured for me the services of a Mututsi Christian, a cousin of the King of Ruanda, who will help me to learn the language in its purest form. Just at present, until I know more of the language, I get most help from him when Dr Sharp is able to be with us. Already some extremely interesting facts about the weird ways of the Lunyaruanda verb have come to light, and I am looking forward eagerly to fresh discoveries.'

Beatrice Martin, the nurse, was also observing and learning about the people: 'Several of them [the hospital workers], not being natives of Rukiga, are not used to eating peas, beans, magusha or buro flour. At every turn I meet them with the same pained expression and a tightening of the belt to show me how empty of food they have become. I love the work here and the people, too. They are most fascinating mostly because, I suppose, one never quite gets to understand them. I long to become one of themselves for a time, just to know their mind ... They all wear charms against evil spirits, and each kraal has a devil-hut into which food of some kind is placed to appease the spirits. They only laugh and mumble something unintelligible when asked about it, not being at all conversational, and they have a most annoying way of always agreeing with one by repeated grunts and broad smiles, which prevent one from getting further. One has times of depression ... We need your prayers that we may be kept enthused and daily refreshed with Christ, never to get weary in his work, and so to give out as to receive continually the abundance of life with Christ.'

In his capacity as Government Medical Officer, Dr Sharp, with his wife and baby Mary, visited the people by the lake for signs of sleeping sickness in September 1925. 'We covered nearly 200 miles,' Dr Len reported, 'and at nearly every place we camped, we found a witness for Christ being made, sometimes by very youthful Christians. ... It was clear from this journey that our greatest need in Kigezi today is for native Christian leaders. Among all the 50 churches in these two counties, there seemed to be only one who could be regarded as an outstanding leader; his name is Bartholomew. We spent a clear day beside Lake Edward, bathing and paddling in the waves that beat upon its sandy shore, and tried to imagine ourselves on the South Coast of England; only all the time we could see numerous hippopotami about a quarter of a mile out, and at night, thousands of white pelicans sailed past over the moonlit waters.

'On the way back we came to a cluster of small grass huts used by the District Commissioner when visiting, so we camped there. We had just settled in when the kitchen hut caught fire and as there was a wind all the huts went up in flames. We managed to save the tent but lots of things were lost, including the microscope, Mrs Len's precious book of supporters' addresses and most of the food. Just some dried milk and porridge were rescued. We sent a message to Kabale for supplies to be sent out to meet us, but it was about 200 miles away, and as we had to walk all the way, we had to do with what we had got. The next morning we set out and after we had gone quite a long way, we decided to stop near a big tree and have some breakfast and for the porters to rest, but they had nothing to eat and needed meat. There were some buffalo in the distance so I went after them.' After he had gone, Mrs Len saw that there were lions in the grass near her. She quickly put Mary and her African nurse up a tree and after sending a message by a porter to Dr Len, she and the men who were with her sat on the grass to wait his return. She could see Dr Len in the valley below walking in the opposite direction until her message reached him.

'After a while,' said Dr Len, 'I saw a man tearing along towards me and he held out a piece of bark and on it written in charcoal was "Lions here. Come back quickly." Of course I ran back like anything. "Where are the lions?" I asked when I reached her. "I was just feeding the baby and when I looked round there were two, there in the long grass. They sat up as they were disturbed by us," she replied.' Dr Len continued, 'I went to see if I could drive them away. There was a huge lion, and a lioness which ran off. I took careful aim and fired and he fell dead. We then went on our way and a week later we were getting towards Kabale when we met the supplies sent to us.'

On their return to Kabale, Dr Len found that their second head hospital dresser, Peter, was dangerously ill. He wrote of him that 'he was one of the first to be baptized at Kabale, and had worked faithfully in the service of his Master for four years. He was in addition no mean athlete. We shall always remember his beautiful full back kicking in soccer matches and his tremendous turn of speed. But God knew best, his work and play among us were over. We shall meet him on the other side.'

The weekend of Saturday 14th to 16th November was a memorable one. The Bishop was coming to inspect the hospital and lay the foundation stone for the new church. Harold Guillebaud set off to meet Bishop Willis at Lutobo hill and while they were away a great storm burst over Kabale: peal after peal of thunder right overhead, and flashes of lightning, and the hospital was struck. Papyrus, unlike grass does not catch fire easily but the ferocity of this storm was exceptional. Dr Len described the scene: 'A tremendous crash told me that lightning had struck the hill not far from our house, and a moment or two later, I heard a whistle, and rushing out saw smoke coming from the roof of the top hospital block, which houses about 50 sick men. One of these men had been struck in the face and shoulder, and was dragged out by the heels in an unconscious state. (It was remarkable that this man was struck in the eye which was already blind). This block was cleared of sick and furniture as rapidly as possible, and we made frantic efforts to demolish the verandah which connected this block with the next by tearing out the thatching. The axes I sent for came too late, and I had reluctantly to give orders to clear the next block of its sick and beds, and abandon it to the flames, while we concentrated on destroying the second corridor, that so we might try and save the rest of the hospital. By this time there were hundreds of people on the spot, most of whom worked hard to help, and a few to plunder. We were all soaked to the skin, and scorched by the flames, which leaped 60 feet into the air, and to which the torrents of rain made no difference. The sick in the second block, which was specially built and dedicated to the memory of Dr Wallace Hillbrook, were all of the most serious cases. Many had had operations, and some could not walk at all, and pathetic sights were witnessed, as some of these were carried, and others crawled out into the soaking rain.'

Rev H Guillebaud added, 'The verandah between the second and third wards was at last broken, mainly owing to the magnificent effort and strength of Dr Sharp himself, who with nothing but a long log which he used as a lever, broke one of the immensely strong posts and made it possible for a breach to be effected.'

Dr Len continued, 'By this time it was difficult to get intelligent assistance from many owing to everyone's frenzied excitement, but as we worked we prayed and, thank God, just succeeded in saving the rest of the hospital. It was an anxious time, but we have to thank God that the fire was stayed and no lives lost. It was a picture of desolation and disorder and smoking ruin that night, and, as bedraggled and exhausted we returned home to change our clothes, we could not help thinking how many self-sacrificing gifts and efforts had been swept away in an hour. Since then we have crowded all the sick into the dispensary and every odd corner we could find. The women's ward, which was designed for 18 beds, is accommodating 70 patients.

'No one who has witnessed or fought such a fire would want to run the risk of it again, and it therefore appears the only right thing is to rebuild with a corrugated iron roof instead of thatch. This will cost between four and five hundred pounds for the part destroyed, and to render the whole hospital safe, £1,000. The day after the fire the patients and staff offered praise to God, and prayed that he would supply our need, and he has given us great encouragement already, for with in a week £100 was subscribed

with the help of the Bishop, and by the same post we notice that
£200 had been sent out for the hospital by some dear Friends
of Ruanda.'

The following Monday, 16th November, the main event of the
Bishop's visit took place, the laying of the foundation stone for
the new church. Jack Warren had set his heart on the construction
of a church building and the Kigezi High School pupils under
his direction had previously prepared the site. He commented,
'When the two doctors started their work here getting on for five
years ago, there was scarcely a communicant in the country. Last
Sunday the Bishop laid his hands on 92, making now 200 com-
municants among the 200,000 of the Kigezi district'.

Gradually the other buildings at Kabale were also re- roofed
with corrugated iron. Mary Sharp remembers praying, at family
prayers, for a new roof and cement floor for their house, and
her delight when it could be afforded in 1930. She was nearly
6 years old.

Through all the problems of the past twelve months, Margaret
Davis had not only pursued her work as dispenser, accountant
and book-keeper; but because of her very good command of the
language she was able to visit local churches. There she saw the
desperate need for books — prayer books, Gospels — which,
although in print, were not available. 'You remember the young
teacher from a little church near here, who was so anxious to have
a prayer book? I paid a visit to the place not long ago, and found
another young teacher installed in his place, who also wanted
a prayer book and hymn book. He was having a game of ball
with some of his young readers, and you should have heard the
expressions of delight when I told him he could come up and get
the books. We were escorted homewards by a very lively and
excited crowd of small boys, one carrying a baby on his back,
who lined up to salute us when we parted.'

Harold Guillebaud was progressing rapidly in learning the
language of Ruanda, 'I receive a constant flow of pure Lunyaruanda from Samsoni, and I have to find out the meaning of each
new word and construction. He knows Lunyoro and Luganda, (the

languages of Bunyoro and Buganda) and refers constantly to the Bibles in these languages, from which he in fact translates. Then I have to find out the meaning of what he says. He is very clever at conveying the meaning of words by explanations and gestures; and if he seems to be off the track, I have to explain somehow the meaning of the original to him, and when he has caught the idea he puts it into good Lunyaruanda. It is fascinating work, especially when one has the thrill of discovering, and verifying a new tense, which I have not heard before. As the number of Lunyaruanda tenses is legion, I may have a good many such thrills before I have done. At present the Gospel revision is temporarily suspended, and we are working at the Adult Baptism Service, for my wife and I are shortly going on safari to Eastern Ruanda, that I may have the great joy of baptizing the first converts.'

Dr and Mrs Len happily welcomed the arrival of their second daughter, Joy, on 19th December 1925.

The beginning of 1926 saw the welcome arrival of another recruit to the missionary team, the Rev Herbert S Jackson, known as Bert. He had spent preparation time in Brussels, though at that time it was not compulsory for non-Belgian missionaries. The recognition granted to Bert Jackson by the Belgian Colonial Office was to prove an invaluable asset in the years ahead. After a period of initiation at Kabale, he left to join Geoff Holmes in Ruanda.

Before returning to Kabale from leave in England at the end of April 1926, Dr Algie laid before CMS proposals for the future of the Ruanda Mission. The doctors felt it was vitally important to be working in a group whose members would be united on a basis of faith and doctrine which all of them could accept, and in connection with the theological controversy within CMS earlier referred to, they now felt it essential that their position within CMS (which they had no wish to leave) should be both safeguarded and defined, so that the witness of the Ruanda Mission might be united and unchanging. The General Secretary of CMS, the Rev W Wilson Cash, was very sympathetic to the idea, and helped with the drawing up of a constitution, which on

26th May was passed by resolution of the Executive Council of CMS. The Council unanimously gave them the assurances they had asked for, and so the work in Ruanda was fully safeguarded upon definitely Protestant, conservative evangelical principles and the Ruanda Council came into being as an auxiliary of CMS, with Mr Cash as an ex-officio member.

Besides making clear these doctrinal principles, the Council's formation made possible the necessary reorganization of the home end. The valiant work of individual Friends of Ruanda, mothers of missionaries and others needed to be co-ordinated, and permanent home staff gradually came into being. 'Without this, the rapid expansion which lay ahead in Ruanda and Urundi could never have been accomplished and new resources at home could not have been tapped, nor could the growing circle of praying friends have been kept in touch with the workers on the field.'

Back in Gahini, a crisis arose because of restrictions imposed by some Belgian officials. The original verbal permission for the work of the Mission in Eastern Ruanda to continue after it had reverted to Belgian rule in 1923 had not been followed by an official recognition of the Mission. Belgian administrators interpreted the permission given in different ways, so Dr Algie and Captain Geoffrey Holmes travelled by foot and motorbike (a six weeks' safari there and back), to Usumbura in Urundi, to see the Governor. He, while removing the hampering restrictions to the work at Gahini, was not able to give consent for the development of other centres until the Mission's position was regularized in Belgium.

Once more it was a test of faith, as the missionaries now saw the whole Land of Promise stretched out before them, but had only limited freedom to enter it. A few months later an international missionary conference was held at Le Zoute, to which the Belgian Minister of Colonies was invited. Among the subjects discussed was that of CMS work in Ruanda, and as a result of the Conference, suspicions that the Mission represented political infiltration were removed. Monsieur Anet, who six years before had so warmly encouraged them, was told at this time that the Government wanted to mark its appreciation of his public services. 'The best thing you can do for me,' he replied, 'is to let the English missionaries into Ruanda.' But it was another four years before, in 1930, *personalité civile* was granted, giving the Mission full Government recognition and freedom to expand.

Meanwhile there was more difficulty. 'Just as Dr Stanley Smith and I returned from Usumbura,' reported Geoffrey Holmes, 'we learnt that the Roman Catholics have just asked permission for, and had been granted sites for four or five out-schools in this territory North of Lake Mohasi. These are located in the most strategic positions in this area; and one of these was a site I had asked for six months previously and been refused. We would specially ask for guidance about the location of further out-schools.'

In Kabale work was under way in rebuilding the burnt wards and re-roofing the whole hospital with corrugated iron. On 4th July 1926 the Sunday morning service was held for the first time since the devastating fire of the previous year, in one of the newly built wards. It had taken seven and a half months to rebuild this block and it was hoped that the second would be completed within a few weeks. All the hospital was re-roofed by November 1926.

Commenting on the hospital work, Dr Len recorded how 'six months ago Capt. Holmes sent us a Mututsi lad of about 17 for training as a hospital assistant. He was a typical heathen Mututsi, who had never done a stroke of work in his life for anyone. He had no objection to standing about in graceful attitudes, and looking handsome; nor did he object to anyone teaching him to read or write. But the unpleasant and menial tasks in the hospital went sorely against his pride. Yet now, though he makes no pretence of liking what is nasty, he is willing, when told, to wash feet, or worse, the feet of the Bahutu in hospital — the Bahutu who for generations have been all but the slaves of the ruling Batutsi throughout Ruanda. This lad is returning to Ruanda, and wants to give his life to God's service in a new hospital to be opened there shortly by Dr Church. When I asked him two nights ago whether he would not be ashamed of Christ when he had to face the jeers of his Batutsi friends in Ruanda, he replied, "No, they may have chieftainships and much cattle; but I possess more than they do." So he has discovered that Christ is a treasure more desirable as a possession even than his cattle are to a Mututsi — a great discovery!'

While the hospital was being rebuilt, progress was also being made on the church building, eagerly watched by Jack Warren who wrote, 'Of the £550 already collected, over £300 has been collected by boys and girls and so, by whatever other name it may be known by Europeans or Africans, to me it will always be the First Children's Church in Central Africa.'

In November 1926 Dr Algie saw encouraging signs of progress in Ruanda. Despite all the 'enemy action' which they encountered, 'The outstanding feature of the past three months to my mind has been the turn of the tide in Ruanda,' he reported. 'Under God the change has come since the visit to Uzumbura. Here at Gahini where our workers had been holding on with dogged determination, there is now new hope. My wife and I have come here on a month's visit to help to establish the medical work and to lend what aid we can.' With them came two builders, two brickmakers, a carpenter and eight new teachers. 'Our journey here was quite thrilling. On one section of the road we had to cross five rivers in flood. In one a porter slipped and dropped a precious suit case, full of books and photos and films, into the water; and in another we had to form a living chain across the torrent along which the porters were warily escorted.

'We were cordially received by the Belgian Délégué at Rukira, and he urged us to take openings which were awaiting us in many places entirely destitute of the Gospel. His evident friendliness and sympathy were a great cheer. The attitude of the chiefs is still what you might call shy. They are afraid that any show of friendliness towards us, as asking us to come to their villages, might be construed as having a political meaning. So it is a matter for great thankfulness that the Belgian officials are making the way open.' The Mission even had a Tutsi evangelist, Zekeriya

Masozera, in Gatsibu, the district Government centre between Gahini and Kabale.

Dr Algie, accompanied by Bert Jackson, then visited the Kagera region. Pursued by ticks, mosquitoes and the tsetse fly, one morning they woke to find that half the porters had abandoned camp in the middle of the night. Another day a sudden storm brought their tent about their ears and sent letters and papers flying into the long grass in the pouring rain. Such was the life of pioneer missionaries, and all recounted without any hint of surprise or complaint.

Concerned for four teachers who went to work in this unhealthy area, Bert Jackson and Kosiya Shalita revisited them a few weeks later. All had been ill. 'One a lad of about eighteen was a living skeleton and could hardly walk four yards without resting. Without quinine he could never have survived. I wanted to bring him back with us but he refused saying he was through the worst. In spite of this he had gathered twenty boys together and was teaching them in his hut. A wonderful example of pluck for a young Christian, who has but a bare saving knowledge of the Gospel; so young in the faith yet willing to suffer. People say the day of miracles is past! What but the miraculous power of Christ in that lad's life could keep him there', wrote Bert.

In November 1926, St Peter's church in Kabale was completed. As Veronica Madeley (née Guillebaud) remembered much later, 'Dr Sharp designed, built and erected the steeple — an amazing feat of engineering at that time. The erection of the steeple, so huge on the ground, so small in position, was a major operation with, of course, no cranes or mechanical help. I remember Dr Sharp in control of a big team of African helpers with scaffolding, ladders and ropes, and the thrill with which we watched the steeple, teetering to one side or another as directions were shouted by Dr Sharp, balanced on the slippery roof. But finally it came to rest in position and all the Africans gave a mighty yell of triumph.' The spire reached sixty feet from the ground. And Jack Warren, delighted with the achievement, commented, 'Only one service is to be held in the church before the consecration in June, and one that forms a climax above one's rosiest anticipation. I am to be married there on New Year's Day.'

On the 1st January 1927 the Rev Jack Warren was married in the church to Dr Kathleen Ardhill. Unfortunately, it started to pour with rain soon after the beginning of the service, which rendered the latter half almost inaudible. The service was in English except for the reading of the Bible which was in Luganda and the sermon, preached by Dr Algie in Lukiga. The reception arranged by Mrs Len in her garden was soaked. Happily the rain stopped by the end of the day and the 'happy pair drove off in their little car, decorated with hearts and arrows and "Just Married" with the time-honoured accompaniment of tin cans, wired on by the indefatigable best man, Capt Geoffrey Holmes.'

Returned from his honeymoon, Jack Warren reported on the progress of the Kigezi Boys' School at Kabale: 'It is a wonderful encouragement to me that of the four senior boys who have left the school since January, 1925, three are workers for God. One, Yeremiah Ziralushya, a Munyaruanda, from being second prefect became a junior master, and has been invaluable to me this last year. Erenesti Nyabegabo, a Muhororo, head prefect in 1926, starts a school among the Bahororo in Ruzumbura this month, and the third, Bulasio Lwampiri, a Munyaruanda, junior prefect in 1926, is starting a day-school in the Bufumbura district this month among his own people.'

Reinforcements for Jack Warren came when a Muganda missionary, the Rev Semei Mugandawasula, arrived to be his curate. He introduced himself in a letter to *Ruanda Notes*: 'I am your friend, who was sent to this country (Kigezi) to work for our Lord Christ. I was ordained deacon on April 25th, 1926 in the Bishop Tucker Memorial College, Mukono. I left Buganda on the 8th of May and reached Kigezi on the 8th June, together with my wife, named Victoria, but we had many troubles on the road.' It is interesting to hear from an African from one part of Uganda, who came to work in another about 300 miles away, and to read of his impressions in his letter: '(a) Hills and nothing but hills stretching everywhere; (b) Bitter cold exceeding that of Buganda and elsewhere; (c) The food, consisting of two kinds of flour, peas and beans and a few potatoes, but this food gives us no joy like that obtainable in Buganda. However, we look not for earthly joy, for ours is a heavenly joy in Christ Jesus.' Another Muganda missionary who arrived at the end of the year was Ham Lule, a Lay Reader, who while at the Bishop Tucker Memorial College volunteered for Ruanda. He and his young wife went straight to Kisoro, 'where he will be in charge of the work. He is eager to start his missionary activities and learn the language.'

Dr Len and Dr Algie travelled to Bufumbira at the beginning of 1927, and were very encouraged by the growth in the churches. The two doctors were never normally able to travel together, owing to the shortage of staff, and so were particularly pleased to be able to do this trip together, and to see the things they had prayed for ten years before, becoming fulfilled. On this trip, 'We spent hours at a number of places arguing with old heathen parents in efforts to keep Christian girls from being married to heathen — among the heathen it is all a question of how much they can get as a dowry. The dowry is usually a number of goats, and these the parents may demand years in advance, indeed the whole lot may have been eaten years before the girl is old enough to be married.

'Bufumbira is a country of great hills and lakes, but high above them all rise the Mufumbiro mountains. Three of these great mountains are on the British border, and one called Mt. Sabinyo forms the boundary pillar where Ruanda, the Congo and Uganda meet. Sabinyo means "father of teeth" from its jagged summit, blown to pieces in an eruption long ago. We determined to try and climb Sabinyo, if possible, though attempts by others had so far failed. On the second day we reached the summit of the mountain, though not its highest peak, and we had some magnificent views from about 12,000 ft. How small everything of earth looked on the mountain top, the hills that troubled us yesterday appeared as nothing, and we could see into the furthest distance. So it can be with our spirits. There is a place where all the vexations that troubled us yesterday are found to be nothing, and from which we can look at the face of him who will welcome us home when our safari on earth is over.'

The following month, February 1927, Geoffrey Holmes announced the good news of 'the official sanction by the Belgian Government of Gahini, and their permission for us to go ahead and develop the work. This is a wonderful answer to our prayers, and a further sign that God has his hand on this work here in Belgian Ruanda.'

In May 1927, Dr and Mrs Algie together with nurse Beatrice Martin, visited Belgian Ruanda. At Gahini they laid the foundations of a new hospital on the excellent site overlooking Lake Mohazi. At the Government post of Gatsibu, north of Gahini, with the good will of the Belgian Administrator, 'We took Perezi Senyabatwa and his wife Tezera, an ex-hospital girl, to start a small dispensary there. They seemed to enter into their work full of the joy of the Lord. Perezi is supported by the contributions of the patients in our hospital, who have been stirred for those in need who have no helper. It would have touched your hearts as it touched ours to see, at the hospital service, when we first had the collection for this work, one poor old woman, her face mutilated beyond recognition  by disease, coming forward to put in her little mite for the healing of others.' Captain Holmes visited Gatsibu when he could leave Gahini.

'We camped at Nyagasiga, halfway between Gatsibu and Gahini, where lives the dancing troupe of one of the biggest chiefs in the country. Here a Mukiga teacher, Stefano Lukwira is installed, and has just started a most hopeful work. These dancers called *intore* are all young lads, trained to the highest pitch of physical fitness in war-dances and jumping. The leader of these young bloods is the champion high jumper of Ruanda, and we went to see him jump. He cleared 7 feet 10 inches, taking off from a small ant hill. I reckoned that his actual jump was 6 feet 4 inches, and he can do better than that. Four of these young lads about 16-18 years old are really anxious to learn of Jesus, but it will only be possible in the face of fierce opposition.

'We visited a very gracious lady, Nyirabalera by name, an African princess in manner and appearance. She and her handmaids gave my wife and Miss Martin a most attentive hearing to the Gospel. Three little girls from among them accompanied my wife for miles along the road learning some simple choruses, and a few facts of the love of Jesus. Sad to think that for all these women and girls there is no woman worker.'

Meanwhile, Dr Len was delivered from almost certain death. 'Returning from the sleeping sickness area, early one morning we had seen many tracks of lions in the wet grass, then the game scout pointed out the tracks of a very large lion, which he and I decided to follow, accompanied by two or three men, while Esther went on to find a suitable camping site. We followed the lion's tracks to a clump of elephant grass when suddenly it leapt out and bounded away, waving its tail, and into more high grass. We followed it again, and then suddenly, there it was crouching low, just in front of me. The lion sprang with its mouth open and claws ready. I fired at it at the same time as it knocked me down. The bullet went straight through its open mouth into its head. It sprang right over me and landed on the man behind. I was on the ground but it had not hurt me, but I felt at that moment that an angel had put his hand over me. But it was on the next man and I heard his call for help. I got up quickly. I could not find my gun so I snatched my second gun from the man who was carrying it. The poor fellow was lying with the lion on top of him holding him with his head in its mouth, a terrible sight. He said, "Shoot it, my friend" which I did. He had some bad wounds, so I tore up my shirt and we bandaged him as best we could, then breaking and binding branches together we carried him to where Esther had already camped.

'It must have been a terrible shock to her to see the wounded man carried in, and I dare say that from a distance she had wondered if it was me. He was a Christian called John. We got out all the things needed to treat him, but he said, "Let us thank God now before you do my dressings", so we did. It was a good testimony to his deliverance, but I am afraid that in those days

I ran a lot of risks which I should not have done, and caused a lot of anxiety to Esther which was not right. The man made a good recovery but it was a horrid moment to see this lion coming straight for me. I felt that a hand had been put over me, and it is really an unusual thing to be attacked by a lion and yet not be wounded.'

The last month of 1927 saw the eagerly awaited arrival of a doctor for Gahini, Dr Joe Church, a newly qualified doctor who had offered for missionary service while Dr Algie had been on leave and on being accepted had taken a Tropical Diseases Course in Brussels, where he had stayed with M. Anet. Joe Church then spent five months at Kabale for an introduction to the work with the two doctors.

Five years after the work began at Kabale, Dr Len again spelled out their objectives and noted, with great thankfulness to God, the progress that had been made. On the medical side, he said, 'The Gospel stories lead us to think that the Lord Jesus Christ gave many hours a day to relieving suffering. He not only thought it worthwhile but he could not see suffering without relieving it. The aims of the Medical side of the Mission are:

To relieve as much suffering as possible.

To draw people under the influence of the Gospel who would never think of going to a village school.

To house and care for the incurable and dying so that they finish their last weeks and months in hospital where the daily uplifting of Jesus Christ as the Saviour may draw their hearts to trust in him.

By healing the sick to help break down barriers of opposition to mission work in general. To fulfil these aims our policy is:

To build hospitals at the main stations.

To establish dispensaries (cottage hospitals) under African dressers at sub-centres.

To undertake medical itinerations in which sub-centres can be visited and many out-of-the-way villages reached with medical help, where native medicines and witch doctors hold sway.

'In the Ruanda Medical Mission we have at present one large hospital in Kigezi and two dispensaries in Ruanda staffed by Christian dressers trained in Kigezi Hospital. These dispensaries are at Gahini Mission Station and at Gatsibu Belgian Government Station, and a third dispensary is to be started at once at Rukira Belgian Government Station. In addition to these strictly Mission dispensaries the last three years have seen the opening of four cottage hospitals in the Kigezi district, which although supported by the Government, are under our medical control and relieve an immense amount of suffering.'

There were Church centres in most of the regional areas and they were benefiting from pastoral visits and from the training of evangelists at Kabale. Schools for boys at Kabale, Kisoro and Rukira were well attended but facilities for girls' education faced problems from parents reluctant to let their daughters attend school. Encouraging initiatives had been taken in the translation of the Scriptures and the production of other Christian literature.

1 *Meg Guillebaud, Ruanda p.24*

## Chapter 8

# An open door
# but many adversaries
## 1928

'A great door for effective work has opened to me, and there are many who oppose me', quoted Dr Len seven years after God had begun to open that door in 1921. (1 Cor.16.9) The period from 1928 was marked by two significant features: the great visible social and spiritual progress of the people of Kigezi and Ruanda, and the great power of the adversary the Devil.

'There is really only one adversary, the Devil, but he works through many channels to close the door of opportunity, or so entangle our feet that we fail to enter in, or hinder one another from entering in. God has wonderfully blessed his work in Ruanda, but we can only hope to enter successfully this open door if the Holy

Spirit is made our guide, and his wisdom and his companion-
ship our daily experience. The Devil can only be defeated in the
lives of the African Christians, and in our own, by the power and
presence of the Spirit of Jesus within us. Let us unite in seeking
a fresh anointing for ourselves and fresh outpouring of the Holy
Spirit on his work in Kigezi and Ruanda.'

One sadness was that Jack Warren was taken seriously ill
again and had to be invalided to Britain. He had recovered wonderfully from his serious illness soon after arriving at Kabale,
but 'his enthusiastic and conscientious nature did not allow him
to spare himself. The prayers of us all will go out in sympathy
with them, that God may be pleased to restore him once again,
and plan his future for him.' The arrival of a recruit, the Rev
Lawrence Barham to carry on Jack Warren's vision was a great
encouragement to them all.

Surprising events were reported at this time, with people
coming in thousands to hear the Gospel. Old men and women,
mothers with babies on their backs, and young girls and boys
began gathering in many places in Rukiga. As Dr Algie told the
story, 'There is a little village far off the beaten track in a valley
ringed round with precipitous hills... where lived a woman, fairly
young in years, but who had already sold herself to the practice
of the occult arts, and was frequented by the local inhabitants as
a witch doctor of some power.' He went on to tell how one night
she woke up at midnight and said to her husband, 'Let us go and
worship God.' 'Are you mad?' he said. 'What have you to do with
the worship?' In the morning she went off with her husband to
the local chief, where she said again, apparently almost in the
language of the possessed, that she was going to follow Jesus;
and she exhorted all the people to do the same. They said to her,
'What do you know about Jesus?' And she replied, 'Was it not he
that came to call me at midnight?' She then began threatening
her devotees with dire punishment if they did not go to worship.
As a result, she was hauled before the District Commissioner.
He asked her if she were a teacher; and she replied, 'We are all
teachers, all who know God must tell of him.' So with a caution

that she should refrain from violence, she was allowed to go, and carried on as before, exhorting all her people to come to worship God.

Dr Algie commented on these developments: 'Towards the end of February, we had our week of prayer in which many of you at home were pleading with us for an outpouring of the Holy Spirit. One week later, our native workers began to get reports of increased attendances at the churches; and this has continued until the present time. One of our native clergy two weeks ago went out visiting, and at one important centre he had over 1000 people at the morning service; and the next Sunday at another main centre over 1,100'. Dr Algie went on to describe how, just as in the time of Jesus the crowds sat on the grass and he fed them, so these great crowds were gathering in the open air to be fed with the Bread of life, as the churches were utterly inadequate to hold them. 'We most urgently need your prayers and thanksgivings. To those of you who pleaded with us in February, this news will come as a cause for humble and adoring thankfulness, that he should have so wonderfully heard our prayers. But it is a movement fraught with great spiritual danger. We need to plead that the whole work may be guided and controlled and energized by the Spirit of God.'

From the beginning of the work in Kigezi, the doctors were aware of the power of evil. In one case a severely burnt boy, the only survivor of a terrible case of arson, was brought to the hospital. His father, one of the teachers returning from his local church council, saw his house in flames across the valley. As he tore up the hill in the darkness, to his horror he saw his wife struggle out with their baby in her arms, only to be thrust back by a man outside, and when he got there the murderer was gone, leaving his home, wife and baby a charred ruin.

'Nyabingi is the most powerful of the evil spirits the people worship here, and the people attribute great power to her witch doctors and sorcerers', explained Dr Len. 'A Christian here, if true to his Lord, has to contend with the fear of witchcraft and the power of Nyabingi. These things may be no terror to us, but for generations here they have spelt life and death.' One person who made a lone stand against witchcraft was Eriya Muzungu, a teacher, and the only baptized Christian in a distant village given over to witchcraft and drink. He had denounced a heathen seance, and had also been threatened with death by witchcraft for opposing the chief's sacrifice to devils,

On another occasion a plot was hatching in a lonely valley on the shores of Lake Bunyoni, and would have matured in three days, in the shape of hundreds of thousands of devil-inflamed Bakiga armed with spears swooping down on us and the Government station... This plot was revealed by one of our evangelists, Abraham, who reported it to a young Christian chief called Zabuloni. These two with the help of others, made a surprise visit at dawn and captured 70 people including the witch doctor himself. Nothing can shake our faith in Christ's power to save and keep.'

This power to save was demonstrated in the lives of two Batutsi male nurses from the Gahini area, who were converted and baptized while working in Kabale and who wrote this testimony: 'We are so glad to have the joy of writing this letter to you. In the first place we confess that we left our country very wicked men, not knowing God who loves. We found the Bakiga preaching to their countrymen, and then you preached to us the gospel of Salvation through Jesus. We find that he is more beautiful than anything. Further, Sir, we know that any man who has tasted the words of God must go to preach to his countrymen that Jesus is our Saviour. It is in our hearts to draw our own people, who speak our language, out of the darkness of death and Nyabingi, and we want to tell them how we have found that the word of God is true.' Soon these two young men, Eriya and Erifazi, would move on to work in the new hospital at Gahini.

New missionaries usually spent a few months with the doctors, who introduced them to the medical and church work, gave them a start in language study, and shared their vision of medically-led evangelism. So in April Dr Church went with Dr Algie visiting churches in the Bufumbura district, marvelling as they went at the view from Behungi ridge over the mass of extinct craters, said to be one of the most wonderful sights in the world. At night beside the campfire they sang songs and hymns with Joe's ukulele and talked with the men sitting all around in the darkness. They visited the Kisoro School and many of the churches dotted here and there, each with its little community of readers and Christians. Over 100 were present at one little church on Good Friday morning when Dr Smith spoke. Then a week or two later Joe set off by motorbike for Lake Edward where Dr Sharp was on safari. Punted down a rapid river in a shaky canoe, he was stunned by the beauty of the pale blue shimmering surface of the lake, with hundreds of pelicans and kingfishers around the sandy shores, while, forty miles away, towering up on the other side, were the Rwenzori mountains, the snow-capped summits buried in cloud.

Dr Len wrote, 'Dr Church joined me on safari and we saw many elephants. There was one with a single huge left tusk; it was a rogue, having been injured fighting another elephant. It was very aggressive and bad tempered and I knew it had killed a chief a while before, so I was determined to kill it. We followed it up and down some steep places and were coming up a very steep incline, not being specially quiet as we did not think it was near, when suddenly I looked up and saw the elephant above us at the top of the hill waiting for us. It gave a scream and started down the hill. It is very difficult indeed to shoot an elephant when it is straight in front of you. Its skull is one mass of bone. I fired in the hope of stopping him somehow but it came straight on. My friend dodged behind a tree and all the men with us disappeared into the bush and I was knocked down. Mercifully it was rushing down hill so fast that it could not stop and went by into the valley below. My friend fired a bullet at it as it went by. We could hear it crashing around breaking branches in the valley.... The men warned us against going down to there as it was too dangerous and was a killer. But we knew it was wounded so had to follow it up next day. We found it standing by a tree and so I fired killing it. Remember the promises of Jesus to keep us from evil, and in the Lord's Prayer to pray "Keep me from evil." He can keep us and he has purposes for us. As his children we want to fulfil these purposes because we belong to him. 2 Timothy 1.9 reads "God has called you and saved you according to his purpose in Christ Jesus." That means he has a purpose for us all.'

The tusk was over 6 feet long and weighed 82lbs. Missionaries' personal circumstances differed, but for Dr Len, ivory was seen as a special provision from God and its sale used for many vital necessities, such as the education of his children or replacement of a car.

With Dr Len and Joe Church back at Kabale, Dr Algie and Rev Lawrence Barham visited the district in which the movement begun by a sorceress was drawing thousands to worship. 'Great crowds came at nearly every church we visited' wrote Dr Algie. 'We arrived at a place called Kitanga, the home of the fine young chief, Andereya Lugasira, in a triumphal procession of nearly a thousand people. The change in the attitude of the people was most striking in contrast to our safaris in early days. Then they would not go a step out of their way to see us, and now in some places women cultivating in the fields would throw down their hoes, snatch up their babies, and come running across the fields to greet us as we passed. Andereya said they would do that for no one, European or chief, except for the preachers of the Gospel.

'The movement is largely among the old people and women, proving that no case is too hard for the Lord, not even a grey-haired old granny, bound sixty years or more in Satan's thrall. It was thrilling to see these old people learning the catechism, and getting a grasp of the way of salvation, which many of the younger adherents had not got. Nothing could have wrought this change but the power of the Holy Spirit.' (In Africa at that time, it was usually the men who would gather in groups and respond to new ideas).

'There is a man in one of the villages we came to, a patriarch with grey hair. He has four wives, fourteen daughters and five sons; every evening and morning he leads his family in worship to the Throne of Grace. In another village there is a young lad of about seventeen years of age who has been deaf and dumb since birth. He has, of course, never heard a word of any language, nor expressed himself by an intelligible sound, and yet he is an intelligent lad, and does everything in the home and in the field like the rest of his family. And he is said to be a convert, and the other Christians think he ought to be baptized. They speak to him by signs and he is a never failing attendant at the little village church and copies all the movements of the others. It seems difficult to understand, but who can say that some whisper of the "still small voice" may not have made itself heard in the empty silences of his heart.

'To attempt to meet this great opportunity, and ensure as far as possible that they hear the simple Gospel of a present salvation, we have been sending out volunteer preachers to most of the churches each Sunday, picked out from among the maturer Christians. Each Thursday Dr Sharp has been teaching on simple Gospel subjects, and so God's word has been proclaimed in almost all these crowded churches.

'It is not often that one is given such a handy illustration for a talk as we had at one church we came to. I had wondered whether to speak on John 3.16 or on Zaccheus. The people came to sit out on the grass, for there was no room for them inside. Just as they were sitting down, a section of the crowd suddenly jumped up with cries of "Snake!" The offender was soon dispatched with a stick, and it turned out to be a very deadly snake, red in colour, rarely seen in Rukiga, and I suppose a close relative of the fiery serpent in the wilderness. It took only a moment to hook it over a pole and give out the text, "As Moses lifted up the serpent in the wilderness, even so must the Son of Man be lifted up." (John 3.14) I have hardly ever had a more attentive audience. Many of them said that it seemed as if God had specially spoken to them that day.'

Mrs Len and Mrs Algie concentrated on work among the women and girls. At Kabale a women's meeting was held every week on Mondays in the old thatched church. A visitor — Mrs Stather Hunt — described it, 'I went with Mrs Sharp to a mothers' meeting. There were about thirty of them there, mostly with infants, so far as I could make out each was clad in two skins. Most of them had about thirty thin wire bracelets on each arm and even more on their legs. After the meeting the main topic of conversation was the arrival of triplets in the hospital. There were two girls and a boy, weighing 6 lbs, 6 lbs, and 5 lbs. Mother and family all well!'

Zöe Stanley Smith had introduced the Mothers' Union to Kigezi and described its progress: 'There are about twelve regular members, the majority of whom have come from Miss Hornby's school. We meet each Wednesday afternoon, and any who come by 2.30 sit and sew until 3 pm when the meeting begins. We sit in an informal circle, and after prayer and a hymn, there is a short Bible talk, and then we have open prayer for any who like to take part. Very often we have scattered members coming in from the villages. Some of them have classes on other days for the heathen women around; but we long to see a real burning love for the souls of others among these young Christians. It is there in some but others, alas, are only lukewarm. These young wives keep their homes and babies beautifully clean in comparison with their heathen sisters who live in utter filth and misery.'

It had been planned that Dr and Mrs Algie would accompany Dr Church to Gahini in Ruanda, but as Dr Algie wrote, 'Time after time our plans for going down to Gahini were frustrated, first by Mr Warren's illness, and then by heavy rain. The roads in April were reported impassable, and on the very day we had intended to go, the bridge over the river that drains all Rukiga was swept away in a torrent of flood-waters. The reason of it all was made clear, when about three weeks ago my wife was taken ill with acute appendicitis. Here at Kabale she was treated with all possible skill by Dr Cook and Dr Sharp, and thank God she is now convalescent. But had we been at Gahini, we would have been alone, cut off from outside help, with no facilities for operation, and absolutely no skilled assistance nearer than ten days away. The possibilities of such a situation make one shudder to contemplate. But God's mercy endures for ever. We have never felt more his nearness than at this time of trial and anxiety.'

So on 1st June 1928, Dr Joe Church set off from Kabale without Dr Algie as planned, to establish a medical work at Gahini, taking over the hospital building and medical work from Bert Jackson, leaving Bert to concentrate on church work and boys' school building. In July Dr Algie and Zöe joined them there, and found the work at Gahini had been brought almost to a standstill by famine. Unlike the hilly Kigezi district where there had been heavy rains and flooding, here almost all the crops had failed for two rainy seasons, so Dr and Mrs Algie stayed at Gahini helping to relieve the situation. It was a very hard time, which brought Joe to the verge of despair. Sickened with horror at the state of the people, he wrote asking for help in the local Press, an appeal which was taken up by The Times newspaper in London. He was grateful for the response, and to 'the Stanley Smiths, who gave five months of unstinted brotherly love to us'.

Dr Algie himself described, 'The whole work in Ruanda is being haunted by the spectre of famine. Two seasons' crops have practically failed and our hopes that now the rain would fall and save these hungry multitudes from still more hopeless destitution seem, at Gahini at any rate, destined to be disappointed. You have to live in a famine area, besieged all day and every day by starving women with their emaciated babies; and then to see day by day, when rain should fall, blue skies and clouds without rain, the crops sprouting only to wither away, to appreciate what famine means. The Belgian Government has risen to the occasion and is sending us tons of food a week to save the worst of the famine victims; and more than 400 people a day, all desperately hungry, are being saved from certain death. Under such conditions the work generally has of course suffered; but in the village churches there are not lacking signs of the working of God's Spirit. At Gahini the hungry crowds are daily being fed with the Bread of Life; and it has given my wife the opportunity of starting work among the women.'

From there in November, Dr Algie wrote: 'Dr Church and Capt Holmes have both been wounded by leopards, fortunately not seriously. Dr Church was called out to kill a leopard which had been responsible for many lives at a village near Gahini; and though he wounded it badly, it got him down and, but for the courage of Kosiya Shalita, it would have badly mauled him. As it was, Kosiya got the leopard off him, and gave him the chance to shoot it dead. The manager of the tin mines near by, Mr Newport, came to the rescue, and took him on an epic ride in a lorry without brakes or lights all night to Kabale. Twice on the journey the car ran back downhill, and they all had to jump for their lives. Thanks to my wife's thorough cleansing of the wounds here and careful treatment at Kabale, he has made a splendid recovery.

'Capt. Holmes at Gatsibu went out after a leopard which had attacked a little lad and mortally wounded him. But it tricked him in some rocky country, and attacked him at short range. His wounds too, though deep are healing fast. Hunting leopards is dangerous work; but no man who can shoot, could refuse to risk even life itself to save these helpless people, children mostly, from such a treacherous foe.' Dr Len also commented on an unusually large number of cases brought to Kigezi Hospital of patients attacked by wild animals: 'We have had three men mauled by lions, one girl and three men wounded by leopards (one of the latter being our brother, Joe Church) and one man ripped by a wild boar. I am thankful to say that all have made good recoveries. But for Kigezi Hospital they could not have done so. Our beautiful new operating table has just arrived and is the last word in convenience for every kind of operation.'

When going on safari again in October, Dr Len was asked to locate a grave in Kinkizi. 'We had been asked to erect a bronze tablet and tomb to the memory of Bernard de Watteville, father of the authoress of *Out of the Blue*, a recent and fascinating book on African adventure. De Watteville was killed by a lion and buried under a tree by his daughter, who then alone in the wilds found her way back to Kabale and subsequently wrote her book. We were punted in a small fleet of most rickety and leaky canoes, the boards of which were tied together with native string, along the shores of Lake Edward. Our safety at numerous places was threatened by large schools of pugnacious hippopotami. At other times we were creeping along silently in the hope of approaching near enough to elephants or buffaloes to obtain good photos.

'We found the grave "out in the blue" and there, with the help of the cement we had brought for the purpose, made a rugged but durable memorial to a very brave man, and it was fitting that while camped there our sleep should have been constantly disturbed by the roaring of lions on all sides of us as they sought their meat from God, and by the moan of hyenas and the horrible noise of hippos fighting quite close to the camp. Mercifully the children slept through the noises of the night and so were not frightened.

'On our way back we had great difficulty in keeping the hippopotami away from our frail craft, but the children took the great beasts as a matter of course and were quite happy, not realizing the danger. We had also to face a considerable storm which made landing through the breakers a risky affair, but we got ashore damp but intact. The hippos seemed innumerable and were quite prepared to resent our invasion of their home waters. Alas ! My beautiful Airdale fell a victim to one of these great lake monsters. He was fearless in hunting all forms of game, even buffalo and lion, and we had great difficulty in holding him in the boat when hippos approached. He longed to go for them in defence of his master, and when at last he had his chance he bit his giant enemy in the tail and ear, before he was engulfed in those terrible jaws from which rescue must always be too late.

> "Constant to do his master's will, eat simple food,
> Boundless in courage, love and gratitude,
> Happy the man if there be any such
> Of whom his epitaph can say so much."'

Regardless of his own safety, Dr Len plunged into the water in an attempt to save his dog, but when pulling it from the hippo's jaws, he found it was already dead. Sadly, Fatty's little mate had to be led away, frequently turning to look back as the journey continued, and she died a few days later from a broken heart.

What were they like, these two doctors who shared the same vision and who complemented each other so well? John Bikangaga, who had first met the doctors as a young man in 1927, observed that he did not see much of Dr Algie's work as he was in Ruanda a great deal, but he knew Dr Len well. 'Their characters were very different,' he said, 'but they combined so well. Algie was a public relations person and Len seemed to be a worker, whether it was his medical work or putting up buildings, or dreaming, planning something. One the diplomat, and the other doing the work. The Africans found it easy to get to know Algie but harder with Len because he was quiet. You had to know him well. Once you became friends, you stuck. Len was completely loyal to his friends.'

Veronica Madeley (née Guillebaud) recalled, 'As a child I think that we knew Dr Len, (as we were allowed to call him) better than Dr Algie as the Sharps' house was nearer than the Stanley Smiths'. Dr Len had a very dry sense of humour and never talked down to us children. I know that I liked him very much. He was always so kind and interested if we asked him questions. Mrs Len was very warm and loving to us children and used to talk to us and take trouble to see what interested us. I remember she took me and my twin sister to see the beautiful little grave in the centre of the station, of her son Robin who died soon after they arrived there.

'Dr Algie was one of the humblest men I have ever known. He was so able, so gifted, so loved but he never assumed or pushed. He would defer to others far less qualified on many occasions. I have heard him talking to his grandchildren just off to school — talking so naturally of the things that really matter. This was always in the forefront of his life — the desire to draw others to Christ. It showed in his face.'

Mr Ken Jones remembered similarly of Dr Len: 'He had a great sense of humour, always a sparkle in his eye. His focus was on Christ, he radiated faith and sound wisdom. I remember talking to him about young people, and he said, "Tell them about

Jesus: who he is, what he said, what he did." We felt it a great privilege to meet and get to know a great man of God.'

Canon Bill Butler knew Algie well: 'I first met Dr Algie just forty years ago at one of the very first Ruanda Conferences ever held in England. I was a raw young missionary recruit at the time, feeling somewhat strange and overawed by the company in which I found myself. Dr Algie typically went out of his way to make me feel welcomed and wanted and part of the "family".

'Later I came to appreciate his encyclopaedic knowledge of Bantu languages, used almost to the day of his death. He was never seen to better advantage (and how few there are of whom this can be said!) than in his own home, with his beloved wife and helpmeet Zöe, who so perfectly complemented him. Always one met with the same loving joyous welcome, the sense of being really wanted and appreciated, and loyally backed through thick and thin. No mention of Dr Algie would be complete which failed to take into account his puckish sense of humour, or his tremendous energy and vitality. More than anything else, he will be remembered for his Christ-centredness and Christ-likeness, whose love, courtesy and humility he unconsciously reflected.'

Dr and Mrs Len loved animals, and always had dogs besides a variety of other creatures. On Dr Len's first tour when in Toro district in Uganda, he owned a monkey. His monkeys were always called Cuss. This one was named Wee John Jamieson Cuss after the Bishop. When Dr Len was posted to Mbarara in 1916 he reared a lion cub, but this he had to put to sleep when he left as he heard that others would shoot it once he moved from the town. Other pets over the years included a leopard cub reared by one of his bitches, cats, baby otters, monkeys, small buck and a civet cat. At Matana he had two donkeys for his children and Mrs Len kept rabbits, chickens, turkeys, ducks and pigs.

Dr Len's Irish wolfhounds enjoyed a cabin to themselves on the voyage back to East Africa in 1930 after being almost washed out of their cages during a storm in the Bay of Biscay. These dogs were the first of the breed in East Africa and they were much sought after by many for their courage and fearless attacks on leopards. The last of Len's dogs, two small Jack Russells were killed by a puff adder on his veranda one evening at Mombasa, causing much sorrow.

Dr and Mrs Algie returned to Kabale from Gahini on Christmas Eve to take over from Dr and Mrs Sharp who were due to go on leave in February the following year. There was much to discuss and pray about before they left.

# Chapter 9

# Jesus, Master, have mercy on us
## 1929-1932

News reached Kabale that the Rev John E L Warren ('Jack') had died on the 20th January, 1929. A memorial service was held in the Church at Kabale which he did so much to build. Hundreds of people came from the surrounding villages to show their appreciation of his work for them, which had overtaxed his strength.

From the time the doctors arrived at Kabale, an ever-increasing number of people with leprosy had been coming for help. Soon they were treating an average of 30 with the latest methods and drugs available, and as the hospital developed, a ward was set aside for them. But large numbers in Kigezi District, estimated to be about 2000, were beyond the reach of treatment and were also constantly infecting their children and neighbours. The thought of all this misery challenged the doctors to meet the need by providing a separate leprosy hospital.

Six miles from Kabale, on Lake Bunyoni, were many islands, one large and some smaller ones, all of which were uninhabited. The largest island, Bwama, had a sinister past as a centre for the cult of the female evil spirit Nyabingi, and a witch doctor named Ndabagera had lived there. About six years before the doctors' arrival, a rebellion took place in which Ndabagera was heavily involved. He and his followers had resisted capture by retiring to the islands taking all the lake canoes with them, and it was not until the police had secured a canoe and conveyed it by head porterage from a distant river, the Kagera, that law and order was restored. To prevent this happening again, the people were banished from the islands, which soon reverted to jungle, only the sacred Nyabingi trees still marking the sites of the frenzied orgies which used to take place there. This seemed to the doctors to be the place for a settlement, and if they could obtain the beautiful Bwama Island, with some of the smaller ones, they planned to build a hospital for 50 inpatients and large numbers of out patients; model villages where patients could live; a house for two missionaries, one a trained nurse; staff houses and a children's home and schools.

Patients would be selected after a full census and examination of all cases in Kigezi, and admission would be voluntary. All this needed careful planning, not only of the buildings but of boats, road transport and much else. Then after a preliminary survey of the extent of leprosy, Dr Len submitted the plans for consultation with the medical and administrative departments of the Uganda Government and also with the British Empire Leprosy Relief Association, B.E.L.R.A. The plans were approved and the site granted, with some initial financial grants. This development had a profound influence on the Africans as proof of God's power to overcome the forces of evil, and evidence of his love and mercy towards them.

One small island was selected for a doctor's house. Preparatory work on the construction of buildings began before Dr Len went on furlough in February 1929, confident that it would progress under the supervision of Dr Algie during his absence. And in March, at Kabale, a second son, James, was born to Dr and Mrs Algie.

In Ruanda, the New Year was dominated by the famine which taxed all the resources of the new centre at Gahini. Despite emergency supplies from the Belgian government, the situation around Gahini, as elsewhere in north Ruanda, was still desperate. The famine also affected Kigezi. As Dr Algie wrote in April 1929, 'The last three months have been "just carrying on". And this they faithfully did, coping with hordes of famine refugees from Ruanda, praying a devil-possessed woman to freedom, welcoming the all too rare thanks from a patient with the recognition that it was God who had healed him, 'for wasn't it he who gave you the wisdom?' and rejoicing in some social and spiritual progress among the people. Nonetheless, 'The work in Kigezi is passing through a time of testing...A good deal of what was unworthy and unspiritual has come to light, and many have fallen away. One realizes more than ever the utter worthlessness of any work which is not the work of the Holy Spirit. But the testing time is proving the reality of those who are true; and when they are tried, they shall come forth as gold.'

To give one example, 'As a fruit under God of the hospital work, we are happy over our ex-patient and hospital boy, Perezi by name, who had started a very hopeful work at Gatsibu. Owing to certain difficulties there however he had to leave the work, and went back to his home in Belgian Ruanda under the mountains near Lake Mulera. In due course he was given a small chieftainship, and there "he could not but speak the things which he had seen and heard". False accusers quickly reported this to the Government official of the district, saying that he wanted to entice them over to the British. The official, a most sympathetic administrator, sent for him and said that he had been told that Perezi was teaching them the words of the English. So Perezi said "No, it is not the religion of the English that I teach, but the religion of Jesus. You have in this country many heathen but they are free to practice their religion; there are Mohammedans too, and they are not stopped; there are Roman Catholics and Seventh Day Adventists, and they too are free to worship God. May I also not worship God in my way?" This simple pleading gained his ready consent, and Perezi is now witnessing for Christ in Mulera.'

On a further visit to Gahini, Dr Algie wrote: 'Every visit here makes one thank God for the evidence that slowly but surely the object of our Mission is being furthered. The incredible disappointments and hardships of more than a year of famine might have daunted the stoutest hearts; but not only have our workers hung on, but there is continual and definite progress in every part of the work, even though the gaunt spectre of famine is not yet wholly laid. It thrills me to see the prosperous little village beginning to spring up on the Mission concession, of people who have come for refuge and food to the missionaries, and whose huts are now dotted in delightful symmetry along the lake shore. May God send rain and so assure a fruitful harvest.'

Back in England on leave, Dr Len explained to supporters, in answer to their questions, that leprosy sufferers in Africa were very like those of Bible times; in need, in faith, in gratitude, and in service, they are the same, 'Jesus, Master, have mercy on us', being their cry; 'If thou wilt, thou canst make me clean', being still their prayer of faith. He explained, 'Leprosy is one of the most terrible diseases, which causes suffering with a combination of loathsome disfigurement and slow torture. Leprosy affects the skin with ugly patches, swollen lumps and sores: the eyes, the lips, the tongue, the throat; so that to eat, speak, or even to see causes pain. In addition the nerves are involved resulting in constant pain and as time goes on and they get paralysed, so does the hand or foot concerned lose its power, its sensibility and vitality. Then if gangrene sets in, the surgeon's knife is the only remedy. All cases are not so bad, others get worse until they long that death may end their sufferings.'

Hopes of finishing building work on the island were thwarted by a hostile official. He expressed doubts as to whether there was any leprosy in the district, and if so if it was necessary to do anything about it, and advised the team to find another site. Work was stopped as these questions were addressed. Dr Len returned from leave in April 1930, to find everything at a standstill.

In June, Kabale received a very welcome visit from Dr Albert Cook who noted: 'A marvellous change had come over the almost bare hillside that we saw at our first visit in September 1921, nearly nine years ago. Mr Lewin had done some useful and pioneer work in Kigezi in placing out teachers before this, but the extraordinarily fruitful work of the Kabale and the Ruanda Mission will be for ever associated with the names of Dr Sharp and Dr Stanley Smith, backed up, as they have been by the devoted labours of their wives and also Miss Connie Watney, Miss Hornby, Miss Martin, the late Mr Warren and many others.

'We wandered through the wards of the spacious hospital, and noticed the details that would hardly strike the casual visitor, but meant so much to our professional eyes: the operating room, the leper ward, the dispensary, the ingenuity underlying so many makeshifts, which told of every penny put to good use, the beds crowded together which told their own tale of the demand for room, as we noted the ingenious way in which a maximum of work could be performed by a minimum of staff. Then as we went higher up the hill, and saw the large church, and to the neighbouring spur of the mountain and went through the large girls' school, we could indeed thank God and take courage.' His assessment of Bwama was different, 'Here we came face to face with a serious check. The foundations of the nurses' house were laid and the hospital foundations were complete, but no busy hum of labour filled the air. The workmens' camp was laid out, but the workmen away. The answer was simple. Recent criticisms, based it seems on insufficient data, had induced the Government to suspend their grant, despite the fact that the special expert of B.E.L.R.A. had reported favourably.' Shortly after his visit, the restrictions were lifted, presumably due to his influence, and work resumed, a year later than planned.

Miss May Langley, a nurse for Bwama, arrived in May 1930 and she worked in Kigezi Hospital for seven months among the general patients and in the leprosy ward. As she described, 'Miss Martin went for her holiday about the middle of July, so I have been carrying on single-handed after barely two months. Naturally the language presents difficulties. ... I have a great admiration for Dr Sharp and it is a real pleasure to work with him. We have had a hectic time the last three weeks.... Last Sunday a terrible 4th degree burn turned up with her arm a mass of sepsis and heavy solid brass rings around, which we tried in vain to remove and eventually Dr Sharp spent the morning filing them off. She is progressing well.' Commenting on the leprosy patients in their own ward in Kigezi Hospital, she said, 'Frankly I have never seen such a collection of maimed, halt and disfigured humanity as were gathered for prayers in the leper block. Even I who love them for God's sake, shuddered: handless, footless, featureless and yet his children. ... On Saturday afternoon Dr Sharp took me to Bwama Island to see my house, it is looking splendid. He is hoping to start on the hospital soon.'

Having received news that the Governor of Ruanda-Urundi, whom they had recently visited, was in favour of the extension of the Mission work, the two doctors visited Ruanda in order to find and request sites for new mission centres. It had been arranged with Monsieur Anet that the Mission should continue to develop their stations in Central Ruanda to Lake Kivu, the hope being to open one new station in the North and one in the South. 'With this in view' wrote Dr Algie, 'we set out early in July, after having sent a letter to the new Governor who had succeeded M. Marzoratti, asking for his sanction, and hoping that he would take the same attitude as his predecessor.

'We went down by car. A whole series of facts combined to show us that God's time seemed to have arrived for advance in Ruanda, and that in the smallest details he had prepared the way before us. Firstly without any planning on our part we met the Governor twenty miles from Gahini, on a flying tour round the territory. And we would never have known of his proximity, if we had not heard of it on the very day he was passing by from a friend from Kampala who casually called on us at Gahini on a quite unexpected visit to Ruanda on business. Who was it that planned that the Governor from Usumbura 300 miles to the South, our friend from Kampala 300 miles to the North, and we from 100 miles to the West, should meet at that spot on that one day, and so pave the way for our journey of discovery under full Government sanction?

'Again our visit came at a time when a new motor road enabled us to pass right through N. W. Ruanda to the foot of the great mountain Karisimbi. It was a fascinating journey on what will become a first-class road, following mostly the tops of the hills, and so giving us in one day a comprehensive view of the country, which it would have taken us six days to cover by safari.' Travelling many miles through unknown country, delighted to meet a local chief whose brother had welcomed them at Gatsibu, trusting only God to guide them, and encouraged by their *Daily Light* verse one morning, 'I go to prepare a place for you', they found two seemingly perfect sites. Wisely Dr Algie observed, 'These two sites then are being asked for, but that does not necessarily mean that they will be granted. We must pray them through. But if ever we felt assured of God's guidance and goodness to our Mission, it is now; and what he has begun, he will finish.'

Dr and Mrs Stanley Smith went home on leave in September 1930, leaving responsibility for the two major developments of the year ahead with Dr Len. On their way, the boat stopped at Port Said. The family decided to have a picnic on a groyne that stretched out into the Red Sea. Suddenly there was a shout and a huge splash. 'Dad leapt fully clothed into the sea to scare away sharks', remembered Geoffrey, their son. 'I remember seeing his pith helmet sailing out to sea as he rescued Nora.'

After hearing nothing from the Governor about the sites after four months, Dr Len set off with Rev Laurence Barham in early November for Ruanda, as there seemed to be an opportunity of seeing him. Strangely enough they met him on the road twenty miles from Gahini where the doctors had previously met him in July! The Governor 'showed a strong disinclination to grant the sites and asked us to consider other sites.' So a fortnight later on

24th November Dr and Mrs Len set off again for Ruanda in search of new sites, accompanied this time by Rev and Mrs Harold Guillebaud and Joe Church. Together they travelled over 1000 miles in two and a half weeks. 'In the course of our journeys,' reported Dr Len, 'we were led to two new sites which appeared to us to be ideal and even better than those we chose before. We all feel that the opening of these two new stations (Shyira and Kigeme) is fraught with eternal consequences to the lives of thousands of heathen folk in Ruanda, and God only knows what a work of grace will be accomplished in the years to come, so let us all go on praying that this new venture of faith may exactly follow the line of God's plan from its beginning.'

Meanwhile preparations continued on Bwama Island as Miss Langley described, 'Dr Sharp and I spent a good deal of time on the leper island making a few improvements in the lighting of the house, etc. (I mean natural light, not electric light or gas), then I went down to see the sick people and lepers who are already visiting the island in great numbers, while Dr Sharp planned a woodshed and a boys' house, and readjusted the roof. He is a wonderful kind of person, engineer, builder, gardener, parson, agriculturist, physician, surgeon all rolled into one, truly a "Jack of all trades" and never seems to muddle them up or do them badly. On Monday evening the very first operations were performed under a tree — I wish it was in my power adequately to describe the picture as badly maimed men came up to have pieces of dead bone removed from feet so badly affected by this cruel disease as to cause death of the bone. It just makes one praise God for such opportunities of service.'

The great day that they had been eagerly waiting for arrived and on 3rd February 1931, the Settlement was opened. 'It is a great joy to have been able to open the hospital this month with over fifty patients,' Dr Len wrote ... 'I must say that whereas some people felt that they would be very unhappy marooned on an island, I have never seen them look so happy, and even the most croaky are demanding hoes that they may plant their own food patches, anxious that the stronger ones might get all the best

land first'. Nasaneri, without fingers, begged to be allowed to
ply a canoe in the lake for a month so that he could buy himself
a Bible.

May Langley wrote: 'Miss Horton and I have been here just
ten days. You can imagine the rush settling into our own house
and then receiving the lepers, who already seem to be coming
in with very little persuasion; from 30 to start with we are now
51, and at this rate will soon be 100. Five came in this morning.
My heart almost bled to behold their misery. One little lad about
eight years of age, terribly emaciated, terrified of everything and
everybody, turned out of home because he was a leper!'

Later Dr Len wrote that although, as with every other forward
move inspired by God to save the suffering and the lost, hostility
had arisen to hinder and if possible stop the work, the settlement
proved a success beyond his wildest dreams, and was being cop-
ied elsewhere in Uganda. 'At first I wondered whether I should
have 100 patients but the 100 came then 200, then more, 300,
then they rose to 400. Some people became alarmed but I praised
God for bringing them in and over 150 were children. What an
opportunity to win them for Christ and show that example of love
and self-sacrifice which Jesus commanded, "I have given you an
example, that you should do as I have done".'

The treatment of leprosy, mainly large doses of chaulmoogra
oil administered by injection, was a painful process. For it to
be effective, sufferers had to have regular treatment and this
meant they must live near the hospital. Following Dr Sharp's
plan, Bwama was developed as a settlement with huts arranged
in 'villages', the scrub on the lower reaches of the island being
removed and the ground cultivated by the patients for food. This
ensured some degree of home life, but meant that provision must
be made for the schooling of children, many of whom were free
from infection.

Some of the leprosy sufferers lived near the lakeshore and
among the hills around and so moving to Bwama was relatively
easy. Dr Sharp was quick to see that 'special measures were
necessary in order to bring the benefits of care and treatment

to the many living farther afield, those who through fear of the unknown or from physical infirmity could not venture on long journeys over the mountains without help. A booklet was printed in the vernacular, explaining the nature of the disease, how it was spread, and what could be done to help those suffering from it; a welcome was offered to all who would come to the island for treatment. Copies of this little book were issued to all chiefs, teachers and schools throughout Kigezi, and they proved very effective in arousing public opinion.' Government support was given by the provision of transport by litter for sick people unable to walk, and exemption from poll tax for those being treated on the island and for their carers. But the medical safaris to distant villages, when hundreds of needy people were seen, were the best way of discovering leprosy cases and winning people's confidence, so that new patients invariably resulted.

'I must tell you a little about the splendid staff of Christian men who are labouring together in this corner of Christ's vineyard', Dr Len wrote. 'Prayer is the mightiest influence that men can use…unseen but it produces immense results… what results one realizes when face to face with the reality of the change that Christianity has brought to these people. Our head dresser, Erenesti came to Bwama in 1931, leaving home, relatives, cultivation and friends, a real act of grace as both he and his wife were terrified of infection from this dread disease. They worked in the hospital and laboratory. Nekamiya, Erenesti's assistant, is very gentle and Christ-like. How Christ-like he is one does not realize until visiting his home and one finds his hut filled with sick folk, not lepers, but others who are suffering from various complaints and for which there is no accommodation in the hospital. Sooner than send them away, his hut is open to them. His wife feeds them while they receive treatment in the hospital. I asked him why? He replied "Isn't that the teaching of Jesus?" The lepers love him for his real out and out Christian life, his love for them and his desire to win them for our Saviour.'

'Much building is wearisome', wrote Dr Len, 'I often feel how nice it will be when our buildings are finished, but there seems no end.' In answer to criticism of his building programmes, he replied that it was not in the buildings, but in what could be done in them, that he rejoiced. In addition to the hospital under construction and the house for the two nurses, he built a doctor's house on a very small island near Bwama, which became known as Sharp's Island. They called the house The White Cottage, after his father's house in Shanklin, Isle of Wight.

Dr Len built many boats for Bwama Island, several large ones for the patients needs, one for the lady workers, a motor boat for the doctor, and another large outboard motor driven boat for a variety of requirements, named The Ark. In addition, he owned a small sailing boat made as early as 1923.

'I remember how they used to enjoy life on the lake. He was pleased with his boats, Algie was a powerful swimmer, and Len would drive his boats; all good fun.' said John Bikangaga. The doctors' children shared their birthday parties with their African friends and Grace Bikangaga was one of them: 'When you had birthdays we used to join you. Gifts would be hidden in the trees and whoever found them, kept them.' Another delight was a grassy bank which the children enjoyed, and even Bishop Willis was found taking his turn to roll down it, on one of his pastoral visits.

In England, while on leave in 1931, Dr Algie wrote: 'We have arrived at the third critical time in the history of the Mission. The first was at its commencement. Many doubted if the Mission was to be, but God brought it to pass, and sent us out for the evangelisation of Ruanda. The second crisis was about 5 years ago, when the fate of our work just begun at Gahini trembled in the balance, and few know how near it was to extinction. And now the third crisis is upon us. Are we to advance, or are we to be content to stay in our two stations, with two-thirds of Ruanda still unevangelised? In the faith that this advance is God's will for us, it was decided that I should go to Ruanda to help start the new stations; and I am taking the Brussels Tropical Medicine course for that end. A little difficult to go to school again at 40! We have staff to enable us to start these two new stations. The sites have been applied for, and the localities chosen have been agreed to by the Governor. It simply remains to go and choose on the spot the actual plot of ground which the Government can grant us. It is essential for the cause of Christ in Ruanda that we should go ahead, and there remains only one need to be supplied and that is the need of funds.'

There were still uncertainties about the granting of the sites, which made the missionaries realize afresh how they could not make progress without prayer. Their prayers were answered, for at the end of June Dr Len received another letter from the Governor suggesting that it might be possible to give the sites after all, if they were content with smaller plots of land, and taking Rev and Mrs Guillebaud with him they returned to Ruanda.

'So in July 1931 we set out again, trusting that this time God would prosper our way and give us good success. As before we motored to both sites, a journey of nearly 1000 miles, sleeping at nights in the cars and making what progress the rough roads allowed during the day. We were thankful for the dry weather, for some of the roads would have been unsafe during the rains. As it was, the only mishap was that Mrs Guillebaud's car fell through a bridge which had become rotten. Happily without harm to car or occupants.

'On the night we set out God gave me the promise, "I will send my Messenger and he shall prepare the way,"(Ex.23.20) and we were very conscious all through our journey that God was fulfilling that promise. At every Government centre we were treated most courteously, and at the actual sites the officials were kindness itself. Certainly the Messenger had been sent and had prepared the way.

'We were deeply touched at passing again through those densely populated regions in northern and southern Ruanda, as we realized afresh the unutterable need of these multitudes. At Shyira in the north the crowds of sick and suffering kept us occupied for hours. How could a Christian man or woman better spend the one life God has given them than in bringing light and life to these millions for whom Christ died? We got back to Kabale

at the end of July, having completed our fourth journey for the
sites, and having covered 3,000 miles in efforts to get them, and
now we are waiting for news and trusting to hear at any time of
a successful result. We have all been praying for these sites, but
we remember that they will bring fresh responsibilities to send the
Gospel, fresh opportunities to save the lost, and fresh privileges in
consecrating our lives and possessions. Our Mission is entering
a new period in its history; a period when financially and in other
ways it will be called upon to stand alone, as a distinct Mission
within the C.M.S. If our Mission is to go on advancing, and it
must do that, it can only do so by a living faith and prevailing
prayer. It must be a faith Mission in the truest sense.'

On 20th August 1931, Dr Len informed their friends in England, 'My wife and I rejoice to tell you that God has given us a
son, John. How good of him to give us back what he was pleased
to take from us ten years ago!' Little Dr Sharp, the Africans said!
Six months later, Esther wrote, 'Baby John is an all smiles baby
and scarcely ever cries. I am so very thankful to our Father for
this precious gift. He was baptized by the native clergyman with
Erisa Mutyaba's baby Rebeka, who Lawrence Barham baptized,
and Erisa stood godfather to John. We are all one in Christ Jesus,
and Erisa will really pray for the little fellow's conversion later
on. In your prayers for us do please remember the little ones who
make it home in this far away land.' Their children were taught
to pray from a very early age, and in 1931 were praying for a
baby brother, some puppies and a cat with two kittens. Dr Len did
not want a cat, and the children were told that not all prayers are
answered in the affirmative. In August John was born, followed
by puppies, and lastly in December a stranger called and asked,
'Can you give a home to my cat and two new-born kittens, as I'm
leaving the country'. With all their prayers answered so exactly,
the cat and kittens stayed.

At the end of the year, the two new sites, Shyira and Kigeme,
had both been granted, and Rev Jim Brazier left Kabale in December to represent the mission in Shyira, living in a tent, until
Rev Bert Jackson returned from UK leave in January 1932.

A few days after Jim's arrival he was joined by Dr Len for a two day visit 'to go over the concession seeing how the various departments would best be fitted in.' The Rev Geoffrey Holmes, still on leave, was to go to Kigeme in January 1932, pioneering once again.

The news of the Belgian approval of the new sites was received with great praise by the Ruanda Council, but there were financial difficulties. So far only about half of the sum required for new work at Shyira had been provided, and the Council were therefore unable to sanction the further expenditure necessary for Kigeme. When they heard this, all the missionaries at Kabale met together to consider and to pray, as a result of which they wrote home informing the Council that they were more convinced than ever that God's will was for them to go forward without delay at Kigeme, and that while continuing to pray for further gifts from friends at home, they themselves were prepared to make a sacrifice. They decided unanimously that all the members of the Mission should give one-seventh of their monthly salary for one year, starting in March, so that work at Kigeme could start. They added that it was a great joy to feel that they were counted worthy unitedly to share in the planting of the Cross at this new station.

'When we remember that the salaries paid to missionaries are really only maintenance allowances, calculated in accordance with the actual requirements of the field in which they work, it will not be difficult to imagine that this decision must inevitably involve very real sacrifice on the part of them all. Surely we at home, in the light of this noble example, must ask God what more we can do to back them up so that what the missionaries in the field feel to be God's will may be fully achieved', wrote Mr Webster, the Organising Secretary of the Ruanda Mission (CMS).

Dr & Mrs Stanley Smith returned to Uganda from leave in January 1932. 'Our journey out was a very happy one,' wrote Dr Algie, 'without any incident beyond the consciousness that God was making our journey easy in answer to many prayers from you at home. At Nairobi we had to part with Nora and Eve, who entered the splendid girls' school at Limuru, and for the first time in their lives were separated for any length of time from their mother. The great compensation lies in the fact that we can have them for the holidays.' It was a tough settlers' school, and missionaries' children were bullied. Nora and Eve started a Bible group there, and Nora's strength protected Eve.

Some time earlier Eve Stanley Smith had prayed, 'God bless Daddy and make him into a little pilgrim.' Her prayer was answered when Dr and Mrs Algie, though based in Kabale, spent most of the year visiting the centres in Ruanda one after another: Gahini, Shyira and Kigeme. Of Gahini, Dr Algie wrote: 'I cannot crowd into a letter anything like an adequate description of the work there. The hospital was full, and a great and deep work was going on there, and this in spite of the fact that the hospital is still far from finished. White ants have made great havoc and are now at last just getting under control. But it will require at least £50 to repair their damages and to put the finishing touches to the hospital, and so make it in appearance what it is already in fact, a work that we can be proud of. ...

'It was very impressive to me to come to Gahini and see its wonderful development in the eighteen months since I was last there. A really lovely church crowns the hill, and the whole of the girls' work has come into being. Almost every one of those 50 or more girls in the school has a story which would inspire you to hear, how they have in various ways been won out of darkness. They need above all to be kept by the power of God. Some of them won't go home for the holidays for fear that they won't get back.

'Then the Church work, in the face of strong opposition, is spreading out, and over fifty village churches are now established. There is a splendid spirit of courage and devotion and Christ-likeness among the teachers. One of them, when being cross-questioned by a priest, was reviled and hit across the face; news of the affair reached the ears of the authorities, and the case was tried. When the lad was awarded compensation for the assault, he refused it, coveting the honour of being smitten for him "who was wounded for his transgressions . . . and by whose stripes he was healed". (Isa.53)

'As soon as possible I came down to Kigeme, where Mr and Mrs Holmes are holding the fort alone. The last twenty-five miles of road is about as hair-raising as one could wish — not having much to raise, it didn't worry me much. It lies at an altitude of about 7,000 feet, and it is set in scenery of great beauty and grandeur. The hills rise steep and smooth from narrow valleys, and are carpeted with the most vivid living green I have ever seen. There is a fair population around the Mission site, and the country within a radius of three days' march is one of the most thickly populated parts of this populous country.

'I had expected to find our friends holding on in loneliness and trying to break down the intense suspicion and intrigue which had so struck us when we came to look for the sites. But in the few weeks since they have been here, all that has changed. The day after I arrived was Sunday, and nearly 200 people, mostly men of between 18 and 80, were present and were most responsive listeners. In the afternoon we went down to a valley about five miles away, and 1,500 feet below us, and wherever we passed the people came out to welcome us.

'It was delightful to see the way the women were drawn to Mrs Holmes. Already people are coming to us from villages three to eight miles away to ask for teachers. I had about 140 people as out-patients today, and proved once again how the medical work is, in God's hands, one of the best means we have of winning the people to hearing of the Gospel. Mr and Mrs Holmes are living in the cunningest little grass house imaginable, and I would need to be an artist to describe the charm and cosiness with which Mrs Holmes has adorned their simple home. I hope soon to go to Shyira, after a visit to Usumbura where I have to see the Governor and the *Medecin en Chef* about important matters connected with our work. But this will suffice to show you that the  opening we have prayed for so long has been granted, and we who are your ambassadors for Christ have begun to enter in, and are finding it true that "He it is that doth go before you."'

The leprosy residents soon settled down at Bwama. 'Those who are too ill or too maimed to look after themselves are cared for in the two airy spacious wards, one for men and one for women in the hospital. The rest live in comfortable little huts in two villages named Bethany and Samaria, with their families or friends, and they seem very happy. ... At present this is the newest branch of our Mission, and frankly perhaps I was a bit pessimistic as to its success, but the lepers seem so happy and new patients are coming to this refuge, so that now a new and third village, Galilee, is being built to accommodate them.'

One excitement, in April 1932, was the arrival of two R.A.F. seaplanes, which suddenly appeared over the hills flying at a great height, and then, swooping down, circled round Lake Bunyoni and over the leper island taking photographs. 'No aeroplanes had ever been over Kigezi before. At first they thought they were looking at great and unknown birds, but when they realized that there were people flying in the heaven, some of the Bakiga thought that it must be the Lord's return. The sudden and miraculous appearing of people in the sky flying with incredible speed and great noise did seem to them at first a sign of his coming.'

In May, everyone gathered for the presentation of watches to three boys who had showed great courage in rescuing their comrades when a storm swamped their canoe. The great event, however, which eclipsed everything, was the unexpected visit to the Island of His Majesty King Albert of the Belgians. King Albert was travelling incognito on a short holiday to visit that part of the Congo which borders Kigezi. He had flown from Brussels to Uganda and was returning, but his route home lay across Lake Bunyonyi and through Kabale.

'You can imagine the flutter of excitement that spread like wildfire through the island, when it was known that King Albert had disembarked from a native canoe and was anxious to see the hospital and leper villages. Miss Langley and Miss Horton received the King and showed him round. The King evinced a genuine interest in all that he saw and seemed particularly impressed with the happy expressions of the lepers, and remarked with surprise that so many lepers could be induced to live together like this on a voluntary basis. After signing the visitors' book the King returned to his camp across the water, and in the morning I had the privilege of conveying him and his party across the lake in our motorboat. The lepers will always remember him by his gracious and kindly manner. This sudden coming of a king was another reminder to all that in such an hour as we think not our King cometh! (Matt 24.42)

'Since last writing, fifty new lepers have migrated to the island. Some of these have come from having heard from friends of all the sympathy and care that they receive there; others have joined us as a result of a series of leprosy safaris. We have been greatly encouraged by all the happenings and developments of the last three months, but now we have had the news that Sister Horton has to leave us at the end of this year for family reasons. All will miss her greatly. Who is to take her place?'

Towards the end of 1932 Dr Len wrote: 'Both Kigezi Hospital and the Bunyonyi leper settlement have just come to the close of record years. Kigezi Hospital has tended more than ten thousand people as outpatients, all hearing of salvation through Christ. The wards have been crowded, a thousand having been treated as inpatients, where they have daily been shown the good things which the love of God has bountifully prepared for all those who respond to that love. The leprosy hospital and school have made remarkable progress in 1932. The number of lepers resident on the island has doubled. The hospital, in addition to the treatment of all the lepers, attended to the ailments of ten thousand outpatients annually who came to the island in their little canoes seeking help.

'The school also has steadily increased until there is no longer space in our one classroom for all our children and fresh buildings are required. We have 80 leper children as well as a number of untainted ones [healthy children of leper parents]. We hope during 1933 to be able to build and equip new school buildings which will meet the need of all. Last October we set off on safari round the villages in British Ruanda with the object of seeing as many lepers as possible, although many stayed in their huts and others were too weak to venture away from home. We saw about 60 ranging from infants in arms to very old people. Many of them were maimed and in a pitiable plight from the dreadful ravages of disease. About 30 of them have now, however, found refuge on the leper island.'

Mrs Len, writing on behalf of her single-handed husband, said that all 120 beds were full, so that with the leprosy work, as well as preaching, teaching, planning and accounts, he was unable to write his regular letter. Kigezi Hospital was also suffering a severe staff shortage. Now that Dr Algie was in Ruanda, Dr Len was the only doctor for Bwama Hospital and for Kigezi Hospital, now enlarged by its Asian and European beds - a new development made possible when the leprosy patients moved to Bwama. The message was, 'It is not possible for Dr Sharp to continue thus single-handed much longer — the burden is altogether too great, and the supply of another doctor and also a nurse for Kigezi Hospital is one of our most urgent needs.' Reinforcements were not expected before the end of the year.

Leprosy safari, 'Many, after a quiet talk, were only too glad to leave their misery ... and come to the Leprosy Mission. pg137

Welcome break on safari for Mrs Len and her daughters pg 137

Patients on arrival  pg136

Christmas at Bwama 1932

Kigezi Hospital 1932

Road to Ruanda

Searching for mission sites in Ruanda  pg133

Dr Len speaking to men at Shyira 1932  pg141

Sunday Service at Kigeme 1934
I had the privilege to preach to ... about 1500.' pg159

'Who would have conceived it possible that Mwambutsa, King of Burundi ...
would assist us choose our first site in Burundi.' pg160

Buhiga. Paul Muhutu & his wife
1935 & 2005 pg161

Buhiga. Titus Sempayore & his wife
1935 & 2005 pg161

Dr Algie & family at Kigeme
pg170

Start to occupy sites in Burundi 1935
Rev Kosiya Shalita & Dr Bill Church pg164

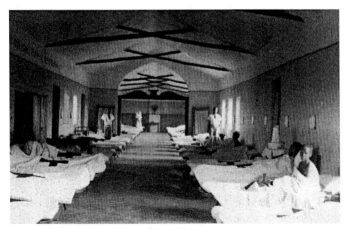

Matana Hospital opened 1936  pg176

Mwambutsa's dancers celebrate the opening of the hospital  pg176

Murundi
dancer

Temporary
wigwam theatre
Matana 1935

The lake built at Matana  pg176

Christ Church Matana 1939  pg183

Rev Kosiya Shalita

Sports at Matana

# Chapter 10

# And every victory won
## 1933 - 1938

Looking back to the start of the Mission twelve years earlier, Dr Len wrote in 1933, 'How could we guess or imagine that in twelve short years God would have brought into being a complete self-supporting Mission backed by a devoted Missionary Council and more than 5,000 praying Friends in England; that he would in twelve years have called out no less than 36 missionary workers for Kigezi and Ruanda; that there would be five mission stations, with evangelistic, medical and school work at each, and that he would bring thousands out of darkness to light, and of these raise up hundreds to be active witnesses for him.

'As we think of these and many other works of the Lord which we have seen and are seeing, our hearts are too full for words of praise, and we wonder how it has all happened. Our Lord speaks of faith as a grain of mustard seed, so small yet having within it power to grow and do great things. And I believe that this Ruanda Mission has been made to grow from such a little beginning only because God planted in the heart of each of us that little mustard seed of faith in him and faith in his word, which makes us love him and long to carry out his plans for a lost world.

"For every virtue we possess,
And every victory won,
And every thought of holiness
Are his alone."

'On November 9th of last year the C.M.S. Executive Committee approved the Ruanda Mission being constituted a separate self-administrating Mission within the C.M.S. The first meeting of our Mission Executive Committee under this new constitution was held at Gahini on February 9th, when we unitedly committed our future way into God's hands, claiming his promises to be with us all the days. This new constitution puts fresh responsibilities upon us, but we feel that these only bind us all together the closer in mutual dependence on one another, and on him who has cared for us so wonderfully these past twelve years.'

The ordination of the first Ruandan clergyman, Kosiya Shalita, took place in 1933. He himself describes this. 'God brought me to work in Kabale for a year, and now I am living in Gahini, which is about twenty-eight miles from my birthplace. Who knew that I was going to work to tell my own people near where I was born about God when I did not know him myself when I left the place? God knew that he would use me to do so, and he took me out of my own country for that purpose. He took me out for good, which my people called danger.'

Dr Len wrote, 'Kosiya, with the love of his own race in his blood, and the love of God in his heart, fought a great fight that his own people may come out of darkness into light. Early in 1928 Kosiya married Irene, one of Miss Hornby's girls, and in February, 1929, Noweri, their little boy, was born. In 1929, the famine year, Kosiya was in the thick of the grim fight. A little daughter Janeti was born in October, 1930. Surely God, who has so marvellously prepared his servant in many places through long years, has some great work for him to do. Perhaps the greatest of all, to lead, one by one, quietly and unobtrusively, men and women into the Kingdom of God.' (After serving God for many years in Ruanda and Urundi, Kosiya returned to Ankole, Uganda, where he was made Bishop of the Diocese of Ankole and Kigezi.)

Dr and Mrs Sharp remained at Kabale, responsible for Kigezi Hospital and the leprosy settlement, where the work continued to grow as more and more patients came to them for help. In September 1933, a reporter of the Uganda Herald visited Bwama. He was impressed, and reported: 'There was a fine school, playing fields, completely equipped hospital with several wards, native crops growing in abundance, goats, sheep, etc., in fact all the amenities of native village life. And the lepers themselves — they were forgetting their terrible affliction under the kindly ministration of Miss Langley, and actually they were living their usual normal village life, but at the same time they were apart from the rest of the world.

'The lepers come to this island voluntarily. Dr Sharp makes periodical trips into the hinterland, and the chiefs call up the lepers, then this Christian worker talks to them in their own language about the island and what it means to them and the future generation with the result that usually after a visit several lepers find their way to the island. The Native Government in Kigezi has long realized the great value of this work and do all they possibly can to help it along.

'Men and women, children and babies, lepers all, who in normal circumstances would be leading the life of outcasts, uncared for, neglected, and the very epitome of misery were here. But on Dr Sharp's island these poor creatures, to a large extent, had rehabilitated themselves. They had some definite interest in life, a will to live: they were all human beings although they were all suffering. Few people can have any idea of this work. It is not large in kind, yet it is of untold value — the saving of future generations. Dr Sharp, with that unfailing optimism of his and stoutness of heart, has overcome innumerable difficulties and objections, and now he has proved his case up to the hilt.'

'This work of compassion was made possible through the unselfish labours of those African Christians who offered to come and help us,' said Dr Len. 'As time went on many of the patients themselves learned to love the Saviour and took over the staffing of the hospital and schools.' He told, for example, of 'Sedulaka, hovering at death's door for months, who said, "Talk not to me of getting better but rather of heaven where I am going." 'He has lost his wife and has been giving his last remaining strength to teaching Biterahoga, a small boy of ten who lives with him, so well that he was top of his class last term. It will be Biterahoga's last term as he is very ill with lepra fever and will not live long, but it will be all right for him *over there* because Sedulaka was faithful. God used Paulo with his evangelist's zeal to cast out a devil in his home village and Nathanael, even more crippled, goes off in his little boat in all weathers twice a week, to a distant village where he was born, to teach his home people of Christ. When I visited him there, I found the tiny grass church absolutely crowded. All Nathanael's work — not all his, but the Holy Spirit's as well.'

In 1933, Dr and Mrs Stanley Smith moved to Kigeme. 'Here we are in our new home in Kigeme,' wrote Dr Algie in March 1933, 'built for us by Geoffrey Holmes and Chris Symonds, and, alas, not really occupied by them, after their year of cold and damp in a grass hut. It is exquisitely cosy. And what a work lies before us. Six flourishing out-stations, with crowds of seekers. Then we've got crowds of patients coming and the first part of the new hospital going up.'

In March 1934, Dr Sharp and Esther with their children Mary, Joy and John visited all the Mission centres in Ruanda: Shyira, Kigeme and Gahini. In his review of the trip, Dr Len wrote: 'From Kabale we motored to Kisenyi by the new road which climbs over ridges more than 8,000 ft. high and among the great volcanoes whose forests are the home of gorillas. From there we went to Shyira, which I had not seen for two years. Imagine our joy to be able to motor up by a newly made road to the top of Shyira hill and find there the healthy signs of Christian activity. We found the Rev and Mrs Jackson and little Ruth at their beautiful home, and already with a well-grown garden, the centre of quite a hive of happy work. On the one side the temporary church stands, with many coming daily to be taught the Way of Life. On another side is the beginning of medical work with a well-built dispensary, and further down the hill the boys' school with already 18 boarders, who, we pray, may one day be messengers for Christ among the countless villages which cover the hills and horizons in all directions.

'From Shyira we travelled south to Kigeme. Again, deep thankfulness to God at the sight of missionary houses and commencing hospital and school work. Dr Stanley Smith's fame as a physician and surgeon is fast spreading over the country, and important chiefs are coming from great distances for treatment. What a pity it seems that he has no adequate hospital for the full exercise of the skill which God has given him. Hundreds come for treatment every day. And the little ward is so crowded it is impossible to examine one patient without stepping over others. There is a spirit of great joy at Kigeme, and it is infectious, so that from further and further hills people are coming to ask for teachers who can bring them the same joyful news. On Sunday I had the privilege of speaking to a congregation of about 1,500 people gathered in the open, there being no room for them in any building.'

As Urundi is only about 30 miles as the crow flies from Kigeme, Dr Len and Dr Algie crossed the border and covered nearly 300 miles of Urundi roads in three days. Longing that the people of this beautiful and thickly populated area might also be reached with the Gospel, their tour led them into a determined effort to find suitable mission sites in Urundi: 'Should not our hearts burn within us, burn with shame that these people still do not know the way of salvation, burn with longing that the Ruanda mission might have twice its present income and missionaries to bring Christ to them?'

Dr and Mrs Len returned to Kigeme in June 1934 and then set off with Dr Algie, Kosiya Shalita and Samsoni, the translator, to search for and try and obtain sites in Urundi. 'We crossed over the Kanyaru river and, travelling south, reached Gitega, 108 miles, by tea-time. As we got out of the cars, in front of the very dirty little inn there, another car came for petrol, and the man who drove it was Mwambutsa, King of Urundi! This coincidence led to friendly relations and further contacts. After tea, we ran into the Administrator who proved to be an old acquaintance. He was friendly to our project and gave us advice which proved to be of the greatest value. The next day he kindly arranged for the King to go with us in our search for our southern site.' Very conscious of God's presence with them, 'from beginning to end of that two thousand mile tour we had a series of wonderful experiences of divine intervention and providence. For instance, who would have conceived it possible that Mwambutsa, the king of Urundi himself, should actually come and assist us choose our first site in Urundi? But so it was.'

The party drove along narrow winding roads until they reached what Dr Sharp referred to as a 'Batutsi plateau'. However every hill appeared occupied, with one exception called Matana. This proved to be a very suitable site for a mission station. As the doctors and the King stopped there, the people came running to greet them, especially as they saw their King in the party. Having eventually returned to Gitega and said goodbye to the King, the doctors returned to Matana next day and were warmly welcomed by the local people. They had prepared five small huts to receive them. The welcome was marred only by the removal of some important items from the doctors' baggage. Dr Algie's only suit of clothing and his false teeth were missing. On the Monday morning, the doctors travelled some 70 miles to the northeast. After looking at a number of possible sites, the most promising seemed to be Buhiga. A series of cascading waterfalls would supply water and a hydroelectric source of power. The doctors waited two days for the chief to come. 'To our amazement,' wrote Dr Sharp, 'he was quite willing for us to have the site we desired.'

Many years later, in February 2005, Dr Algie's son, Dr Geoffrey Stanley Smith visited Buhiga. Two men who had been in the crowds following the two doctors on their first visit told him their stories. 'One of those men was a very slight, short and malnourished Tutsi, with a withered arm, probably from childhood polio. His name was Fyoto, meaning sickly. Dr Algie had asked the crowd, "I am looking for a hill with lots of rocks and running water. I want to build a hospital." Stephen Fyoto immediately led him to such a hill — hoping for a magic cure for his arm. The hill was Buhiga. The doctor was unable to heal his arm, but Fyoto was captivated by the Gospel. He immediately responded to the Lord Jesus Christ, eventually becoming the first local Murundi Tutsi pastor at Buhiga, which was a Hutu area. Targeted years later by the Tutsi Government Army for ethnic cleansing, which was always followed by Hutu revenge attacks, Titus Sempayore, a Hutu pastor and Stephen Fyoto moved into our house with their families, welcoming in up to 40 people, young and old, Hutu and Tutsi, so that whoever came, Tutsi army or Hutu revenge killers, they were told, "We are all brothers and sisters." Now they are in heaven. Stephen Fyoto was the only Tutsi pastor who refused to flee.

The second was a very tall young man who had kept as close to Dr Algie as he could. Seventy years later Paul Muhutu came with his wife to see Geoff Stanley Smith on his visit. He recalled clearly Dr Algie's question, 'Do you know that the God in Heaven loves and hears our prayers?' Paul never forgot that truth, and throughout his long life it was crucial to his ministry in the young church at Buhiga, and was passed on to the next generation, as Geoff's story of Penelope shows: 'In 1955, twenty years later, I was posted to Buhiga, and a young married woman came to me complaining of sterility, in spite of medical help. Then on my recent visit in 2005, Penelope came to see me again reminding me that we had agreed to pray, as the medical help had failed. Soon she had had four children, and she never forgot the answer to prayer. She bled heavily after the 4th baby and required intravenous infusion, which became infected, and she was seriously ill. Her trials started as the ethnic conflict began. Her village was targeted by the army. Her husband was killed and her house ransacked and burnt, but she never forgot to pray. Gradually her infection improved, and the family managed to escape. Her testimony to the Lord's faithfulness in constant answers to prayer, food provided, shelter and protection from the army covered one cassette side as I recorded what she told me. Her song of thanksgiving and praise for answered prayers was unforgettable.'

Back in 1934 a letter had been received saying that the Mission would have to leave Kigeme and Shyira. This and the prospect of advance in Urundi led the doctors to arrange special daily prayer meetings. Quoting the biblical event when 'Moses held up his hands Israel prevailed, and when he let them down Amalek prevailed' (Ex 17.11), Dr Sharp wrote, 'We determined to obtain victory in all these by prayer.'. The doctors remained in Urundi to complete the formalities, anticipating a difficult interview with the Governor but found him very friendly. Not only were the sites granted but also the threats to Kigeme and Shyira were lifted. They returned to Ruanda with thankful hearts and wonder at the way God was in control in all they did.

In the early days at Kigeme the chiefs were reluctant to listen to the Gospel, but slowly this changed. Years later, Dr Algie wrote the biography of a great friend, Semugeshi, the paramount chief of the Kigeme area. The title was *'An African Nebuchadnezzar'*, since as Nebuchadnezzar fell into pride and lost everything, including his sanity, so Semugeshi fell into corruption, lost his status and wealth and went to prison. But for both of them there was hope. Dr Algie visited his friend in prison frequently, pleading with him to turn to Christ, and eventually he did. In the book Dr Algie quoted the hymn, which became his testimony,

> 'My chains fell off,
> My heart was free,
> I rose went forth,
> And followed Thee.' [1]

In August 1934 Dr and Mrs Len returned to England on leave and Dr Theo Goodchild, who had recently joined them, took over the medical responsibilities of Kigezi Hospital and the leprosy settlement. Travelling widely in the UK, bringing news of their work, 'It is with hearts deeply conscious of God's bountiful goodness, both to ourselves personally and to our Mission as a whole, that we have returned to England again after these four and a half years in Africa,' wrote Dr Len. 'We most thankfully record that these years have been to us among the happiest that God has given us, and they have certainly been blessed years of advance for the Gospel. But as we turn our thoughts back again to that great field of opportunity and need, and we think of all that waits to be done, we feel weighed down by the immensity of our uncompleted work. Our Lord Jesus Christ said, "My meat is to do the will of him that sent me, and to finish his work". We have but begun the work that he has given us to do.'

He then explained to supporters some of the realities of a pioneer mission, 'We start with getting a suitable site. This involves finding a place near plenty of people on good soil, with water, not occupied, free from native rights (which it never is). The chiefs and administrators must be willing to cede those rights (which they won't be to strangers). It means endless correspondence, exasperating delays, and repeated journeys only to have the whole thing wasted owing to R.C. intrigues. Having acquired sufficient French to cope with Belgian correspondence and sufficient native language to make yourself understood and able to teach, you can make a start.   The station must be carefully planned, roads made, buildings marked out...Hundreds of workmen obtained, controlled, trained, supervised and kept content, and daily taught from God's word... Trees, plants and flowers obtained and planted. The sick arrive before you have a hospital. At Kigeme hundreds come every day. Then they ask for teachers...

'Later will come attacks from the enemy with persecution of adherents and Christians by R.C. chiefs. People will lose their land, their cows, their position and attempts at redress will be unsuccessful. Slanders will be started against the missionary or prominent Christians to bring their name into disrepute among the natives or cause political trouble with the Belgians... In all these things patience, courage and endurance are needed.

'Attacks on the missionary which come from outside at least drive us to our knees and bind us together if we are loyal hearted. But dissension among missionaries, jealousies and disloyalties are the devil's favourite weapons, these and slackness in your personal walk with God. How many missions have these not ruined. We wrestle not against flesh and blood alone but against the prince of this world's darkness.' After emphasizing the necessity of absolute dependence on God through prayer, trust in him leading to contentment, loyalty to fellow workers, endurance and the willingness to be spent in God's service, Dr Len ended, ' Count the cost. There will certainly be weariness, loneliness and disappointment. There may be illness, pain. There may be bereavement, or an early grave. Face it. Is it worth it? And I would like here to add my testimony, that not one good thing has failed which the Lord spoke. He has been faithful to his promises. He has never failed me or left me alone.' [2]

The move into Buhiga and Matana in Urundi took place at the beginning of 1935, the pioneers this time being Dr Bill Church, Joe's brother, who had worked at Gahini for the previous four years, and the Rev Kosiya Shalita. The party, led by Dr Algie, spent the first night at Musema, a Danish Baptists' centre, where they were kindly welcomed by Mr Jensen whose hope was to develop work where a large population lived on the steep slopes of the escarpment leading down to Lake Tanganyika. They also met Mr Haley of the Free Methodists of Canada and Mr Chilson of the Friends. It appeared, then, that the Ruanda Mission would be working in Urundi with the Danish Baptists, the American Friends under Mr Chilson, and the Methodists under Mr Haley. This was something they were very thankful for, as all were closely united in the fundamentals.

At Buhiga, where Dr Bill Church was to be based, there was a good rest-camp, which he was allowed to use till his own house was finished. The next day Jim Brazier arrived on his motorbike, which he lent to Dr Bill, as it wasn't possible to manage the two bases, Buhiga and Matana, without some motor transport. They went over the site carefully, deciding where to place the first buildings, in line with Dr Sharp's plans. The same day a Roman Catholic priest arrived and camped on the same hill, having come post haste to Buhiga on learning of their arrival. He was not very welcoming, and sadly it was what they had come to expect. They then went on to Matana where Kosiya was left in charge. He had a tough time at first, in a tent, cold, wet and lonely. Soon he built a round brick house for himself, and a mud and wattle church as well as a school of grass. Several chiefs asked for village churches and he opened four village schools. His wife and family were able to join him after a few months.

Dr Algie reported, 'Next week we are going to a conference of all the protestant missionary societies working in Ruanda-Urundi, to prepare a statement of the difficulties under which protestants are working under the Belgian mandate. It is felt that such a statement coming from the united body of protestant missions working in the area would have more force than any sectional complaint. Whether the effort will have any effect is open to question. But I am quite sure that this first conference of all the missions should be a landmark in the history of the Ruanda work. If we can get together for spiritual fellowship and counsel, the whole work will begin to be knit together and will be greatly strengthened. We believe that we are on the threshold of a great forward move, though we are still so weak.' This meeting led to the formation of the Protestant Alliance, which included all the protestant missions working in Ruanda-Urundi. It provided invaluable co-operation, especially in translation work. Its secretary was the Danish missionary, Hans Jensen.

In August 1935, Dr and Mrs Sharp and John now aged 4, returned from the UK to work at Matana. There they joined Kosiya Shalita who had spent a pioneering year there. Before leaving, Esther Sharp left a farewell message: 'It was a great joy to see so many of you, and we are being upheld by your prayers and know that you will follow us all through the voyage and journey to our new home and work. We have left Mary and Joy at school, but are looking forward to being reunited in May, when they are (D.V.) coming out with a governess whom we feel sure God has prepared for our need, Miss Winifred Cox. The children will be with her at Christmas time, their first Christmas without us. When we said good-bye to them yesterday, Mary gave me

one of those texts that children paint: "I will not fail thee nor
forsake thee", and it has come to me as a message straight from
God.' (Deut. 31.3-8). The day before they left for Africa, the
gift of money for the construction of a hospital at Matana was
withdrawn through a misunderstanding, so they went, dependent
as always on God's provision.

With the coming of the Sharps and a Swiss nursing sister,
Berthe Ryf, the centre at Matana began to develop further. More
buildings soon went up and trees, lawns and flowers were planted
which, against the wide-stretching blue distance, were to make
Matana one of the most beautiful mission stations in the country.
Still evident today, but very much so in the early days, were the
gardens planned and laid out by Mrs Len, and her example was
followed in other places. Even Belgian officials commented on
the green lawns and colourful flower-beds of the protestant mission centres as compared with the wholly brick Roman Catholic
compounds. The greatly needed medical work met with such
a response that the first grass shack was soon hopelessly inadequate. The Belgian administrator visited Matana in the autumn
and asked when Dr Len would start building the hospital. Dr Len
replied in faith, 'In the middle of next year'. It was another two
months before the first seven shillings of the money needed for
a permanent building came from two little girls in England who,
having received a book at Christmas on the theme of giving a
tenth, entitled *Jill's Red Bag*, by Amy Le Feuvre, immediately
brought the tithe of their Christmas and birthday money 'to build
the hospital at Matana'.  When the story was told in *Ruanda
Notes* it was not long before the children's gift was multiplied a
thousandfold, and work on the hospital began in June 1936.

Dr Sharp wrote: 'Our journey from London to Matana occupied two months of almost continuous travel, of which the
journey from Mombasa to Matana, a distance of 2,000 miles, we
covered by car. We were greatly cheered during the few days we
spent at Kabale by the loving welcome back, and by the number
of keen Christians from the different departments of the work
who volunteered to go with us the long 400 miles from Kabale

to Matana. On the Sunday before our departure we were deeply touched by the service of farewell in the great Church, where all of us who were to go, were 'commended to the grace of God for the work to which he had called us.' We felt that we were doubly commissioned, first in England, and then by the young but living Church in Kigezi, where our life and home had been for nearly 15 years. These reinforcements for Matana have proved a great encouragement to Kosiya and his small band of teachers who have been holding the fort at Matana, and they will enable us to expand the work and spread the Gospel further abroad.

'So now we are here at Matana. Our home is a tent and a wigwam made of bamboos and grass. Life in this part of Urundi is still anything but peace and prosperity. There is a semi-famine and many people are just skin and bone — too weak to cultivate their crops or to work for wages. The children are the chief sufferers and we see them pathetically searching for and eating little roots of the weeds which grow among the grass. We are able to give milk to those who come to us, but we shall be very thankful when these people have enough food, which we hope may be in about six weeks. Our food stores are raided at night if not watched. These people are so wonderfully friendly and approachable, that it makes one long that their thought and affections might be turned to the unknown Saviour and Friend of their souls.'

He added, 'Sister Bertha Ryf has just joined us. It will be a great comfort to have her, as she is not only a nurse, but also speaks perfect French, and I now look forward to the time when I shall be able to understand and use this very necessary language.' This highlights an important factor in the work of the Ruanda Mission, the fact that as Dr Algie explained, 'With the exception of Kabale and the leper settlement all our work is in Belgian mandated territory, under the Administration of the Belgian Congo. We have to realize that we are guests of another Government, and socially all our work must be carried on in loyalty to it. It is no end of a strain to achieve this, and we still haven't got very far. The only language permissible in our schools is French.

Everything we can do to give our work a Belgian rather than a British setting is of value.' So it was a real triumph when they struggled to welcome the Chief Medical Officer to the strains of the *Brabançonne*, the Belgian National Anthem.

Dr Len did not say much about the housing situation, but the Rev Kosiya Shalita added interesting details: 'I am glad you do not see me in my brick house, while Dr and Mrs Sharp and young John and Miss Ryf are living in damp wigwams, draughty and full of ants; it is only that Spirit which was in Christ which makes them so happy as they are. One day rain surprised us by coming from the unusual side where these wigwams face; it is hard to explain what happened without being called an exaggerator. Now the doctor's house is on its way towards completion of the brick work.' Milk was brought to the missionaries' doors in pots each morning, but before accepting it, it was examined for pollution — smelt and specific gravity taken in case water had been added — then strained and boiled. On one occasion the milk brought to Bertha Ryf was decidedly pink, and on inquiring the cause the milkman replied scornfully, 'Everyone knows the water in the river is red at this time of the year!' (The African soil is a red brown and this is swept into the rivers in the rainy season). Even more alarming was the way the milk-gourds were sometimes washed — in cows' urine straight from the tap…

Prior to the arrival of missionaries at Matana, the RC priests had so frightened the people that they were reluctant to come near them. 'They were pygmies who would eat them' among other threats. This particular fear was soon proved false by the first missionaries they saw, Dr Len 6'2", Harold Guillebaud 6'3", Bishop Stuart 6'4"! However women were still shy. Mrs Len hung her full-length mirror at the entrance of their wigwam, and the antics of their pet monkey were an attraction. Accompanied by Irene Shalita, she used to visit the women in their homes. The women were fascinated by children who did not have curly black hair. Mary's and Joy's plaits were undone many times for them to handle. These small things helped to break down barriers.

In March, 1935, the Rev Arthur Pitt-Pitts, a friend of the two doctors since Cambridge days, was appointed to the dual post of

Archdeacon of Ruanda under the Bishop of Uganda, and also as Field Secretary of the Mission, with a view to steering Ruanda towards the ultimate goal of a separate diocese. That December, Dr Algie reported: 'These last 6 months have been perhaps the most important in the history of the Mission. First I would mention the fact that at last we have been given full liberty of religion by the Government. I tremble to think of the reams of execrable French I have written trying to get justice and true liberty for Protestantism in Ruanda. At length all the protestant missions united in a final memorandum to the Government exposing our difficulties, which, meeting with no response from Brussels, formed the basis of an Appeal to the Mandates Commission. This was prepared by the Home Councils and actually presented at Geneva. At the last moment we heard of the coming of the new Governor General of the Congo, Monsieur Ryckmans, and with one last hope of fixing things with the local Government in preference to any appeal outside, I cabled asking for the appeal to be withdrawn. On November 27th he met us, and in the frankest manner set all our anxieties at rest by a statement of policy which assured to us the fullest liberty.

'Then came the visit of our Archdeacon. With his great experience in Kenya he was able rapidly to get a grasp of the situation here. He has an astonishingly wide understanding, wholeheartedly in sympathy with the basis and purpose of the Ruanda Mission.The whole work now demands a man to lead it, free from the distractions of station work; and we look forward to his return next year. One felt that even his brief visit of inspection lifted a great burden off the shoulders of those who had been trying to direct the work till now. With this increased efficiency we are convinced of the urgency of increased expansion. North Urundi demands a station.' Dr Algie mentioned too the recent inter-missionary Conference of the five Protestant missions working in Urundi, rejoicing in their sharing in the one Faith whilst respecting one another's differences. 'For all these things we thank God and take courage.'

Christmas 1935 was a happy time for the Stanley Smith family, as Dr Algie explained, 'We had an unforgettable Christmas with the family all complete. When I think that I only saw my father on an average at intervals of seven years, it makes one realize what a wonderful privilege it is to be able to have one's children for the holidays.' Maybe it was this Christmas when, as Geoff Stanley Smith recalled, on the way home for the holidays 'The 800 mile journey (400 by train, 400 by car; a journey of about a week) was nearly over. We had a live turkey as it was Christmas. It was raining and late. Suddenly Dad saw a string across the road. He stopped just in time. The bridge was in the river. A passing African took a note to Mum. Nora climbed a tree with the turkey and tied it to a branch to stop a passing leopard having a snack. We children slept in the car and Dad underneath. In the morning our gardener brought a loaf and a bottle of milk, and a crowd of Africans sent by the local chief cut the right trees to make a bridge. Nora climbed the tree to get the turkey, then home at last!' Geoff remembered too 'the fun and games that brought happiness to all of us children, especially at Christmas time: archery, pillow fights on slippery pole, sack race, three-legged race, water bottle on head race, football etc. The archery once nearly led to disaster when an archer's arrow hit a post supporting the target and was deflected, hitting the left arm of a watching girl. It was only inches from her heart, but she was rushed into the hospital, the arrow removed and all was well.' This was one of many deliverances experienced by the Mission and by the families, including countless narrow escapes on the roads.

In many ways life was fun for the children of both doctors' families. Geoff Stanley Smith described a picnic place where a road was being cut through the jungle-covered mountains: 'Eve, Jim and I wandered down the road. Huge vines hung down from the giant trees. I thought it would be fun to swing out over the road and the canopy below it. Eve said she must do it first to see if it was safe. (What if it wasn't?) I was next, missed landing coming back, but was OK. Eve tried to stop Jim, "You might fall into the canopy and we would not find you!" Jim insisted and landed safely.'

There were problems: lack of privacy was one. The families were observed whatever they were doing. There was rarely any 'off-duty' unless they were able to take a holiday together in some distant place. And then, 'Our children! Here lies one of the greatest problems of the missionary calling. All of us have known the apprehension of taking children to Africa and the haunting thought of separation as they get older.' Through the generosity of friends the Sharps were able to have a governess from 1930-34 and from 1936-40, and in one way and another, with good schools in Nairobi or back in England, both families found that God met their needs.

And now it seemed that God was doing something new. 'It began, says Dr Stanley Smith, 'quietly and almost imperceptibly' among the African staff at Gahini hospital and in the deep brotherhood discovered in mutual confession by Dr Joe Church with two African teachers Blasio Kigozi and Yosiya Kinuka. In 1933 'Bible teams' had begun to go out from Gahini led by these three and by Blasio's brother, Simeoni Nsibambi, whom Church had first met at Mukono in 1929. In December 1935 Bishop Stuart invited a team from Gahini to lead a convention at Mukono. The missionaries' annual conference and retreat, and the retreat for African clergy in January 1936 both had 'the general subject of life-changing'. They felt themselves called, the bishop wrote, to self-examination about faith, prayer, preaching, and about bringing souls to Christ by individual work, visiting and open-air witness. In 1937, to mark the diamond jubilee of the CMS mission to Uganda, a campaign of evangelism was planned throughout the diocese. 'Messengers' were chosen in every parish and Canon Herbert was released from most of his other work to go round to every deanery and hold missions for clergy and teachers. Joe Church held a ten days mission at Mukono and three area missions for the chosen messengers. The staff and students of Bishop Tucker College, Mukono, took responsibility for the diocesan mission in two districts.

Revival is a spiritual renewal of believers by God, and is preceded by faithful prayer and Bible teaching, sometimes over a long period of time; it is also a time when unbelievers may be brought to faith in Christ. From Gahini, revival spread as men and women became convicted of sin and confessed their sins publicly with great emotion and distress. Whole congregations were sometimes trembling and weeping: other people saw visions or fell to the ground, and then found forgiveness and joy. There was renewed zeal to witness to others and a desire for fellowship and holiness. The revival had a revolutionary effect on many Africans. Festo Gakware had been a house servant for the Stanley Smith family. He married Julyana and was later ordained. He was 'saved' in the revival. 'I rushed home,' he said, 'and, for the next meal, laid the table for two.' When Julyana came in she asked him whom he had invited for the meal. 'From now on,' he replied, 'we will always feed together' a small sign of a great transformation in their husband and wife relationship due to Jesus entering their home. The two doctors welcomed the revival for which they had prayed so long.

Meanwhile Kigezi and Bwama hospitals had come under the care of Dr T Goodchild and Dr J Symonds and more nurses from England. At Bwama there were leper orderlies who, though infected themselves were devoting their lives to helping others in a more advanced state of leprosy. Outstanding among the hospital staff was Simeoni Ngiringuba, a Christian from Kigeme, where he was senior orderly in the hospital. To everyone's dismay, he contracted leprosy and was advised by Dr Algie to go to Bwama. His wife Edreda, who had been operated on for osteomylitis by Dr Algie and cured, refused to be parted so they went together to Bwama. They were welcomed by Miss Langley and given a house and land to cultivate. Simeoni became a valued member of staff at Bwama hospital. Six years later he was symptom free, but they felt that God wanted them to stay and continue their work. Simeoni and Edreda remained at Bwama until the 1950s when they moved to Urundi to help set up a leprosy centre there. Erisa had lived at Bwama since 1933 and was awarded a Certificate of Honour for 20 years of faithful service in the Coronation Honours list.

On 8 December 1936, Dr Len wrote, 'As we look back over the last twelve months we can indeed thank God and take courage at all that he has done here during this year. In every direction and in every branch of the work there has been blessing and progress. The revival work of the Holy Spirit, which has been so powerfully felt at the older stations has reached even to us and among our small community of Christians several have received very real blessing, some have confessed and made restitution and others are filled with fresh zeal for preaching and evangelizing among the Barundi. There is also, thank God, the beginning of an awakening among the Barundi themselves which shows itself in larger numbers coming to be taught and in appeals coming in from outlying parts for teachers to be sent to them.

'On the first Sunday of each month all the village congregations from far and near come into Matana for a special Gospel service. This gives us all a chance of seeing each other and also of making offerings for God's work, some giving small coins and others little offerings of food. It has been difficult to know how to find shelter for these increasing crowds in the rainy season, but this problem has now been solved for the time being by our being able to meet in the main wards of the new hospital which is now approaching completion. It was a great joy last Sunday to welcome into the hospital over 1,200 for our united service. Those who have so generously given for the building of Matana Hospital will rejoice with us that even before we could use it for the healing of the body, so many should be hearing the Gospel under its roof. It has been a big job, all the building this year: our house, then the hospital and Miss Ryf's house. Much time and constant supervision has had to be given, as you may imagine!

'The medical work has proved of the greatest value for, quite apart from its direct witness for Christ and relief of suffering, it has been the instrument which has most influenced chiefs and others in authority from an attitude of indifference and opposition to one of friendliness and helpfulness. Preaching the Gospel and healing the sick is the Christ-ordained way of reaching the hearts of mankind, and we have proved again and again that in following this method, especially in pioneer work, we have something supremely useful, which meets human need.

'On September 22nd, the Bishop of Uganda visited Matana and baptized the first ten Barundi converts. It was a great and joyful day for Matana. Great crowds gathered and several important chiefs were present. Of these ten young fellows, seven are at this moment among the hills preaching the Gospel to their fellow Barundi and teaching the children of Jesus Christ. It is this work of supreme importance — the evangelizing of Urundi — that I want you especially to think about. The missionary can do a little, but it is essentially the work of Christian Barundi and Banyarwanda. This week I have been out twice with Kosiya to villages about 20 miles away to see what we could do to meet their need. People from these villages had walked many miles to be taught and the evangelist who went to visit them wrote to me, 'I write to tell you that I have arrived here and find very many people who want to be taught. They are oppressed by Satan. I find people in great distress. I see how many they are and they are troubled. How can I leave them as they are? It cannot be right just to leave them. It hurts me. They must not be lost.'

Dr and Mrs Algie left for leave in the UK on 18th January 1937. Before leaving, Mrs Algie wrote, 'I know you will be glad to hear that the Lord is working in a special way still here and numbers are turning to him with all their hearts and are absolutely changed. There is a real conviction of sin and confession of it. One little girl came with tears and told me that she had stolen a long metal needle (used for making baskets) and she wanted to work for me to repay it. Another brought me an egg, saying that long ago I had paid her for five and she had given me only four. And, of course, in the case of grown-ups more serious things have been told. But everywhere there is a joy and fellowship unknown before. It reminds one of the days of which we read in Acts, so many seem to have had an actual vision of Christ, but there are still multitudes in the valley of decision (Joel 3.14), so do go on praying that this movement may spread throughout the land.'

A new development in 1937 was the opening of a new mission centre at Ibuye, in northern Urundi near the Ruanda border. Ten years earlier, while still at Kabale, Dr Len was sitting one day talking to several of his fellow-missionaries. Spread out between them was a map of Ruanda and Urundi. He pointed to a spot in the middle of the map where he thought a centre should be established to link up with others. This was Ibuye, and now in February 1937, the concession of the land having been granted, Captain Holmes and his wife, once more the pioneers, with Graham Hyslop, Mission accountant, came to occupy the hill and began building what came to be an important centre of the Ruanda Mission.

Two events, one in June and the other in July 1937 brought special joy to Dr Len and Esther.

'When I wrote my last letter we were being given the first drops of blessing before the shower. God had brought one by one to realize their personal need of the Saviour and we had had the joy of seeing these Barundi and Banyaruanda find salvation in Christ. But God had prepared a messenger to visit us at the very time when many at Matana were feeling the convincing power of the Holy Spirit in their hearts. An old friend of Ruanda, A.W. Baker, of Johannesburg, was with us for five or six days, preaching the Gospel by interpretation. On Sunday, June 13th, many came under deep conviction of sin and about 60 stayed on to the after-meeting, where one by one each confessed aloud to God and sought his mercy. Several of us had the great joy and privilege of explaining the Way of Salvation and inviting all to accept in faith Jesus as their own personal Saviour and find in accordance with his promise, pardon, peace and newness of life. Then, as we knelt again, we had the still greater joy of hearing each one after the other accept Christ for themselves and thank and praise him for his gifts of forgiveness and salvation. Never shall I forget June 13th. Truly Christ was exalted on that day among the heathen Barundi, and we were all able to enter into the joy of our Lord as he received so many lost sinners to himself and made them his.

'With so many young Christians just born again, it was most important that there should be no delay in feeding these lambs and helping them to grow in their new-found faith. Here again

God had prepared another messenger, Mrs Guillebaud, who with Kosiya gave time for the next two weeks to this important work.' As a result of this and another time of special blessing in November, it was decided to have evangelistic missions like this once or twice a year.

Then, 'On July 14th His Excellency the Governor of Ruanda-Urundi did us the honour of coming to Matana to open the new hospital officially. A number of important Belgian officials also came. The King of Urundi arrived and many of the most important chiefs accompanied by their war dancers in full dress. The ceremony consisted of a speech of welcome in French and Kirundi, an answering speech by the Governor in which he spoke very kindly of the Government's appreciation of the work of the Mission, and prayer by the Archdeacon. Then a bandage, stretched across the hospital porch, was cut by His Excellency and the hospital was inspected. The schoolboys and girls were also inspected and a fine demonstration of war dancing was given on the football field to the great enjoyment of the thousands of Barundi there.'

There was a small valley with a natural spring nearby which Dr Len realized could be a useful source of food if stocked with fish. It could also provide a pleasant place of recreation. To this end, he built a dam across the valley. The completion of the dam and the rising water level of the new lake was an object of local curiosity and amazement. Small tilapia fry were collected from Lake Tanganyika, and carefully transported to the lake at Matana. The overflow from the lake was used to run a small generator to charge 6 volt batteries. A home-made boat and a grassy space made a pleasant picnic site and the Sharp children learnt to swim there. While Dr Len was at Matana, cattle were not allowed to cross the dam but had to use a crossing lower down the valley, below the dam. As time went on and the Sharps were no longer there, lack of maintenance and failure to observe the regulation weakened the dam. Cattle were driven across it which resulted in its gradual destruction. One night, 25 years later, after heavy rain, the dam gave way and the water rushed down the valley leaving a trail of beautiful tilapia fish. A young VSO working at Matana at the time was so upset that he travelled 2,000 miles to Mombasa to ask Dr Len how it could be rebuilt. It was never done.

On 6th December 1937, Dr Sharp was taken seriously ill, and neither Dr Hindley nor Dr Bill Church could find the cause. Blood tests were negative. It was only after several weeks of fever and increasing weakness that Dr Len was able to diagnose himself from the pattern of his fever on the temperature chart as having relapsing fever - a tropical disease caused by a certain type of tick. It is extremely difficult to diagnose, and as Dr Len had already been through three increasingly severe cycles, a fourth would have killed him. Immediately life-saving treatment was given and he began to recover. However complications had occurred, great pain followed by paralysis of his arms, shoulders and part of his diaphragm.

At this time of crisis, Esther Sharp's mother, Mrs Macdonald died suddenly. 'It is just twelve years since Mrs Macdonald had to give up her work as Secretary and Treasurer and Editor of *Ruanda Notes*. She had then an acute attack of iritis and the doctors forbade her to touch the Ruanda work again. Up to that time the whole of the work on the home side of the Ruanda fellowship was done by Mrs Macdonald, and she gave practically her whole time and energy to it. Since then, though unable to take any active part, her interest and sympathy have been unfailing. We are thankful to know that she had not to face a long and painful illness.' wrote Mr Webster in *Ruanda Notes*.

On 25th March 1938 Dr Len wrote in pencil, 'I am afraid we all missed writing to the *Notes* in December, so you had no news, but that I was ill with relapsing fever. It is not very easy to learn the lessons which come through suffering, weakness and disappointment, but they are things we cannot learn when we feel full of life, strength and joyful achievement. I don't want to say more about myself, but I must say how deeply touched I have been by the many letters of loving sympathy which have been received from dear friends in England, who have helped us in our hour of need by prayer. We do thank you very much indeed and hope that you will continue to pray that, if it is God's will, I may be healed of the paralysis and weakness which persists in hands, arms, and shoulders. Also, I cannot leave this subject without acknowledging most gratefully the great debt I owe to those in the mission who have ministered to me and mine during the last three and a half months.'

Dr Len's condition required further treatment and on the advice of now, Sir Albert Cook, they left for UK in April, by sea-plane. Their journey home was hazardous. First at Athens bad weather prevented the flight over the mountains and when the pilot attempted it, flying through cloud, the sun suddenly came out to reveal they were flying straight at a mountainside! A quick U-turn was made and the plane returned to Athens. Two days later, a fuel stop was made at Bordeaux, and Dr Len was permitted to stay on board. Suddenly he smelt petrol, and aviation fluid was pouring down the inside of the cabin. In spite of the danger the pilot, anxious to get home, proceeded with the flight but took the precaution of seating the steward facing the passengers, in case one should light a cigarette. It was Dr and Mrs Len's first flight.

In March 1938, Dr Algie wrote from the UK, 'By the time you read this, I shall be on the way back to Ruanda. My work this time is to carry on with Mr Guillebaud's translation of the Bible into Lunyaruanda. It is a great privilege to be allowed to attempt it, and a heavy responsibility. We, who know Mr Guillebaud's work, realize how incapable I am of attaining his high standard; so I need more than ever the "wisdom that is from above". Added to that, I shall not have the advantage of having Samsoni as my native collaborator, for I hear he has dropped out of the work. A new man will have to be chosen. We must pray that the man chosen will be the one of God's choice, spiritually as well as mentally equipped for this exacting work.'

As they had decided that Zöe should remain in England to provide a home for their children, he continued, 'Many of you have been praying for my wife and me as the time of separation draws near. I can't tell you what we owe to your prayers. Day by day God has given us messages of comfort from his word. When you pray for us, will you remember our children for they, too, share in the testing. Nora is at home and hopes to come out eventually as a nurse. Eve and Jim are at school in Croydon, and Geoffrey is at Monkton Combe Junior School.'

After intensive treatment Dr Len's arms began to improve and Mrs Len wrote in July 1938, 'The knowledge of your prayers has been very precious to us during all these months, and we do want to thank you so much for them. They have been a wonderful help, and my husband is now much better but still some of the muscles are not making progress, though some of them are back almost to their normal strength, and we should still value your prayers for his perfect restoration if that is in the line of God's will. It may be that like St. Paul he may be left with a thorn in the flesh and will then find out still further the truth of the promise, "My grace is sufficient for thee, for my strength is made perfect in weakness." (2 Cor. 12.9). Anyhow he is wonderfully better and we have much to praise God for. Mary has arrived home (for schooling) and is a great comfort to us. Joy and John are still at Matana with Miss Cox and their Uncle Algie so we feel that they are in good hands, but you can imagine how we are longing to get back to them and our dear African home. We hope to start immediately after Christmas and to be quite fit by then.' But clouds were gathering at the start of the New Year.

1. See the tribute by Mrs Dolatiya Rutwe and An African Nebuchadnezzar
2. Rest of text in appendix

# Chapter 11

# Gathering clouds
## 1939 - 1945

Dr and Mrs Len returned to Africa with Mary at the beginning of January 1939. They had intended, reluctantly, to leave Mary in England for schooling, but the ominous signs of war and the possibility of years of separation changed their minds. Mary and Joy became boarders at Limuru Girls School, Nairobi, where their cousins had been, and John Sharp, Noweri and Janeti Shalita continued their lessons with Winifred Cox (later to be editorial secretary, Ruanda Mission).

As war loomed, spiritual clouds were gathering as well. The revival in Ruanda, which brought much blessing with many turning in faith to Christ, was experiencing problems. As with all great movements of the Spirit of God both before and since, where there is blessing there will be counter attacks by the devil causing disunity and division, and the Ruanda revival was no exception. Among the revivalists, many who were young in their faith insisted, in their enthusiasm for God, that their experiences at revival or on conversion must be the pattern for everyone. Many insisted that detailed, public confession of sin, demonstrated by tears and great emotion, was essential for conversion, and the key to deeper fellowship. In their zeal and concern for others, they pointed out their faults to them. In some cases this was a blessing, but it also led to false accusations, distress and potential harm. African Christians and missionaries alike became divided. As one missionary put it, the question was, whether people are 'building their lives on experiences or on daily union with Christ. At the end of the month all our evangelists are coming in and we want to make it a time of instruction, "not laying again the foundation of repentance from dead works and faith towards God." (Hebrews 6.1.)'

In January 1939, Dr Algie outlined the situation, 'As I look back over my diary for the last three months, by far the biggest item in it has been the stages towards reconciliation between the two parties in the Church. It has been extremely instructive. The two parties are the abaka or keenites on the one hand, and the 'orthodox', on the other. The one, fired with a great zeal for God born in the manifestations of his power in the revival, have no use for anything less than the really victorious life; while the other, seeing the dangers of extravagances, have felt that they had to be the custodians of sound doctrine. It should have been easy for the two to be complementary, but the devil has got them divided. The Abaka have been harsh in their dealings and their criticisms, and have tended towards the idea that only their party are real Christians. The orthodox have been resentful of criticism, quick to see the inconsistencies of the Abaka, sometimes only too obvious, and they have often sheltered behind their orthodoxy so as to go on comfortably at a low level of Christian living, and sometimes in secret sin. And both sides have indulged in definite misrepresentation of the other.

'Efforts by Europeans and native leaders at bringing about reconciliation have conspicuously failed. But the Lord is now doing what we have failed to do. The tide began to turn, when we learnt that it was only he who could do this, and that our part was to cease seeking to establish our own righteousness, but in real humility see how far we were from his ideal for us. If any of you doubt this read as I did John 7. 38. This overflowing spontaneous life is the promised result of believing in Jesus, where he so fills every part of our being that he can pour himself out through us to others. All of us who have been public school boys know the blighting effect of the public school spirit on any enthusiasm in religion. It simply isn't done! The outcome of this is an orthodox but dilettante form of Christianity, which is simply put to shame before the openness and keenness of these Africans. Lord, set us on fire again, and give us an enthusiasm which is inspired and controlled by the mind of Christ. I believe that we are near the end of these troubles; but don't pray that things may settle down. We never want to go back to the old complacency. Pray that the fire doesn't go out.'

When God is working in reviving power, many Christians sense a very powerful conviction of the holiness of God and a strong desire not to tolerate any sin, however seemingly trivial it may seem, either in themselves or in others. In themselves, there had to be repentance and a seeking for God's forgiveness. In others, there had to be 'light' where what was seen as sin in someone else was pointed out to them with the sincere prayer that they would repent and know God's forgiveness. In many instances the oneness which this concern for each other brought, resulted in very deep fellowship and this in turn led to the conversion of others. However, zeal in 'putting others in the light', needed to be tempered with discipline for two reasons. Firstly, no one could know another's thoughts, and outward expressions, such as public confession of sin, were not a sure guide as to another's spiritual experience, and, secondly, the act of 'being in the light' with another could easily appear as, and sometimes actually was, harsh criticism and false accusation.

On his return to Matana from sick leave in January, Dr Len had found much disunity. In May 1939, a request was made in *Ruanda Notes* from Ruanda office in England for prayer for 'Dr Sharp's efforts to establish peace among the African workers at Matana. Nowhere in the Mission has the revival movement caused such difficulties. However recently Dr Sharp got them all together and a new and more hopeful state of things is reported by him. By July, Dr Len wrote, 'In the early part of this year we felt rather like the faithless disciples in that little boat on Galilee, when the storm of wind descended upon them, and the waves beat into the ship. Waves of difficulty had arisen and winds of controversy had been raging for months both at Matana and indeed throughout the Mission. How could the little ship make progress in such a sea? But the Lord Jesus was in the boat. He answered your prayers and ours. He rebuked the wind and waves, and there was a great calm. We thank you for your prayers. And now for the last three or four months God has given us rest from these troubles, so that we have a new spirit of unity and trust and have been able to press forward.' The two doctors' calm and wise leadership had been essential at this difficult time.

A good deal of Dr Len's time that year was also spent supervising the building of a fair-sized church, to hold 2,000 people, to accommodate the huge crowds who came from about 50 smaller churches, once a month, for a united Service at Matana. Most people on the mission hill helped carry the bricks from the kiln to the church site, including the future Archbishop Samuel Sindamuka, then a schoolboy, and Dr Len's daughters.

Bill Church said of Dr Len, 'He was a born leader and pioneer. He was a man of vision and at the same time a man of action. He was sustained by a faith that was undaunted and he made light of difficulties. I found him a delightful companion. He had a great sense of humour, which was a saving grace amidst the stress of pioneer life. Often I saw him wipe his eyes after a good laugh. He was a clever mechanic, which skill he used in constructing vital equipment for boats, windmills for pumping water for Bwama and water wheels for generating electricity at Matana. He was a good and careful surgeon. I can picture him now standing on top of Matana Church tower directing the building of the turrets. A nurse arrived and shouted. He let down a string. The message came up, "Obstructed labour." He sent down a reply, "Cook instruments. Down in ten minutes."

'He had a deep knowledge and love of the word of God and used every opportunity to give systematic teaching in Rukiga and Kirundi. He wrote a small booklet called *Great Truths from God's Word*. This pocket sized booklet contained subject headings with a few supporting Bible references, to help evangelists prepare a range of basic Christian teaching for their villagers. It was first printed in Kirundi then in English, Rukiga and other African languages. (A Professor at Mukono Theological University still treasured his little copy, many years later in 2004.) 'When we faced difficult problems in committee, we came to rely greatly upon his judgement as he was a wise missionary statesman.' Bill Church added, 'In all these labours, Dr Len managed to maintain a balance. When on safaris he was in the habit of taking a week off for relaxation.' Len was aware that mission workers too needed a healthy balance in their busy lives, with times of recreation. He encouraged weekend breaks, picnics, sports and other activities. Wherever he worked a tennis court would be constructed, and these were popular with the missionaries and also as friendly contact with government officials. One Belgian who enjoyed tennis was dreaded by the lady missionary who partnered him, for his shouts of 'Quelle faiblesse' when a shot was missed as he rushed, poaching from side to side of the court.

The mission held their annual conference for missionary personel in July 1939 after which Dr Len wrote, 'Our 'Keswick Convention' at Kisenyi is just over. We all came oppressed by the knowledge that though God had granted stretches of sunlit water and calm patches here and there, yet as a mission we were passing through rougher seas and more threatening clouds than ever before. But again the Lord Jesus saw our need. He came into our midst and commanded peace. So we are returning to our stations with a new trust in him and in one another, and with renewed confidence that in spite of every difficulty, financial and otherwise, that may lie before us, he will fulfil his purposes through us in a united mission and Church, which the Evil One will not be permitted again to divide.'

The financial situation of the work was weakened by the war, but there was another difficulty. Much of the recent expansion had been made possible by a remarkable gift of £30,000, made in 1934 and payable in five annual sums of £6,000. By 1939 this sum was used up, without enough extra income being available to sustain the work. After much heart-searching, the decision was made at this conference to close Kigezi hospital, as a Government hospital was now open nearby, and so to free resources for the newer work in Ruanda and Burundi.

Despite their faith and optimism, the conference was a difficult one for all the leaders of the mission. Both doctors were marginalized, criticized and their efforts ignored. It was to be cause of deep distress and heartache in both couples. This situation was to last for many years, especially for Dr and Mrs Len. Both responded with love and forgiveness, prayer and patience for their friends and colleagues (Matt. 18.21-23), Dr Algie working to counsel and restore broken relationships and Dr Len, to encourage others and preach the gospel, teaching the importance of personal conversion and spiritual growth, and opening up the meaning of the great truths of God's word.

Immediately after the Conference, Dr and Mrs Len were miraculously protected from injury and possible death. They took a short break to a nearby Belgian game park, where they met a party of students with their professor. It was arranged that the next day the party should visit the game park and as they were short of transport Dr Sharp was asked to take his car and lead the party. Early next morning Dr Sharp found that the rim of the hub on one wheel had split away as though wrenched up with great force. No similar occurrence had ever been known or has been since, and no explanation could be found. The party set off without him, and were attacked by a lone elephant which charged the first car, which would have been Dr Sharp's, thrusting its tusks in and turning it over just as the professor was trying to escape out of the car on the other side. It broke both his legs. Hours later, the elephant was found dead of natural causes. Was it angelic intervention, Dr and Mrs Sharp wondered, behind the remarkable damage to his car wheel, which protected them from harm?

At Kabale Miss Hornby commented 'A wave of revival came here and the school did not miss it. These revivals are all right, but when you get people who work themselves up into a frantic state, I do not feel it right just to leave them unguided in such matters as singing hymns far into the night and attending prayer meetings at all sorts of times. To give an example, one teacher who was in charge of the dining room just came in for meals and then went off to pray. If you know anything about a community dining room, with 85 boarders and 14 day girls, you can imagine the state it was in, so I said to her, "The girls have not swept and tidied the dining room." She replied, "I've no eyes for this world, I only see the things of God." This sort of thing went on for 2 weeks. I felt inclined when pay-day came to say to her, "Of course you will not want your pay as it is of this world."' Similarly when one of the abaka, noticing that Dr Len did not confess his sins publicly and with tears, questioned whether he had been born again, his reply was firm: 'Young man, I was born again before you were born.' Dr Len was particularly encouraged when the church leaders at Matana realized that deep sighing during prayers was not, as some had begun to believe, evidence of the Holy Spirit, and they themselves, finding that the Bible did not teach this, put a stop to the practice.

Len was single-handed as doctor in charge of Matana, although his arms never fully recovered from his illness, and during long operations he sometimes needed a dresser on each side to support his arms, leaving his hands free to complete the job. From there he wrote in October 1939 to the supporters in the UK who were facing war, 'I think these days of trial and war have brought us nearer together. In past years we were always claiming your loving sympathy, help and prayers. Now we and the Barundi Christians feel we can help you by prayer for your comfort and protection, and so offer some small return for all you have done for us. The war means for us all a tightening of belts. But God uses these things to help us to grow in grace, and indeed this has already been apparent here. For, when our African brothers and sisters learned that they would be asked to share in carrying on God's work in reduced circumstances, they accepted this without grumble or complaint for Christ's sake. A striking sign of growth in grace. I believe these days of stringency will prove a blessing in many ways, not only in strengthening their trust in God's providence, but also in helping to make them more self-supporting, and more determined to grow their own crops instead of just buying food with their surplus wages. We arranged a Convention for our Evangelists and other Christians last week, which was very well attended, four to five hundred daily, though many had a long way to come each day and all had to provide their own food. Judging from the praise that went up on the last day it had proved a time of help and encouragement to many.'

Writing from Gahini, Dr Algie echoed Dr Len's concerns. 'The effect of the war out here was to put an immediate embargo on the export of English money. So the church has had to face up to (a) the certainty of being cut off from most of the financial help which they had been receiving, and (b) the possibility of losing many of its European leaders. Such a test must demonstrate the strength or the weakness of the foundations on which this very young church has been built. There is more than ever need for prayer for these African Christians, but there is a great deal to praise God for. All through the Mission, wages have been cut twenty per cent, in order to compensate for the fall in the value of the shilling. It has been accepted everywhere without a murmur.' He went on to say that where it seemed as though some churches would have to close as the teachers could not be paid, in practically every instance the teachers who had been told to leave the work had refused to leave their flock, and were going to carry on without pay. He was sure that the spiritual blessing of the revival had prepared the people to cope with the material testing.

The outbreak of the war ushered in a period of particular difficulties for missionary activity linked with Great Britain in every part of the world. Travelling overseas became severely restricted if not impossible, and the movement of funds from country to country was severely curtailed. In October 1939 Archdeacon Pitt-Pitts, the Field Secretary, hoped to fly to the UK for treatment of very painful arthritis of the spine, so severe that he could not sleep at night without sedatives, but since war had just broken out in Europe, Imperial Airways would take no passengers. Also, while in Kampala, he learnt that 'It is forbidden to take any money out of the Empire, and therefore we cannot touch any of the Mission money or our own money which is in the Bank in Kampala. The Manager, who was most sympathetic, promised to help me in every way possible. He saw at once the difficult position we were placed in, and he advised me to do two things, write to the CMS at home and get them to help, and go and see the Manager of the Belgian Bank in Usumbura and see how much he would allow us to over-draw our account till we could get permission to have our money.'

This led to many long, very painful and frustrating journeys between the two capitals for the Archdeacon. His work for a separate Diocese continued, and in January 1940 he was able to convene their first Diocesan conference, after which he went on holiday in Kenya. There he was suddenly taken ill and died of a blood chemistry imbalance on the 22nd March 1940. The Mission at home in Great Britain and in Africa was shocked to hear of the death of Archdeacon Arthur Pitt-Pitts, affectionately known as 'Pips'. It was a great loss to the Mission and a particularly sad personal loss to his friends. Sir Albert Cook paid tribute, 'Arthur Pitt-Pitts fulfilled St Paul's description of a true minister of God, "In much patience…in afflictions…in necessities…in distresses…in weariness…in painfulness." (2 Cor. 11.17). Doctors Len and Algie paid similar tribute to their old Cambridge friend, who had supported and encouraged them so faithfully in their work for God.

At Matana Esther ran a weekly shop, supplying a range of items for the needs of local people. She developed frequent debilitating migraines which continued to trouble her for several years. Writing from Matana in May 1940, Dr Len reported : 'At Christmas, at the consecration of the church at the end of January, and at Easter the church was absolutely crammed, including the aisles, the chancel, the vestry, the porch, the gallery, while others were at the doors and windows. A very moving spectacle to those who had the privilege of being present and who remembered the small beginnings of the work at Matana a few years ago.'

A Keswick Convention was held at Matana in August 1940 when Sin and Repentance, Salvation and Assurance, Temptation and Victory were the main subjects.

In August 1940, Dr Algie became Field Secretary of the Ruanda Mission — the Mission's official representative in Africa, based in Ibuye in Urundi. In this role, while awaiting the return of Zöe from the UK, he wrote: 'During the last three months I have been able to go round all the stations of the mission, and it has been a most inspiring experience. It is an amazing thing to think that with a war on, and the probability of diminishing resources, God has allowed our numbers to be increased by no fewer than eight, including the Guillebauds and Zöe, now on their way. We have the quiet conviction that God means us to carry on and to go ahead. We have had to face up to the possibility of home supplies being cut off, and I have found a wonderful unanimity in the way we should meet it if it comes. With most essential foods locally produced we could live on the land, and we reckon we could then keep going with no further outside gifts for a year. So we are in a land of peace and all necessary comforts. Meanwhile our African Christians are responding splendidly to the inevitable economies, and becoming increasingly self-supporting. The Danish Mission has given the whole Church here a splendid example. Cut off from all home supplies in April, their Church, spiritually prepared by the revival, immediately took on full self-support and has since then opened sixteen new village churches. Their increasing expansion compelled their courageous and resourceful missionaries to open boarding schools for boys and girls.

'I can't tell you how much it means to me to have the prospect of Zöe rejoining me in a few weeks. Two and a half years is a long time, and, apart from the joy of being together again, it is going to make all the difference to my work to have her with me.' Zöe sailed in convoy at the height of the U-boat attacks. She wrote, 'I do want to thank you all for your prayers which surrounded us

on the voyage of three weeks to the Cape, uneventful though we
were very conscious of our invisible convoy. I was marvellously
kept too on the long three thousand mile trip alone up country, by
train and river-steamer to where Algie met me at Albertville on
Lake Tanganyika.' She had written in her Bible, 'Perplexed but
not in despair. Sailed to join my darling. Put our four precious
children in God's hands.' Happy to be back in Africa again, she
witnessed to the peace God had given her as she trusted God's
promise for the children 'My Father who gave them me is greater
than all and no one is able to pluck them out of my Father's hand,'
(John 10.28-29). Each of them by now had responded personally
to God's call, and Zöe knew that he would look after them. But
the children remained very conscious too of their parents' love for
them. As Geoff remembered many years later, 'Because several
missionaries had joined up, Dad was doing several jobs, but he
never failed to answer Jim's letters full of questions. Mum wrote
to the rest of us regularly. All their letters were full of concern
for us, and no mention of the trials and difficulties that they were
going through came to us in England.'

Mr and Mrs Guillebaud were welcomed to Matana, after
several years in England. Harold Guillebaud took over as Archdeacon after the death of Arthur Pitt-Pitts, but in just over a year
he died of a heart attack, following acute bronchitis. Having translated the whole Ruanda New Testament previously, he had just
embarked on its translation into Kirundi. Quoting the words of
Jesus, 'I have given them thy word', Dr Algie wrote, 'What more
precious and fitting epitaph than this for Harold Guillebaud! God
had endowed Harold Guillebaud with an able and clear-thinking
mind; he had also a balanced and accurate way of expressing
his thoughts. These talents he consecrated to the service of his
Saviour. He gave to the peoples of Ruanda-Urundi, both present
and future generations, much of the Scriptures and many beautiful
hymns, besides other valuable books. What greater gifts could
he have bestowed upon them?' Harold's work on the Kirundi
Bible was taken over by his daughter Rosemary, while Dr Algie
continued translating the Ruanda Old Testament.

Dr Len's daughters Mary and Joy faced a 1,000 mile journey to Nairobi at the beginning and end of every school holiday, 600 miles by car to the railhead in Kampala then 400 by train. On one of these journeys, trying to cross a flooded river where there was no bridge, the car sank in the riverbed and the water rose to window level, flooding everything inside with swirling water and mud. With the help of men and ropes they got the car out, but all the machinery was full of mud and it took three days cleaning everything before they could proceed. Mary and Joy and other missionary children in the school faced bullying from the settler children. They were not at school long before Italy came into the war, and Italian propaganda led to fears of an invasion of Kenya from Abyssinia. They went back to Matana and continued school work there. Dr Len helped with their maths, and Lindesay Guillebaud with literature until they could return the following term.

In October 1941, Dr and Mrs Len spent two months at Kabale while Joe Church was away. 'After a lapse of seven years since we left the work at Kabale and the leper island, we have had the joy of returning to it... and so were able to meet many old friends. What struck me perhaps most was the evidence of God's grace among the lepers, many of whom through long years of pain and suffering have been kept with their faith in Christ strong and bright. There are many Africans who are readily moved by religious enthusiasm for a short time, and in time of testing fall away, but our Lord said "He who stands firm to the end will be saved". (Matt. 10.22.) Here we see the keeping power of the Lord Jesus over many years.'

At Matana there was encouragement, with over 100 children in the Sunday School, Mrs Guillebaud turning out hymn sheets on a printing machine, and Rosemary continuing the translation of the remaining half of the New Testament with the help of her father's Barundi collaborators. 'In August', Dr Len reported, 'a party of Christian workers from here, at the request of the neighbouring American Mission at Kayero, in Rutana, held a mission there for their people. God gave great blessing to many, and there was a great burning of heathen charms in public.'

In 1942 Dr Algie wrote, 'We are back in our old home at Kigeme, fragrant with memories of the children. The post of the hanging cupboard in our bedroom, where we marked their heights as they grew up, is still there to remind us of the happy family life we lived out here together. We are glad to be among our old friends again. In spite of the extra work I'm still keeping on with the translation, and in a few days' time hope to begin on the wonderful 40th chapter of Isaiah.' The growth of church membership was remarkable: 'There is now a Christian community of over 20,000, with adherents totalling altogether nearly 50,000. Last year there were over 2,200 adult baptisms. These people are grouped together in well over 700 village congregations and they are ministered to by nearly 1,400 trained workers, of whom 5 are now ordained. The Church work is rapidly becoming self-supporting. Taking the Church work as a whole, the self-support proportion is now 50 per cent.

'Two and-a-half years have passed since we missionaries met in conference. The distances between the stations made such a big meeting costly and difficult, but we were impelled this year by a sense of deep personal need to meet together at all costs to receive from our Father his reproof, his correction and his renewal, to enable us to bear the burdens which were becoming increasingly heavy in the deepening shadows of this terrible world-war. Some of us came weary and discouraged, but we have gone back to our stations knowing that "His strength is made perfect in weakness." We had hoped to come home this year, but the door is closed. We are perfectly content that it should be so; but we would be grateful for your special remembrance in prayer for our children.'

In August 1942, Dr and Mrs Sharp returned to Kabale but before leaving Matana, Mrs Sharp wrote: 'It is a long time since I have written to you, but you have been often in our thoughts and prayers in all you have gone and are going through. We follow the news very closely on the wireless, so we know more or less what is going on. We are, indeed, one big family and when one member suffers, all suffer with it (1 Cor.12.26).

'It is with mixed feelings that we shall say goodbye to this dear work and place later in the year and go back again to our old home and work at Kabale. We hope, though, that our going will not mean that any one of you who are supporting the work and praying for it here, will lessen your efforts one scrap. This is a live work, and the people themselves are keen on the salvation of the lost, and that is why it has expanded and grown as it has, all these last few years - from nothing to a very big work indeed. They know the joy of passing on the Glad Tidings and are keenly evangelistic. Mary and Joy are working at their School Certificate examination. They both want to go in for nursing when old enough.    John is at school in Kampala and is doing very well. It is rather a hot place for him, but at present that is the best we can do for him. Pray for him and those with whom he boards, that they may be blessed too…and that John may be brought up in God's faith and fear.'

Kigezi Hospital had closed in 1940. Dr Joe Church supervised this, retaining the administrative block for out-patient clinics only, a few beds and the theatre. The other blocks were occupied by Kigezi High School. Now back in Kabale, Dr Len renovated the out-patients' block and operations were carried out. Government grants were being provided for Bwama, to replace the huts with small burnt-brick houses and to rebuild the hospital. A contract had been made to build some of the houses before Dr Len's return, but he was concerned at the cost. The contract was not renewed and by using the excellent clay on the island and re-employing his own trained carpenters and bricklayers, he was soon building three times as many houses for the cost of one beforehand. This was followed by a spacious new hospital. In the years from 1942 onwards, Dr Len divided his time, five days at Kabale and two at Bwama, except when he had a heavy building programme at Bwama requiring more of his attention. He reintroduced the regular Bible teaching sessions, which he always held in his house once a week. Bible teaching had largely lapsed in favour of twice-weekly fellowship meetings, in which repentance and confession took the major part.

Mrs Len wrote, 'It is a great joy to my husband to be back
with his leprosy patients again. To them he is like their father;
in fact all the people here look upon us and the Stanley Smiths
as their parents because we have known so many of them for so
very long. They greatly appreciate Len speaking their language.
I am no use at it, or at any other language for that matter, so am
glad to be able to take a Bible Class on Mondays for the most
senior Christians by interpretation. I have been finding out lately
the wonderful teaching there is in the Tabernacle and how it all
speaks of our Lord and his atonement. It is a great delight to be
able to pass these things on, and he is teaching me as I study it.
The Christians are simply thrilled and are most responsive. I am
sure that what our people here now need most is regular Bible
classes and teaching; they seem so keen to learn and to have a real
hunger for the word. There is a Bible class some of them have
started by themselves for Bible study and discussion of various
problems on Wednesdays. They appoint a speaker and chairman,
and it is all done decently and in order and is most helpful. They
are trying to get in the outsiders and to bring them to Christ in
a loving way. It is true that our people seem to be growing in
grace and in the knowledge of the Lord and are wanting to learn
more of him'.

A picture of these classes is given by Eli N. Bisamunyu:
'When Kigezi High School became a Junior Secondary School,
Kirungi came to conduct a weekly lesson on the Jewish 'Ark'
(meaning the tabernacle). In our class she often came with a
model, which she placed on the table, and referred to during class.
The lessons added to and enriched our English vocabulary sev-
enfold! The purpose of the lesson, however, had been to channel
our spiritual vision to the essence of Christian life guided by Jesus
Christ. We always looked forward to her lessons on Thursdays
and she was a great influence on all our lives.'

Esther was at heart a very sociable person, and she could
sometimes have been lonely, especially on Sharp's Island, when
Len was busy with his medical work. She took up again her
responsibility of maintaining the Mission site. On returning to

Kabale, she found much of her earlier work of laying out gardens, hedges, lawns etc. had been invaded by a pernicious weed. To remove this weed was said to be impossible without weed-killers. This was, however, to underestimate Esther's tenacity. Within months all the public roads, gardens, under hedges and round buildings were again clear of the weed. Joy remembers too accompanying her mother in her visits to women in their homes, supporting the pioneering work of the Mothers' Union and in the sewing and teaching classes she arranged in their homes both at Kabale and on Sharp's island.

The contrast between Kigezi as it was when they first arrived there and the situation to which they returned in 1942 was a cause of great praise to God. 'In 1921 it was with difficulty that we reached this place, both sitting on a motorbike. The road was little more than a track, ungravelled, and often washed away. Now there are fine motor roads all through the district, and all the important centres can be reached by car within two and a half hours. There were no shirts and shorts in those days for the Africans to wear; they were clad, or rather one would say, scarcely half-clad, in goat and sheepskins. Their hair then was long and matted; now it is either shaved or kept short and clean. They were wild, rebellious and drunken, with frequent murders. Now the whole district is law-abiding, ruled by chiefs educated in the mission schools, and violent crimes are few and far between. What is even more striking is that a country which so recently was wholly given to heathenism and the power of the witch-doctors, now has a strong self-supporting and self-propagating Church, many of its evangelists taking the Gospel all over Ruanda and Urundi. For these remarkable changes we can all praise God, as workers together through prayer and support of all kinds.

'During the last few years some 250 lepers have left the leper colony to return to their homes, either because they were apparently cured, or for some other reason. I had been feeling that it was important to see what had happened to them, whether they have remained well, and which ones might have relapsed. To do this, and in order to see how God's work was going in different parts of the district, we started a series of safaris to different parts of the country. In March 1943, we went to British Ruanda, which is the part where the Mufumbira Mountains form the boundary between Kigezi, Ruanda proper, and the Congo. As in the old days, we did not go by car but over the mountain ridges and through the bamboo forests which separate this part of the district from the parts inhabited by the Bakiga. It was wonderful to camp again on those mountain-tops covered with dense bamboo, far above the plain, and look down upon the villages thousands of feet below, where so many years ago it had been our precious privilege to be the first to take the Gospel. This wild and lonely tract of country is still the habitation of elephants, buffaloes and a few pygmies, but it has a charm and fascination all its own to anyone who is a nature lover. We saw quite a number of lepers on this safari, and many of them were keeping in good health, but we also found many poor creatures urgently needing the care of the leper colony. We met many old friends of earlier days, several of these being among those who were baptized at the first baptism in Ruanda in September 1922.'

Joy recalled, 'We loved the safaris. Evenings in camp were wonderful: the night sky above, the sounds of the night, the men talking round the camp fire, the myriads of strange insects attracted to the lamp. We enjoyed walking, but when we were small we would take it in turns to be carried in a chair slung on a pole if the march was too far.' Mary too remembers the family trying to explore a cave in Bufumbira, taking hurricane lamps, but they could only go a little way as the floor of the cave opened into a chasm stretching from wall to wall.

As Dr Len commented, 'A safari like this gives one opportunities of quiet talks with some who need counsel and help in their spiritual lives. At one place we found some pygmies (the most difficult to reach of all the people in this land), who have now started to learn of Christ. One of these told me that he had first come to trust in Christ because one day when attacked by a wild buffalo in the forest he had cried to Jesus to save him, and the buffalo had then left him. This month we have been to another part of the district called Ruzumbura. Here we were able to use the car to save time over the journey. We did not find many lepers, but there were thousands of other sick folk who came from far and near seeking for treatment. The day after we arrived we found a crowd of over 1,000 people waiting, and it was no easy task to meet the needs of so many in the few days at our disposal, but it was an opportunity to speak to them of the Saviour as well as to help them physically.

'On our way home we camped at the bottom of a deep ravine where a winding river flows among trees and rocks, a lovely spot where we spent a quiet weekend. The children particularly enjoyed some fishing (with safety pins, and locusts as bait) and the bathing, which was especially attractive because hot springs run into the river at this spot. But even here we were not given much leisure for people began coming in bringing their sick and suffering for examination and treatment, and these continued to arrive until we had to return to Kabale. Truly in this land we are surrounded by a great and ever-present need, whether at Matana, Kabale, or any other station. We have great opportunities and privileges. What we need is a daily anointing, renewing, and reviving. May the Lord keep us all daily receiving his abundant grace and claiming his wonderful promises whether it is you in England or we out here.'

At the end of 1942, Dr Algie also visited Kabale, commenting, 'While there I went to a most inspiring convention meeting out in the villages, where hundreds of earnest seekers after full salvation were gathered. God is working mightily in Kigezi. Even those who are critical of the revival acknowledge the transformation in lives. It is an interesting fact that the receipts from the Beer Tax are estimated to be 20 per cent less than before.'

As Lindesay Guillebaud pointed out in her book, *A Grain of Mustard Seed*, the period of the Second world war was a time of consolidation for the Ruanda Mission. It seemed that God had given the vision and the faith for expansion while the opportunity lasted, so that in the years before the war the Mission had expanded rapidly — almost too rapidly for its resources, some thought. Once the war started such expansion was no longer possible, but by then the Mission was established at key points throughout Ruanda-Urundi. Both doctors found encouraging signs of this consolidation as they travelled around, Dr Len observing, 'In many ways the work of God in the Kigezi district is very prosperous. During the last two years there has been an increase in evangelistic zeal as shown by the opening of many new village churches, very liberal giving of money to cover all the needs of the work and salaries of the teachers, and the travelling round of bands of preachers. There is much enthusiasm and large crowds everywhere. Yet one cannot help realizing that there is a deep need among the teachers and evangelists for a fuller understanding of the great truths of the Gospel, a more regular study of God's word, and a more evident pre-eminence of Christ in their teaching and lives. Please pray that the word of Christ may dwell in them richly in all wisdom.'

In 1943, Bishop Cyril Stuart wrote, after a visit to Ruanda, 'As most of you know, there has been a little trouble between me and a few (a very few) of the Ruanda Mission, or more particularly some in Uganda who have been following the lead of a few in Ruanda. I believe that this trouble is now over. There has never been any difference of opinion about our aim here, which is the salvation of souls and the building up of an African Church to God's glory, but there has been some difference of opinion about methods. I found the whole spirit different this year in Ruanda and I came away feeling completely at one with them. We seemed to have come out of a nightmare of misunderstanding to a real union in Christ. On the whole revival question I do believe with all my heart that it is of God, and thank him for it, but, the main trouble has been with just a few Africans, some of whom are good men in themselves but who genuinely feel that no one can be a Christian who has found God in any other way than themselves ... and some who are not so good. ... I look forward to a glorious future and real deep revival both in Ruanda and Uganda now that we have got on to lines which I believe are the lines of our Lord himself.'

During 1944, Dr Sharp was requested by C.M.S. to undertake a survey of mission hospitals and a leprosy settlement in Tanganyika which he did, taking Esther and his daughter Joy with him. A number of recommendations were then sent back to London. A few months later an Australian C.M.S. missionary working in Tanganyika came to Bwama for experience in leprosy care. The Sharps hoped to end this tour with a break in Mombasa, which would have been their only holiday for ten years because of the war, but urgent business intervened, and it was not possible.

The Leprosy Settlement required a constant number of new boats, and building these was an ongoing task for Dr Len and his helpers. Most were constructed from galvanized sheet-iron, cut and riveted together, but on one occasion he made use of the floats of an abandoned seaplane which came down on the lake but could not take off again. These were cut horizontally to make two large boats for Bwama, and two small sailing dinghies with out-riggers for his daughters. The Sharp family spent much holiday time sailing on the lake exploring the inlets and islands. Sometimes Mary would prepare maps, *Swallows and Amazons* style, and they would take food and camp overnight on an uninhabited island. And always there was swimming and diving, and on very rare occasions (because petrol could not be wasted), the treat of water-skiing on a homemade board. From 1942, when John had friends staying from Kampala, Joe and Decie Church's three elder sons would bring their boat out on the lake and there would be great sailing rivalry and races between the families.

As Joy remembered, 'Life on Sharp's Island was wonderful for children. The lake was free from hippos, crocodiles and bilharzia. The hills around were steep and so was the gradient under water so one was almost at once out of one's depth, but this did not bother us as we had all learnt to swim at Matana in the lake my father had built there to provide fish for the local population to eat. We had various boats and canoes on the lake, a landing stage and a diving board, a long rope attached to a tree to swing out over the water and then let go, a tennis court and a pet monkey and dogs and cats, plenty of books and freedom to explore.' During the wet seasons, great storms would descend on Lake Bunyoni with very little warning, tearing roofs off buildings and whipping the calm waters into rough seas which were dangerous for any canoe out in open water away from the shelter of an island. Dr Len's family were on the look out in these conditions, and Mary, Joy and John would sometimes accompany their father on high-speed motor rescues.

But by 1944 Mrs Len wrote, 'Our children are getting horribly grown up. Mary is at present helping the European Children's School as housekeeper, but will be leaving in December. In January she goes to Nairobi to the Lady Northey Mothercraft Training Centre. Joy is already there and is loving it. John is also in Nairobi at a big school for European boys. His letters are full of cricket and about making a wireless set with which he hopes to get London.'

Dr Algie wrote from Kigeme in May 1944 'At last, after four years of war, Ruanda is beginning to have a share in the universal tribulation. With us it is famine. There are many contributory causes, but the fact is, it is the most widespread famine within living memory. The Belgian Government is supplying food and our mission stations are helping in cooking and distributing it to the starving people. One starving child, past the power of swallowing and semi-conscious, was restored by subcutaneous saline and is now saved.' Dr Algie decided to make the hospital responsible for her. Helen grew up a bright Christian. One night her little hut caught alight, and her life was saved by the duty staff, although she had severe burns. Geoff Stanley Smith wrote after visiting in 2005, 'She always considered Dr and Mrs Algie as her parents, so when the duty nurse introduced me, her joy knew no bounds, and her face lit up as she sang her favourite Ruanda hymn, for here was her 'stepbrother' visiting her from England! The nurses' prayer was inspirational, as if we were already in heaven.'

Dr Algie writes again, 'The past year has been shadowed by threatened disaster in the Church from party spirit, as well as by famine. We have been made to realize that only God could help us. And now indefinably we are all beginning to sense the spirit of victory. In a very small way it must be like what you are feeling at home, on the eve of the invasion of Europe. There is a great wave of confidence and affection towards our Mission in Ruanda. It has been partly due to the help we have given to certain people in trouble, and partly due to the spirit of love shown to the starving in famine food distribution. As a result, many have been most strikingly converted. And a second cause for confidence is that God is, I'm sure, beginning to deal with the indefinable things that have caused us so much trouble among ourselves. Spiritual blessing is so easily followed by spiritual pride and the party spirit.  We are beginning to see that the first, second and third Christian virtue is humility, that the only weapon that conquers the world is "faith working by love." This means the Cross, and our method in all things is to be like him whose description of himself was "I am meek and lowly in heart."'

The Mission had recently been granted a site at Nyanza, 'which from the African point of view is of great importance; for it is the King's court and a place constantly visited by all and sundry. The Banyaruanda have a very strong sense of royalty; and we have all these years laboured under the disadvantage of appearing to be a body out of favour with their King. Now we shall have a better chance.'

Dr and Mrs Algie left Ruanda for leave in the UK from December 1944 to June 1946, sailing up the Clyde in glorious wintry weather. A policeman at the docks said to them, ' The old country has suffered terribly, but she still has a kind heart.' Dick Lyth travelled with them on the same boat, and he and Nora were married at York on 15th December. Nora and Dick soon went back to the Sudan, where Dick had served during the war, and he became District Commissioner. After leaving the Sudan he was ordained in England and came to Uganda, where he was appointed Headmaster of Kigezi High School. Later they started the new and wonderful outreach of Christian Rural Service, where together they went all over the Diocese on safari with their team. Dick was then unanimously elected first Bishop of

Kigezi Diocese, and he eventually handed over to Bishop Festo Kivengere.

Mrs Algie wrote, 'It is such a joy to be home again after all these years and we are looking forward to seeing as many of you as possible. I can't tell you how much we have valued your prayers for us and especially for our children during these years of separation, and we would like you to know that the Lord has abundantly answered and has not only kept them from physical danger but "from the evil one" and taught them more of himself as their need of him grew. Geoffrey has passed his second M.B. and is now at Barts, and Jim, who is now 15, is at Winchester. We just got home in time to be able to go there for the end of term gymnastic display and carol singing. He was taking part in both and is very keen on them. We cannot thank God enough for all his loving care of them.'

Dr Algie wrote too in January, 'We who come home have a story to tell you of how the Lord has been dealing with us "in judgment and mercy," of how all these past years he has been making us pass through the crucible of trials within and without until he could give us one heart and one way in the great movement of the Spirit which has for ten years been transforming the Church in Ruanda. As we left Kigeme we asked our people what message we should take to the people at home. "Tell the people in England," they said, "that Jesus saves."

'It is a day of the flowing tide in Ruanda, Urundi and Kigezi and we have to tell you of our needs. At such a time as this it seems madness to expect to double our income, bring back our missionaries still at home, add at least one-third to our staff, and seek for capital expenditure for new permanent buildings costing anything up to £5,000. Yet such are our essential needs if we are to take advantage of the opportunities opening up before us on every hand, and establish our two new stations, Shyogwe and Astrida. To accomplish this we need, under God's goodness, a great increase in the number of our Friends who will pray and work and give.'

In March a further appeal went out to supporters, 'And now as the hope of an end of hostilities brings us face to face with the urgencies of post-war planning, we ask you with us to take stock of our situation and look forward into the future. Africa is being drawn into the comity of nations, and a policy of exploitation has given place, in the conscience of a world saved from the domination of a 'Master Race', to the principle of trusteeship. To take her place in the "brave new world", pagan Africa must be educated, and the colonial governments of the great powers have for the most part never swerved from the conviction that it must be Christian education they give her. For over twenty-five years the Church has been entrusted with the amazing opportunity of moulding young Africa in the impressionable years. What has been the fruit of this great effort? A huge number of children have been educated and passed almost automatically into the Christian Church; and all branches of Church, State and Commerce have benefited by the supply of educated Africans for their various needs. And yet few responsible missionaries would deny that the educational approach into the Church has had one serious defect, in that it has substituted the call, "You must learn," for the challenging word of the Gospel, "You must be born again." The result is that Christianity in Africa from Sierra Leone to Zanzibar is to an alarming degree becoming nominal. Christians of the third and fourth generation are for the most part indifferent to the spiritual truths and claims of the Gospel. And the Church is facing a situation of real gravity. If Christianity on which such hopes were placed fails her, what hope is there for poor Africa, as she plunges with an unregenerate heart into the glittering attractions of materialism, the passionate prejudices of nationalism, and the racial hatreds of the colour bar?

'There is no hope but in true revival. Now God in the very hour of Africa's need is doing this very thing. In many places throughout the great continent the fires of revival are burning, and the Church is finding its true vocation as it testifies to its Saviour and welcomes the sinner to its fellowship of redemption. In all humility we in the Ruanda Mission can claim to have been objects of his mercy and witnesses of his power to save. Already this work of the Spirit is spreading out to surrounding countries; and on many occasions teams of witness from Ruanda have been used to spread the blessing. Here lies our opportunity and our responsibility. This revival movement must be a part of God's plan for the purifying of the Church throughout Africa. What are we to do?'

The Ruanda Council on 13th March reported, 'If we are to fulfil the inescapable obligations forced on us by the very blessing that God has given to the work, then the whole Mission must expand and go forward.' The recognized needs were listed: a Bishop to co-ordinate and lead the whole Church on to fuller effectiveness, clergy, women evangelists, doctors and nurses. There would need to be 26 additional workers, but not all at once. Ten in 1945/47 would cost £94,000, with houses and school buildings needing £3,000 initial capital. Two vital places were Shyogwe and Astrida (now Butare). The Government were willing to provide a hostel for Protestant boys who would learn at the Astrida Educational Centre, where all the future leaders of the country were trained. Convinced of the way forward, the Ruanda Council urged their friends to pray and to give.

Dr Stanley Smith wrote again in October telling of illnesses striking missionaries still abroad, and of Mr Webster, the Home Secretary of the Mission also unwell, 'the price paid in dauntlessly carrying on through the war years, in spite of wounds and sickness, and maintaining the home base.' (His home and the Ruanda office had been destroyed by bombs.) 'Will you unite in praying the Lord to give us a helper for him, one gifted to carry the organization ahead, as a living organism which will be able to bear the increasing load of the mission commitments in the field. One more attack, this time against my wife. Three months ago her right arm was stricken with shingles and paralysis. It has meant three months of pain and helplessness, with all that that means of feeling oneself a burden to others. She has been marvellously helped to take it as one of the "all things that work together for good," though during this testing we have both been tempted to say "Why?"' They had prayed for a temporary home while they travelled around reporting on the work and asking for new recruits, but 'the Lord knowing what was coming (Zöe's disability) withheld it; we would not have been able to manage it. This period of homelessness has made us wanderers from place to place, and here again it has turned to blessing in making us realize in this practical way the love of friends.'

In fact Dr and Mrs Algie did find a base in a missionary guesthouse in Wimbledon. Geoff remembers at the start of Algie's tour round the country, his suitcase was snatched by the doors of the tube train, and he was left holding the handle. Undaunted and sure of the Lord's enabling, he completed the tour without any fuss. A year later the missing suitcase was returned and to his great joy his precious Bible was there. During these 18 months in Wimbledon Geoff was commuting to St Bartholomew's hospital as a student, and Eve was also there convalescing in a complete plaster cast following a spinal fusion operation. Meanwhile Tony Wilmot, recently demobbed from war service in Africa, came to occupy the last room in the guest house. He had prayed continually for guidance about his future wife, and immediately he saw Eve he knew that she was the one. Within a few months they were married, in June 1946. Tony and Eve went out quite soon in secular employment to Ghana, then Singapore and then Nigeria. Always Tony would contact local churches and then work with students, leading Bible studies and speaking at conferences. Finally they went to Nairobi and started the Nairobi Evangelical Graduate School of Theology, of which Tony was the first principal. Now NEGST is fully African staffed and there are graduates in 30 African countries including Ruanda. With both his daughters married, Dr Algie returned to Africa rejoicing.

# Chapter 12

# Sounds of Jubilee
## 1946 - 1955

The Ruanda Mission celebrated its Silver Jubilee, six months after the end of the 2nd World War, with joy and thanksgiving. As Dr Len recalled, 'On 24th February, 1946, it will be twenty-five years since we first climbed the hill here at Kabale. It was pouring with rain, we were tired after a long journey along very indifferent tracks on a motorbike which we rode tandem fashion. The path was very slippery, and my wife, I believe, ascended it on her hands and knees as it was also very steep. The motorbike had to be left some distance away as it was quite impossible to get it up the hill. We had with us a puppy and very little else, as our goods had to follow us by porter across country. And so we entered on the great enterprise to which God had called us. This enterprise was to bring the Gospel to Ruanda-Urundi and to the bordering tribes of Uganda and Tanganyika living in a mountainous country of nearly 100,000 square miles.

'All these tribes and people were at that time without God or hope in the world, and practising every evil work of witchcraft, drunkenness, murder and even in some cases cannibalism. This great untouched mission field was a heart-searching challenge which in spite of our weakness constituted God's urgent call to us to go forward in faith for him. On the human side our resources were very meagre. There were only the four of us, we had few financial resources, we were not gifted with brilliant natural endowments, we had not much missionary experience, and we were faced by an implacable enemy defending one of his age-old strongholds. On the other hand we were possessed of wonderful spiritual resources, indeed those irresistible resources which are at the disposal of every missionary recruit who sets out on his Master's business. ...

'Twenty-five years ago these things were but hopes, dreams, and prayers. Now much has become reality. We never thought in 1921 that God would gather together such a mighty band of praying Christians as the Friends of Ruanda have become during all these years. We never thought that he would call out to work for him over eighty missionary workers, clergy, doctors, accountants, teachers, nurses, translators and home-makers, some sowing the seed, some watering, some reaping as God had appointed them, but God gave life to the seed, God gave the increase and God gave the harvest. A largely self-supporting and self-propagating Church has come into being, centred on every mission station that has been opened. Although we rejoice at the great opportunities presented by the multitudes flocking into the Kingdom, we can never be satisfied with mere numbers or outward success. It is thrilling to see a vast multitude, as we often do, gathered together to hear the Gospel message, but it is only as one by one they come to Christ for cleansing and new life that saving work for eternity is accomplished; therefore it is the manifestation of the work of God's Spirit in the hearts of these people which gives us most joy, and for which we praise God continually.'

Dr Algie added: 'I think the prevailing impression on my mind after these twenty-five years is amazement that God can have done so much through such feeble instruments. Looking back, we recall the way he led us to humble us and to prove us to know what was in our hearts. The years have revealed so much pride and self-sufficiency to be humbled, and so many testings, which have shown up the poverty of our spiritual understanding. And yet God has blessed the work with revival, the priceless blessing which so many earnest Christians are praying for all over the world.' The Silver Jubilee of the Mission also marked a publication relating its story. Written by Dr Algie, it was entitled: *Road to Revival*.

Bishop John Willis, the retired Bishop of Uganda, commented, 'Within the last twenty-five years advance has been almost unbelievably rapid, and it may be doubted whether any other mission field can record so large an advance within so short a time. The single station in Kigezi has now become eight, around which cluster something like one thousand out-stations. A tiny Christian congregation of under thirty members has grown to a total of over twenty thousand in Kigezi alone, while a further forty thousand are said to be under instruction. The furthest station now occupied by European missionaries in Urundi, lies many hundreds of miles to the south of that original station. That all this should have been accomplished within a quarter of a century is a miracle indeed, and the story of that advance affords an inspiring record. Such rapidity of progress carries with it inevitably seeds of danger. Wherever European and African staff alike are relatively young and inexperienced, where converts are so quickly made before qualified leaders can be trained, the danger of a land-slide cannot be forgotten; but we may well thank God for the work already done, and believe that "He that has begun a good work in them will perfect it to the day of Jesus Christ."' (Phil. 1.6)

Dr Algie returned to Africa in June 1946 without Zöe, who again remained in the UK for the sake of their younger children's education. In December of that year he wrote: 'It is almost six months since I left England, once again alone, for Christ's sake and for the sake of our boys. After travelling by a Belgian boat to Leopoldville, I took part in the Equatorial Africa Regional

Conference, where the missionaries and African church leaders who took part came from Angola, Belgian Congo, French Congo and Cameroon. We met to face the problems of post-war Africa and went into them in detail. The key thought was, "I am come that they might have life, and that they might have it more abundantly." (John 10.10). Running through all our discussions was the thought that the vital need of African missions today is the power of Christ, who died and rose again to make a living Church. It is the only remedy for the supreme danger in Central Africa today, the danger of a lifeless, powerless Church, with no witness that Jesus Christ really saves from sin.'

From there Dr Algie drove 2,000 miles east across the vastness of the Belgian Congo to get back in time for a convention in Urundi. This was followed by a conference of the Protestant Alliance, which concentrated on formulating a united educational policy, and meetings of the Ruanda Mission committees to consider the best use of their limited personnel.

Now that the Government had agreed to recognize and subsidize the educational work equally with that of the Roman Catholics, it was necessary to conform strictly to the Government syllabus. Therefore the Mission planned to open a 'Normal School' for training teachers at Shyogwe, and Peter Guillebaud and his wife Elizabeth, now qualified educationists, prepared a syllabus for the training course. Dr Algie wrote, 'As regards personnel, we are in for a lean time next season. A clear proof of this is that I have been located to be in charge of the school. My teaching is limited to French, hygiene and singing, with some supervision of higher mathematics. I am a curious sort of schoolmaster. The staff of the school are grand; they bear many of the burdens. Do pray for this school. Educational work, essential as it is, is almost always disappointing in spiritual results. I am more than ever convinced that revival is the one thing that counts supremely. In essence, what is it? I believe that it means getting back, in experience and reality, to the simplicity of the faith of the early Church.'

In the medical work at Shyogwe, Dr Algie, single-handed, did what he could, reluctant to take on many patients because of shortage of personnel. There was a good Government hospital not far away, but 'A quite undeserved reputation is making people come, so I am trying to give Saturday mornings to seeing them.' By 1947, as with the schools, the Belgian Government was offering support for the Mission's hospitals and staff. And, most encouraging of all, Dr Algie commented on the joy, while living alone, of sharing in the trials and joys of his African friends and marvelling at the unaffected simplicity and consistency of their faith. 'If I ever had doubts of the genuineness of God's work in revival, I have none now. One is living in a community which is simply absorbed in Christ, in the midst of busy and often humdrum lives.' He also mentioned that although still subjected to Roman Catholic opposition, 'The Lord is showing us and the really converted people that the way to win through is not to carry complaints to the Government but to win by patience and prayer and love, willing to be broken to self-justification and to all vindictiveness. When one sees this, it is a very strong proof of Christ-likeness.'

Five Protestant boys passed the entrance examination to the big Roman Catholic college, the Groupe Scolaire in Astrida, and in April 1948, Dr and Mrs Algie moved into the ex-Governor of Ruanda's house to set up a hostel for these boys. Not only did they care for the boys' physical and spiritual welfare, but they longed that through their presence and that of the local evangelist Gideon and his wife Ruth, the light of the Gospel would shine into the town. While at Astrida, Dr Algie was able to pursue his translation work and also seek to establish the church in the area around. In 2005, the present Bishop of Butare speaking to Geoff Stanley Smith paid this tribute to Geoff's father's efforts: 'I thank God for him so much. He worked very hard to get us a new site for the Diocese on which we have schools, houses and especially a lovely cathedral and guest-house. He planted 20 churches around Butare, and in Gisanze we are building a Health Centre which I want to name after him.'

For three of the five years that Dr Algie was in charge of the Home at Astrida, Veronica Guillebaud, now Veronica Madeley, lived with them. 'I was there to help Mrs Algie making new shorts and mending old ladies' umbrellas. The Ruanda ladies really loved her; her secret was patience and real love for individuals. But my main purpose was to help Dr Algie prepare his newly revised translation of my father's Ruanda Bible for the printer. He was trying to fit in three hours a day, in between teaching the boys and secretarial work.'

After the war through the generosity of friends a burnt-brick church with tower and spire was designed and built on Bwama Island by Dr Len assisted by Bwama workmen. The orb on the spire was two of Mrs Len's large kitchen bowls, soldered together, and the family helped cut out the metal lettering for the walls. It was built on the highest hill on Bwama island and named Emmanuel Church. Two nursing sisters, Marguerite Barley and Janet Metcalfe were released from war service, and arrived to join Grace Mash on the island.

Mrs Len wrote, 'Last month the mail brought the astounding news of a huge consignment of goods for the leprosy island, a most magnificent gift, we were almost staggered by it. The freight was paid to the coast but not beyond, so we were faced with a huge bill for carriage of about 1,500 miles and customs. This would have taken all our earmarked money. Of course our Heavenly Father did not want us to have to pay, so he arranged that the Governor should be at the dentist, when I was waiting, with every detail of the consignment in my bag. I was able to put the whole position before him. We are to give one third to other leprosy settlements and will get the rest free of charge. We have proved again and again that God does this sort of thing when it is in line with his will.'

In May 1948 Dr. Sharp wrote from Bunyoni, 'As I was thinking what I should write for this, the hundredth number of *Ruanda Notes*, these words came to my mind: " Thou shalt remember all the way which the Lord thy God led thee " (Deut. 8.2). Dr Len proceeded to do this by contrasting the past with the present, quoting from some of the earliest letters to the Friends of Ruanda.

On **medical work**, he recalled his first patient, the blind old witch-doctor, Mutambuka, and compared with 1947 when over a quarter of a million out-patients came to the eight mission hospitals and there were more than 7,000 in-patients. Similarly with leprosy work, thinking back to the modest start of the venture, he quoted more than 800 lepers treated in 1947 with a promising new drug. Each year about 30-40 leprosy patients were able to return to their homes with certificates of health. For these a thanksgiving service was held and their village chiefs were informed.

For **schools**, the start of Kabale High School with eleven small boys clad in skins and dirt had developed into the present Kigezi High School, which 'has 350 boys, it teaches secondary standards, and is staffed, including the headmaster, by old boys of the Kigezi schools. In addition to this, there are now in the Mission 178 other schools for boys and girls, with a staff of nearly 400 schoolmasters and mistresses. Those attending these schools number over 10,000, and many of them have competed successfully with the best talent that Uganda can produce. God has taken those small urchins clad in skins and dirt to make of them evangelists, schoolmasters, hospital workers and clergy to their own people.'

On the **evangelistic** front, 'When we first started at Kabale, Dr Stanley Smith and I used to go out on Sunday afternoons among the kraals at the foot of our Mission hill to hold open-air services. Owing to the absolute indifference of the people, we had to give up. Last Christmas Day, so vast was the crowd that came to Kabale that the Church which holds over 2,000 was already full two hours before the time for the beginning of the service. As the crowd continued to increase, we all went down to the foot of our hill and there we held an open-air service with a congregation of over 7,000, who listened with deep attention and joyful understanding to the message. We were confident then that "There has been so much prayer in the past that a great harvest is a glorious certainty". That harvest is now being reaped. Last year, there were nearly 5,000 baptisms in the Mission; there are 26,348 baptized Christians in Kigezi, Ruanda and Urundi and 74,817 more are under regular instruction.'

Dr Len went on to consider the **training of evangelists**, started at the very beginning of the Mission. '*Ruanda Notes* No. 1 said: "We have started a weekly meeting which we hope may be of great benefit to the work, a devotional meeting for the teachers and senior Christians, to be held each Saturday morning." This work of training evangelists has grown through the years so that now, from the eight mission stations, over 2,500 men and women are teaching and preaching the Gospel in 1,334 village churches, in hospitals and in schools throughout Kigezi, Ruanda and Urundi. A number of these evangelists are now either ordained clergy, or are reading for ordination, men who can be trusted with the care and responsibility of a hundred or more village churches each.

'**Church Giving**.  When we first came to the country, there was little or no money, and any gift had to be in kind, such as eggs, a chicken or a goat. Last year, the Christians in Kigezi District alone subscribed £3,216 for the support of all their clergy and evangelists and for the building of their churches; so the Church work in this area is wholly self-supporting.

'**Workings of the Spirit**.  In the first letter to Friends of Ruanda even before *Ruanda Notes* No. 1, written as we were sailing for Africa in November, 1920, we wrote: " Perhaps it is hardly necessary for us to say how utterly dependent we are in this undertaking on the power and indwelling of the Holy Spirit." The Church of God in this land is now a truly living Church with many evidences of the Spirit's mighty working. Next week-end, which is Eastertide, there will be in this district of Kigezi alone ten different teams holding missions at important centres. These missions are not dependent on the missionary but are entirely organized and run by the African Christians among themselves.

'Friends of Ruanda, "I thank my God upon every remembrance of you...for your fellowship in the Gospel from the first day until now". The Ruanda Mission has all these years been upheld by prayer, and through prayer God will go on to perfect that which he has begun.'

Archbishop Howard Mowll of Sydney, Australia visited the Mission in 1948, and went to Bwama Island. There he set the example of Jesus, greeting and shaking hands with as many of the patients as he could, whether their hands were bandaged or in whatever condition they were. The patients were astonished and delighted, ' No visitor had ever done that before!'

Mrs Len developed Sharp's Island into one of the most beautiful gardens in East Africa. It was visited by hundreds of day visitors, besides many missionaries and other friends who enjoyed holidays with them or who used a small guest cottage that Dr Sharp built there for this purpose. All were welcomed there. From 1948, Mrs Len began distributing Christian newspapers like *Life of Faith* that were sent to her, to the ever increasing number of English speaking Africans. This was followed by her request for devotional books and commentaries to distribute. There was a great response.

Sadly Dr and Mrs Len continued to be marginalized by some in the Mission. Executive Committees became an ordeal for them both, and the time approaching them a period of stress and apprehension. 'It nearly killed him', admitted one committee member some years later.

Dr and Mrs Len went on UK leave in the autumn of 1948, the first time for more than nine years. Accommodation was hard to come by and food rationing was still in force, but people coming into the country were allowed to bring food parcels up to a certain weight containing tinned butter, sausages and other rarities, hugely welcome to hostesses. The best accommodation CMS could offer the Sharps to rent had a sitting room on the first floor, bedroom on the second, bathroom on the next and an attic to use as a dining room and kitchen with table, chairs, an old gas stove, but no sink, drainage or water. Here they proceeded to make a home where the family could come on days off or weekends. To avoid carrying bowls of water up and down stairs, Len created a system using garden hosepipe, which carried clean water half way up the stairs and dirty water down a pipe along the outside wall into a pavement grill. Almost at once, angry shouts came up from the owner of the house whose basement was getting wet with grimy water — grrrugsome, Len said. Esther seized tins of butter and dashed down stairs. Soon peace was restored and the owner was very friendly for the rest of their stay. This was the worst housing experience they had — a slum, it seemed to Mrs Len — but after that Dr Len determined never to live permanently in England. During this leave Esther was diagnosed as having diabetes.

Dr Len wrote, welcoming the opportunity of meeting old friends, thanking God for the great privilege they were conscious of in serving him and for the precious sense of his presence they had enjoyed over the last ten years. He added, 'Expansion is under way everywhere through the Mission. No wonder we are praying that God will grant us the means to send out those who have obeyed his call and are offering themselves as missionaries. Many of our missionaries are hard-pressed to deal with all the calls made upon them from the many-sided departments of the work. What a welcome awaits returning missionaries and new arrivals!'

He asked too, 'We would like you to remember prayerfully sometimes Mary, Joy and John who are now all in England. Mary and Joy have started nursing training at the Middlesex and St. Thomas's Hospitals respectively, and John is training for a medical degree also at St. Thomas's. All of them would welcome new Christian friends.'

More new treatments were becoming available for the treatment of leprosy and Dr Len was determined to obtain them for the leprosy settlement. Miss Dorothy Lowe was recruited as the pathologist for this work. While in England Dr Len met a retired general practitioner with previous missionary experience in China, who wished to use his skills again for a number of years in missionary work: Dr Parry and his wife Muriel accompanied the Sharps to work at Bwama, when they returned to Uganda in February 1950.

Before leaving Mrs Len wrote: 'The time has come round again to say good-bye to you after this very happy time in England. We are expecting to sail on 4th February on SS Mantola and you will have heard that God has given us partners, Dr and Mrs Parry, to go back with us to the leper work. It has been amazing to see his working over this. We can only marvel and praise him.

'We want to thank him too for many other tokens of his love and care and encouragement. When you are praying for us, praise him for all he has done and ask that he will do greater things in our own lives and in our children, and in the lives of the dear Africans, among whom we shall be working. We want to thank those of you who have been so wonderfully kind to us and our family. Your love and fellowship has meant more than we can tell you, to us all.

'In praying for us and our work at the leper island and Kabale, please remember also the many tired missionaries from different missions whom it is our privilege to have to stay with us. They have come in the past from all sorts of work and places and we do long to be able to serve and help them while they are with us. Pray that each one may come into closer touch with the Lord Jesus himself and that he will lovingly and graciously rest and restore them so that none may go away without a blessing to spirit, soul and body. ...

'Many of you have asked me when to start sending *The Christian* and *Life of Faith* again. Please start as soon as you get this letter and send the current copy. It is sometimes difficult to deal with large parcels of old copies all at once, but a number of small parcels or weekly copies will be more than welcome. You see, these people in the British part of our Mission, Kabale and all the Kigezi District, are learning English fast. Every year we as a Mission, with the help of the Government, are turning out numbers of young people who speak English well. Ian Gateley has told you of the need for a school library and that is a very great need indeed; so please go on sending him books to lend to the scholars. What I have on my heart so particularly is the need of the great many who have left school these last thirty years since we first went to Kigezi. Most read English well, so the whole field of English literature and thought is opened up to them. What are we going to give them to read? We are responsible for this as a Mission. Read they must and will, but what?'

A book on the history of the Leprosy Settlement, *Island of Miracles* by Dr Sharp and Janet Metcalf, was published in 1950.

In letters to her children, who were all in England between 1950 and 1955, Mrs Len wrote, 'We are very busy with books. I've cleared out several bookcases for them. More books keep coming, they are a wonderful lot, very good indeed.' Then later, 'People come at all sorts of times for books. Pray that they get those that will help them most.' 'We are expecting a lot of people for books. They are hiring transport to the lake and two huge canoes to come over here. We are ready for them and will give them tea and cakes.... 35 came.' This book ministry, together with Dr Len's Bible teaching, reflected the Sharps' concern to enrich new Christians' understanding of their faith by teaching, rather than their going over and over, exclusively, the same ground of emotional confessions and testimonies.

Esther requested her daughters to tell supporters, 'People are asking for Church History books, perhaps there are some spare ones at Oakhill Theological College. Do ask. Ask for simply written books but having the whole truth of the life side of Calvary, as well as the death side clearly stated, like *How to Live the Victorious Life* and *Victorious Living*. So many are truly converted and we rejoice but many grow cold or do not continue. Dad says it's because they know the cleansing from sin but not the keeping power of God through the indwelling Christ to keep them, and so far haven't wanted to learn, as they say it is not revival.' As time went on revivalists began to develop sensitivity to the harm done by 'the detailed confession of sin in mixed company and began to check it, while meetings increasingly became times of sharing not only spiritual victories and defeats but also the treasures of God's word' [1]

Interestingly, the Rwandan Antoine Rutayisire picked up these concerns in his book *Faith under Fire*, written soon after the 1994 genocide in Rwanda. He pointed out positive effects of the revival, which might have helped avert the tragedy. 'The revival had some impact on the ethnic relationships as many

Batutsi started repenting of arrogance towards other ethnic groups.' But he also highlighted weaknesses. For one thing, 'the movement was so heavenly-minded that it forgot that Christianity has duties even here on earth. This led to a kind of naïve faith, often irrelevant when it came to dealing with social issues.' And secondly, and this was the particular concern of the Sharps: 'Another characteristic of the movement was the emphasis put on personal testimony. This is very biblical but the weakness in many of our Church meetings was lack of balance: personal testimonies took more time than anything else and finally became almost the hallmark of spiritual maturity. This in the long run has led to a very poor church, with many old people who should be teachers still needing to be fed on milk...Christian babies only able to give old testimonies of how they got saved somewhere in the 1930s! The lack of biblical teaching is still a weakness in the church and will be for a long time as people have not been trained to enjoy discussing and sharing the Bible. Preference always goes to preaching, and this is often done so poorly that no solid grounding in the word of God is provided.' Sadly, Dr Len's prophetic insights based on his balanced and Biblical understanding were not always listened to.

Mrs Stanley Smith wrote from Astrida at the end of 1949 that all their nine students at the Astrida College had passed their examinations, and all nine had now turned to the Lord for cleansing and forgiveness. The translation of the Old Testament was going slowly owing to increasing Government work in connection with the Protestant Alliance. In March 1950 Dr Algie wrote of 'Africa in rapid transition, with the scene often confused, but a pattern of things to come shaping themselves. For me, it has been a year of strange and new work. It seems to have fallen to my lot to be the liaison between the Mission and Government. The latter have launched a big welfare scheme in which they offer to help missions, especially in the domain of education, maternity work and child welfare. On the one hand this has involved a vastly more complicated system of statistics. Even now, three months after the end of the year, we are still getting requests for new facts about 1949's work; the Government, too, are feeling their way. On the other hand I have to draw up plans and detailed estimates, all in French, of all the buildings we have to put up. This would mean even more labour if it were not that the mining company headquarters at Astrida willingly, and for nothing, make all my blueprints. When you think that every request to the Welfare Fund has to go in seven copies, you will see what that means.

'The big problem is, " Where do we go from here?" There is quite a natural fear in the Mission that the lure of grants may be leading us ahead of, or even contrary to, the Lord's will. We need much prayer for that spiritual intuition which only those who really live close to Jesus can have, for I feel so much the lack of it. Then we can be safely guided along this unknown way. Education looms large. Humanly speaking, everything turns on our getting, and getting quickly, some men recruits, who see in education their particular sphere of service. We have grand material in our schools, and, again humanly speaking, the strength and progress of the material side of our work depends on our doing this, and doing it well. So enthusiasts are needed. It is important to realize that it is not only Government who are pushing us; it is our Africans, who very naturally want us to educate their children.

'I feel very thankful for the deepening spirit of mutual trust and unity in the Alliance of Protestant Missions. Hans Jensen of the Danish Mission is back, and he has taken off the main burden of the Urundi Alliance work. We now have nine stations on which Alliance institutions are operating: three of ours, one Belgian Mission, two Friends, one Baptist and one Methodist, and the Astrida Hostel. These Alliance efforts are already a growing factor in breaking down denominational imperialism. Our hostel lads are going quite well. We are fifteen now, and, at the recent test, none failed — in fact, two did brilliantly. Best of all there is evidence that God is working. Our original four are now prefects, and are working loyally and conscientiously for the "Home."

'In translation work, I had to go through all the books of the Bible translated by the late M. Monier. This is at last finished; and there is now a clear field for the preparation of the Old Testament for the press. I have done quite a bit already but far the greatest part still lies ahead of me. I would welcome prayer for a definite solution of the problem of orthography.' Bible translation was another area of co-operation between the different protestant groups, and both M. Monier of the Seventh Day Adventists and M. Honoré of the Belgian Protestant Mission had collaborated with Harold Guillebaud on translation work.

After their return to Bwama, Mrs Len wrote to her family, 'We had rather a knock yesterday in a letter from a member of the Executive saying, we were against revival. It was not a loving letter,...It's unjust... very sad,....but...God's peace is something above circumstances... Don't worry about us... We must wait and pray for his time and his release from this burden.' (1 Peter 4.12-14.)

Dr and Mrs Parry were a comfort and support for them. The remaining outpatient block of Kigezi Hospital was finally closed in 1950, but the people of Kigezi kept on pleading for the hospital's reinstatement, and the needs of the people remained very great. Dr and Mrs Len took the Parrys on a number of medical safaris, one of which was to Rukungiri in Ruzumbira. Mrs Len described it to her family: 'October 1st. We are in rest camp, comfortably settled into tents, Janet Metcalf (nurse) and Dr and Mrs Parry also. It's their first safari experience. We had crowds in the old church. They listened well to Len's preaching. They need to realize the fact that the Holy Spirit's indwelling can keep them from sinning. They lay the foundations of repentance over and over again but need to build a "Holy Temple" of the Lord on them. After lunch we had a special meeting for teachers, followed by giving away books to those who can speak English. We pray the books may help them.

'October 2nd was a terrific morning with patients, there were thousands of them all wanting help. There is a government dispensary nearby, but they come. The crowds were terrific. It was so hot and people grabbed us, all wanting something done for them. The sights which were revealed as dirty cloths were pulled away were terrible. There is so much need here. Samsoni Bafakulira, Blassio, Nekemia and Erisa are all here and dear old faithful Yakobo, all hard at it and Janet, but we could hardly cope. There was a service first, a loud speaker was used. Len spoke and then Shem, the pastor, and the people heard every word and listened well. Then instructions were given to where they should sit for different classes of treatment. Dr Parry took out masses of teeth. Len did the eyes and examinations and saw people who needed injections and I took money and gave out tickets. We explained they could get injections free at the government dispensary, but they prefer us. Len wouldn't let me or Mrs Parry go and help in the afternoon. (Mrs Len's health was not good). People streamed into the CMS site from all sides, over the hills. It was an amazing sight. The need is appalling and we can do so little to help. I prepared hot water and a meal for him when he had finished, but some people came to see him, and he wouldn't wash or eat until he had seen them.

'The Rukungiri people have done a magnificent job building their new church, and after Len's advice they should be able to finish it. They raised the money themselves in all sorts of ways. One poor widow had nothing to give, no food, no money, too feeble to cultivate, only one thing, a precious safety pin on a string round her neck. She gave this treasure into Shem's hand. Others heard of it and saw her joy and it stimulated them to give more. So the people of Ruzumbira who were so dead, that we used to wonder, "Can these bones live?" before revival came to them, have built their own church. Shem is a real shepherd of his flock.'

Dr and Mrs Sharp returned urgently to England in November 1950 as their elder daughter Mary was diagnosed with cancer of the inner ear and given six months to live. Geoff Stanley Smith, meeting them soon after their return, recalled their 'calm, deep peace and great strength, coming from the past.' Mary underwent radiotherapy followed by two operations. Her confidence and courage when facing the probability that these would not be successful and the possibility of facial disfigurement, were to inspire three other student nurses to answer the call to the mission field. Two went to Ruanda and one to the Far East. Mary made a good recovery but it left her with severely and permanently impaired hearing. While in England, Mrs Len was twice in hospital herself, once for urgent surgery.

'Before my wife and I return to Africa', wrote Dr Len, 'we want to send you a farewell message. But first I want to say how deeply we have been touched and strengthened by the loving and prayerful sympathy given to us as a family and especially to Mary. Your prayers have brought peace and quiet assurance when most needed and we thank you. I know you will rejoice with thanksgiving to hear that Mary is now back on full duty again at the Middlesex Hospital. This extra time in England has enabled us to see something more of the saving and quickening work which the Spirit of God is doing in this country through a host of different agencies: keen evangelical churches, conventions and diverse groups of devoted and Spirit-filled Christians working especially among young people. Truly, God is no respecter of any particular persons, nor is he confined to using any specially privileged mission. But in every land the Holy Spirit ever does his saving and life-giving work of grace in and through fully consecrated believers on the Lord Jesus Christ. What encouragement there is for each of us in Romans 12.1-12, and 1 Corinthians 12. Here we see that God has need of all and each of us; that we need one another.'

Mary wrote too, thanking all those whose prayers had made her very conscious of the Lord's presence during her illness, enabling her to keep trusting him through the darkest days and to hear his assurance that his grace was sufficient for her, his strength made perfect in weakness. She added that as a result of their prayers not only she herself, but others too had been drawn closer to him, and ended by thanking 'all the Friends of Ruanda who have remembered all of us, the children of your missionaries, in your prayers from the beginning of our lives. The older ones of us realize that we owe you very much, and would still value your prayers as we serve the Lord, or train for the work he is planning for us.'

Mr Reg Webster, the Home Secretary of the Ruanda Mission, died in July 1951. Dr and Mrs Len with Joy were able to attend the funeral, and in a moving article, Dr Algie, the Field Secretary, paid tribute to him: 'There is a prince and a great man fallen this day.' They had worked together, one in England, one in Africa, for over ten years.

Dr and Mrs Len arrived in Mombasa on 6th January 1952 and after a long and tiring journey were back in Kabale a fortnight later. Mrs Len wrote to her family, 'There are committees at Ibuye next month, it's possible we will not go, Dad dreads them.' (Dr and Mrs Parry went.) 'We found we had been burgled while away. Dad has lost his medals among other things. The other day I lost my keys to the fridge so I prayed about it. Isn't it wonderful how the great God can bother himself over funny little details of our lives, but it is just because he is God that he can and does do so and he cares. Well next day Eridadi got into his boat and looked down and there they were! I praise our Father for his kindness. There has been a terrific storm here. The Africans say it is because the King had died. Dad found a smallpox case in the hospital so vaccinations are going on apace, and so far no more cases. Miss Hornby has been staying with us. She said yesterday, "I'm never ill. I can't imagine how I'm going to die and what of. Someone will have to come along and kill me!" She really is marvellous.'

June 1952. 'Dad will be preaching on Whitsunday. Our trailer has arrived for building a caravan; Dad is longing to get on with it. The windmills are getting on at Bwama. I think he will be able to turn the lower one on tomorrow and the upper one later in the week. It will make a great difference to the hospital and crèche to have the water instead of using watermen to carry it. The back lawn looks like a boat yard. The motorboat stern needs repair and something in the engine has broken, but he has repaired that. He really is clever. Two paddleboats are ready now and the others need their final coat of paint,' Again, 'The new boat is more like a boat now, perfect shape, light and safe. Now it's a case of thousands of rivets. It's the best he has made. The District Commissioner and others are coming over to see it.'

August 1952. 'We have never lacked what we need but have had to be careful. Ruanda missionaries are on a lower scale than other missionaries in Uganda. However we manage and I marvel at it. It has been God's way for us. We are looking forward to safari with you, Joy, when you finish your training; Dad has nearly finished the caravan. He wants to go hunting but I will not mind so much as you will be there in case of need and William Biteye, Saza chief, Kinkizi, says he is going with him.' (Joy spent 3 months with her parents before returning to UK for midwifery training). 'We have had lots of visitors, Algie and Zo, the Guillebauds, Bishop Stuart and Mrs Stuart and others.'

Meanwhile the Stanley Smiths were still in Astrida. Zöe wrote, 'Another year is starting and our small family is growing. Eight new boys have come this term to the hostel; once again, two of ours were bracketed first and second among the other candidates in the entrance examinations. Now we number twenty-two, one of the second-year boys having failed in the yearly examinations, so having to leave. All the boys are kept hard at their lessons, morning, noon and night; in fact, one of the new ones in his first letter home said, "We have no time here, even to take out our jiggers, except on Sundays." Then they are free from the Frères in the College and spend the day with us. Do pray that all this work may not crowd out the spiritual.

'On Friday mornings, we have been having some stirring times in the women's meetings, especially among the older people. One dear old granny, with a beaming face, told how Jesus saved and satisfied her; she said that, when she refused to drink beer with her husband, he said that he didn't want to drink it alone and he has given it up also, and has become a Christian and they have great peace in their home. What strikes me so much out here is the reality and freedom of their witness, and their willingness to ask for prayer if they are getting defeated, instead of being self-conscious and trying to hide it. It is called " Walking in the Light," and it is this openness which leads to victory in so many homes.

A great joy at this time was that Geoffrey Stanley Smith, Algie and Zöe's son, now qualified as a doctor, returned to Ruanda where he had been born, to work at Shyira. Geoff wrote at the time, "'I, being in the way, the Lord led me." Although I have many happy memories of Ruanda, when I left in 1936 I had not let the Saviour into my life and it has been only gradually that I have been willing to face up to " the plague of my own heart." God's call to Africa has come mostly through a sense of gratitude for his wonderful love and patience with me. The great needs in the missionary ranks after the war strengthened the conviction that the Lord wanted me overseas. At first I did not think it was right to go back to Ruanda, partly through fear lest it should be due to family reasons and partly through pride lest people should think I was choosing the easy path! God has shown me that he does guide through natural circumstances.'

At the end of 1952 Dr Algie wrote, 'In July, Veronica Guillebaud, after helping me for two years in the typing of the Ruanda Old Testament (and in many other ways), flew home with the manuscripts, and delivered them to Bible House. It seems incredible that, after the late Archdeacon Guillebaud had translated the Pentateuch, the work on the rest, which began in 1938, should only just now be finished. For long periods it had, owing to overwhelming pressure of other work, to be set on one side. Never in all these years has anyone been able to give full time to it, except when, for a space of about a year, Mr. Monier of the Adventists did most of the prophets and the poetical books. I wonder if other translators have the same experience; but every time I look up some passage, I seem to find something which could be improved. However, the great joy is that at last the Old Testament, our Lord's Bible, is on its way to being printed for the people of Ruanda.

'It has been decided that we should be relieved of the work of the Home, and go to Gahini. Bert and Heather Osborn are to replace us, and they will come young and fresh to the work. These five years at Astrida have been an interesting and varied experience. I have to confess, with much sorrow, that my faith and spiritual life had grown very dim — a lesson to me and perhaps a warning to others, to teach us that however long our service and experience, we can never get away from the need of a daily walking with Jesus. Thank God, he has forgiven and cleansed all this through his precious Blood; and he has restored the sense of his presence and the joy of his salvation and service.'

In January 1953, Dr and Mrs Algie moved to Gahini. Zöe wrote, 'We thank God for bringing us back here where we lived years ago in 1928. Then there was only one European house and that was thatched with grass, and the hospital had not been finished building. With the burdens lightened, Algie has time to get on at last with the revision of the New Testament for Ruanda. He is more than half through Acts and wants to get on quickly before the Old Testament proofs come back for reading. Here, there is much testing for, though rain has fallen all around, just here there is none and many are repenting of fear of famine. We are praying for rain, and for the showers of the Spirit. It is thrilling to hear from those who have come up from Kenya of the power of the blood of Jesus over the blood of the Mau Mau oath that so many of the Kikuyu people have taken. The "saved ones" are fearlessly witnessing for him, in spite of threatened death.'

In March 1953 Mrs Len wrote to her children, 'More visitors. People seem to love coming here and we love having them. The island is getting known as one of the most lovely in East Africa.' Another day, 'We have been to a cocktail party given by the Governor at Kabale, it was a very friendly occasion.' And in September,' We are going on safari to Bufumbira. All the dogs and puppies are going too, and from there to Kinkizi. Dad wants an elephant. Pray he gets it quickly and safely. It's such a risk. The chiefs said, " Do be careful of the Mwami going after elephants, Mukyala (lady)." They will send a good game guard or two with rifles with him. We need a new car, and Bwama could do with the money.' Joy commented years later, 'It is humbling for me to think of the dangers he faced to educate us and provide necessities.' (For a note on the ethics of hunting at that time, see appendix.) In October Esther wrote while on the safari, 'Yesterday Dad was out after elephant with two men for 7 hours without finding any good ones. He saw lots, but only young males with short tusks. It's Sunday, we had a nice service in camp round the camp fire. Leopards abound of course, so the dogs are safely in our tent at night. I can't walk now and have to be carried in a chair slung on a pole. We are expecting lots of patients tomorrow.' October 28th: 'Out again in search of elephants. It's like a needle in a haystack. Dad returned without one.' Soon after they got back they were burgled again. 'The dogs were quiet but the safe was gone. A cloud hangs over the nearby village and everyone is upset having the police and so on. Dad has had trouble with sciatica. It is a comfort that Dr and Mrs Parry are back from Burundi.'

The people of Kigezi persisted in asking for a hospital again, but there were difficulties. Mrs Len told her family, 'Dad was saying last night that he doesn't think that the idea of a hospital will come off'. John Bikangaga, retired elder statesman, recalled to Joy Gower (Len and Esther's daughter) in 2004, 'He had his eye on a flax factory; he wanted it [for a hospital] and so tried to get it but the mission in the field was not behind him and that influenced the whole mission, and they did not back him and he was going single handedly on it....He was alone.' Dr Len continued to go out to the people on medical outreach, and sometimes Mary, now working in Buganda, was able to help them on safaris.

In 1954 Mrs Len wrote, on safari, 'Kinkizi, Patients are coming but not so many, we will be able to manage comfortably. There will be more at Bambura. It's wet and cold but we have our caravan. I had a hypoglycaemic attack and felt queer...There were hundreds at Ruzumbira. Back at Bwama every Friday crowds come across the lake for medicines. One woman said she had come from Mbarara and would rather walk 100 miles than go to the hospital there. Some have come miles for 2nd injections... they walk vast distances. Such is the feeling all over the country. They say they are treated with love by us.' Gradually Dr Len did fewer safaris, because of Esther's health.

Mrs Len described to her family 2nd May 1954: 'We have had an exciting time during the Queen's visit, in Entebbe. We saw the plane arrive with a R.A.F. escort and heard the 21 gun salute… then European and African motorcyclists in white helmets arrived and a large Government House car flying the Royal Standard, then there she was wearing a lovely green dress and a little hat and sitting bolt upright. We then went to Government House and found our seats under flamboyant trees. Sir Andrew Cohen, the Governor of Uganda, greeted her. The Queen was lovely… Nursing sisters in their blue capes lined the route to the dais. There were addresses of welcome from the Katikiro, (prime minister) of Buganda, an Indian from the Legislative Council and the Chief Secretary, then the Investiture.

'In the afternoon there was the Garden Party… all well arranged… Theo Goodchild and Jim Brazier were there and we stood with them. At last she came with Sir Andrew Cohen who stopped and said "Your Majesty, may I present Dr and Mrs Sharp who have been doing leprosy work?" She was charming, "How long have you been out?" "Forty years, Your Majesty." "Oh that's a long time  and where are you doing leper work?" "In the Western Province your Majesty." "How many lepers?" "About 700." "Do you get many cures?" "Yes we are able to send a number home each year." "That's good. Are the new drugs helpful ?" "Yes they are." "I'm so glad." What a thrill, we never expected such a thing! The Duke supports her wonderfully. She then sat and watched the K.A.R.band…

'Next day we went to Jinja early. The Queen was in blue and in spite of the heat, she walked round the parade ground and presented new colours. After lunch we went to the dam, our seats were near the dais and we saw it all. Water was gushing out of the sluices of the great dam but they stopped. The river Nile had been simply boiling but it dropped dramatically and rock appeared and it fell and fell until very low indeed. Then she came. She pressed a button and the sluice gates opened and a huge volume of water rushed foaming and roaring out. She just sat and watched it evidently thrilled. It was an amazing sight… After a picnic and fireworks we went home.'

In October Mrs Len wrote to her family: 'We had a visit from a fellow missionary, still emphasis on repentance, repentance, and nothing further, not on the work of the Holy Spirit and sanctification at all. Things are vastly improved from what they were in the past... There is a loving spirit now, which is a mercy. Pray about the committees: for travelling mercies but also mercies and grace there, love and a positive message. He wanted us to say we praised God for everything about the revival. We do praise God for a great deal, but could never praise for every thing, as much was definitely wrong and has been put right.' And later in 1954 she wrote again, 'Committee meetings. We arrived very weary. Meetings went well. There is a lovely spirit of love, still great emphasis on repentance but only as a means to an end now, and the life of Jesus by the Holy Spirit is stressed as essential. There is a willingness to get Kigezi Hospital restarted. It has been referred to London. The Executive and African Diocesan Council are urging the restart somewhere in central Kigezi. It's a huge answer to prayer and everyone is encouraged. The Ruanda Council may turn it down, but if it's of God nothing can stop it.'

And at the end of 1954, after Dr Len's annual leprosy survey at Bwama, Mrs Len commented, ' He reckons that if things go on as well as they are doing now, leprosy will be eliminated from the district in 15 years. There is a big percentage of arrested cases this time and many can go home and so far, only one of the hundreds he has seen is worse. Then Bwama's work as a mission hospital will be done.' Early in 1955 the Chairman of The Ruanda Council, Rev L.F.E.Wilkinson and his wife, visited all the mission stations. They came to stay with Dr and Mrs Len, who wrote to her family: 'He is most keen on Kigezi Hospital, and on Friday, William Bitye, Saza Chief of Kinkizi, Filemoni Kikabaraza, Saza Chief of Ruzumbira and Blasio Balinda came to tea. Then they got down to it. Out came the map. Filemoni said there was good land that his father Kalegesa, hereditary chief, would give in Rukungiri. Then when the flax factory in Rukiga was suggested, they all jumped at the idea of asking for the site. Though in a hollow, it has good buildings, a waterfall for electricity and land... and they urged Dad to ask for the site. Next day he saw the District Commissioner about it. He was most helpful and friendly. He told Dad to put in an application and gave him other helpful suggestions.' As a result, an application was put in for the flax factory site at Kisiizi.

In June Dr and Mrs Len returned to England for the wedding of their son John to Doreen Harris and they returned to Uganda in October. The retirement of Dr and Mrs Sharp was marked in London by a farewell meeting in C.M.S. House on 13th October, 1955. In his farewell message, Dr Len said, referring to the miracle of Jesus feeding the five thousand, 'He said to Philip, "Where shall we buy bread for these people to eat? He said this to test him, for he knew what he would do." As I have been thinking over the days that are past, it has been very clear to me that the history of our Mission has been one long continuing succession of miracles, which have come about because Jesus saw the need and he spoke to his disciples, whether here in England or out there, of what was in his mind and in his heart, so that he was able to do the miracles.' Then recalling what had happened through the history of the mission, in spite of many problems, and how God had answered prayer, ' I have one personal word. When Jesus spoke to Philip, he said, "What shall we do about all these people?" He wanted Philip to work with him and he wanted to work with Philip. It is like that with us today.... There is one little word that I want to leave with you, and it is *we*. He did not say: "Where are you going to get it?" He said: "Where shall *we* buy bread ?" When Jesus speaks to me, it is *we* — he and me. It means that he has a plan, which he wants to do, something which is on his heart, and he is willing to do it, but he needs you and me. Whether it is here at home, or out there in Africa, let it be "*we*" — Jesus and you, all the time.'

Mrs Sharp who was recovering from an operation, added, 'It's not at all easy (to say the least of it) to 'retire', but we feel it's right to go back and do what we can in various ways. You won't forget us, will you? I think that as we face the many added problems of retirement and approaching old age we shall need your prayers more than ever before. I'm sure we can count on them. I do thank all of you who prayed for me in my recent illness and operation. I am wonderfully better, though so sorry it has curtailed our chances of seeing many of you while we were on this short visit to dear old England.

'Mary is already in Buganda, working as a nursing sister, and making it a real missionary job. She asks for prayer for her Bible Class for African trainees in the hospital, for her Sunday school for white children, and her many contacts for Christ both with Africans and Europeans. She is keeping wonderfully well and we thank you again for your prayers for her in the past. Joy is also going out to Uganda and sailing with us on 26th October, but we are not sure where she will be stationed. Christian doctors and nursing sisters are so badly needed in government service and can in many ways touch people for Christ. It was a great joy to us to see John married and to know that his heart is set on what he knows to be God's call to him to come to the land of his birth and help the people as only a missionary doctor can. I must stop, but I want to thank you and to thank our faithful God for all the way he has led us, both in our personal lives and in our Mission through all these years. He is the God who does wonders and has done wonderful things in and for our Mission in establishing it, caring for it and giving us revival personally, and through the whole work, and to so many other parts of the world as well... So we take courage for the future. We praise him for all that is past, and trust him for all that's to come.'

Dr and Mrs Algie went on a short leave for the summer of 1954. They met Jim at the Billy Graham Crusade at Haringey, where Jim shared his glad news of his love for Edith Wittenbach. At Haringey also Margaret Palmer, Geoff's future wife went forward to give her life to Christ. In 1955 the double engagement of Geoff and Margaret and Jim and Edith led to their weddings in England in the summer of 1956, for which Zöe flew home specially. Dr Algie remained with his newly formed translation team at Mbarara. In the providence of God a double African Christian wedding had been arranged on the same day as Geoff and Margaret's wedding, July 21st, 4,000 miles away.  Dr Algie was asked to speak and rejoiced in both celebrations — God is no man's debtor.

Geoff and Margaret went out to work at Buhiga for 8 years and then at Matana for 4 years before coming back to GP work in the UK in 1969.  Jim and Edith soon joined CMS and went to  a Teacher Training College near Embu in Kenya for 8 years.  Jim was then appointed Religious Education Adviser for the Diocese of Mount Kenya, which involved visiting schools and Christian camps for 8 years. After returning to England in 1975, he was Area Secretary for CMS in Winchester and Portsmouth Dioceses and was ordained and served in the same area.

At the end of 1955, after over 40 years service in Uganda, Ruanda and Urundi, Dr and Mrs Stanley Smith and Dr and Mrs Leonard Sharp officially retired from active service.

1. *A Grain of Mustard Seed, Lindesay Guillebaud.*

Sharp's Island  pg214

Boat building Dr Len Sharp with helpers  pg 199

Sea plane on Lake Bunyoni  pg199

Bwama Hospital rebuilt  pg193

Dr & Mrs Algie at the Home de l'Alliance Protestante,
Astrida 1948  pg210

Bwama Island 1948

Emmanuel Church Bwama pg211

The doctors deep in conversation

Rukungiri. Dr Len safari
'There were thousands of them ... all wanting help' pg221

Kisiizi 1958 pg244

Dr John,
the future Dr Andrew
& Dr Len Sharp

Dr Len & Dr John Sharp
at work with a\ndrew

Retirement

Deep in conversation with Mr E Mugimba  pg255

Eseri Serubibi & her
daughter Margaret Rose
pg277

Dr Algie with emblems of
Kigezi Blood Brotherhood
ceremony January 1968
pg 257

Wedding of Stanley Peregrine
Smith and Sophie Reuter
16th September 1888
pg13

## Chapter 13

# Fruit in old age
## 1956 - 1980

Released from responsibilities, this was a time for new opportunities. Dr and Mrs Sharp continued to live at Sharp's Island for 6 years, and then at Mombasa, Len for 16 years and Esther until her death in 1962, Dr and Mrs Stanley Smith lived at the church centre at Mbarara for 21 years. Many visitors, both old and new missionaries came to see their senior colleagues. Other visitors included many Africans with whom and for whom they had worked during the preceding 41 years.

Kigezi Hospital was closed in 1939. Dr Len and Dr Algie had built that hospital and served in it for many of its almost 20 years, but at that time, under wartime financial restrictions and with a new government hospital a few miles away, the Mission had needed to concentrate its reduced resources in Ruanda-Urundi. Although some missionaries had seen this as a step forward, for the people of Kigezi it was a devastating blow. They had loved and trusted the medical care they had received in the mission hospital and dispensaries, and the government institutions had not yet earned their trust nor covered their needs. Travelling among them as he did, Dr Len was well aware of this. Although the situation was accepted — there was no alternative — the Church and people of Kigezi did not give up hope and prayed that at some time in the future, God would provide a church hospital again. That hope and prayer was fulfilled in a remarkable way.

During World War 2, the British colonial government had built a flax factory at a place called Kisiizi, some thirty miles north of Kabale. Some buildings had been erected and a small hydro-electric plant had been installed. The project was not a success, and the site was left unused. This did not go unnoticed by Dr Len Sharp, and it was thoroughly discussed with the African leaders of Kigezi, as described in the previous chapter. They all saw the possibility for a hospital at Kisiizi to take the place of the closed Kigezi Hospital. Dr Len applied for government permission for the site, its small buildings and the hydroelectric plant in 1955, the plan being to establish a church hospital, backed by the Ruanda Mission.

Objections were raised by various government departments. A long time went by as alternative uses of the site were explored: a tea or pyrethrum processing plant perhaps? But neither these, nor a bark tanning industry, peppermint extraction or even the production of soap, were found to be workable. The local people were eager to grant the land, but the buildings were government property and it seemed unlikely that they would be given to the mission for conversion to a hospital. Negotiations were set in motion and for three years the issue hung in the balance.

As John Bikangaga remembered, talking to Joy Gower in 2004, 'The Government was not keen to let Dr Len have the site, and he shared all this with us. We too got discouraged. I was one of the senior people stationed at Kabale and we tried to persuade him to choose another location and we told him we would try and get it. He said, No. He wanted Kisiizi for the hospital. We were short sighted, but when he got into these problems and shared them with us, he said we should organize a prayer meeting every week about it. So we met every Thursday and we prayed. My impression was that we were praying for the impossible, but we did! That's my impression of Dr Len; he was determined. Even getting Sharp's island, as we called it, for the development of the leprosy work was difficult because the DC had a government camp there and the DC refused; I think he (Dr Len) took it to Entebbe and he got it. So I hope you, Joy, have the same determination. You have your father's character, both quiet. Mary is like her mother all the way. Dr Len encouraged me to join the local government, which I did.' This was the beginning of John's distinguished career.

Many people gave up hope, but Dr Len had an unshakeable conviction that Kisiizi was the place of God's choice. History repeated itself as, in the face of many obstacles, the prayer of faith was first made and then acted upon, plans laid and preparations underway even before the answer was given.

Meanwhile, two of Dr and Mrs Sharp's children had heard God's call to them to serve him in Africa.    Mary was already in Uganda and she explained her call: 'Born in Wimbledon, I was baptized at three months at Crosthwaite Church, Keswick, on 25th July 1924, but I did not know until I found an entry in my Grandmother's Bible many years later, that I was also publicly dedicated the next day in the Keswick Convention tent, to serve God in the foreign mission field, should he call me. After completing my nursing training in 1953, I returned to Africa but because I had had cancer I was only offered short-term jobs, and spent intervals helping my parents. While with them because my mother had been ill, on the morning of 20th June 1956 God clearly called me to full time service through the verse "Go you also into the vineyard, and whatsoever is right I will give you." (Matt. 20.4). That same afternoon a letter arrived requesting my help at Ibuye hospital, Burundi. This gave me the certainty of my call, and my parents great joy and thanksgiving. So I started working for CMS, first at Ibuye and then at Mengo hospital until 1959. Then again with CMS, I was appointed Travelling Secretary for the Kenya Hospital Christian Fellowship 1964-1977, building up Christian fellowships among healthcare workers throughout Kenya, which involved much travelling. I lived with my father after my mother's death in November 1962. He was my best prayer partner during all my many visits to hospitals, clinics and conferences. Since Dr Len's Home Call, God has guided and provided for me and I have inherited a whole lifetime of benefits from him through my parents and other Christians.'

John Sharp, now a qualified doctor, was certain that God wanted him to be a missionary, but when a request came from the Kigezi Church to be in charge of the new hospital, he said no, feeling that this was too much like going home — not the fulfilment of a missionary call. However, when the request came a second time, he realized that this was from God and that the answer must be yes. He reached Africa with his wife Doreen, a physiotherapist, and son Andrew before the Kisiizi site was granted. So while negotiations continued, John and Doreen worked at Gahini, gaining valuable medical experience in the hospital, and for Doreen, excellent training for missionary life in Africa.

Eventually, in March 1958, a telegram arrived for Dr Len from the Governor, ' KISIIZI IS YOURS.' Most of the site was granted for a nominal sum. A miracle indeed! The news brought tremendous joy to the African Church, and preparations for the hospital began. St Thomas's Hospital Christian Union, London, of which both John and Doreen Sharp had recently been members, rallied round and provided equipment. As Doreen described, 'March 28th 1958 was a red-letter day for us. John's parents drove us on the 30 mile journey from Kabale to Kisiizi at the start of the great adventure. We were accompanied by two lorries loaded with hospital equipment and our luggage, and trailing the home-made caravan — our first guest room, where Len and Esther would stay when visiting Kisiizi to assist in the planning and building work. On arrival we found many willing helpers to unload the lorries and to help us settle in.'

Two days later a dedication service was held, led by Kosiya Shalita, Bishop of Ankole-Kigezi, and a crowd of several thousand gathered on the site to rejoice and to praise God. Some had arrived the night before and slept in the disused factory buildings, others walked all night, and one of the sheds was filled with bicycles. Both the founders of the Mission and many leading people of Kigezi were present, and all thought back to the time 37 years before, when the two doctors had arrived at Kabale, and among their many projects was the building of Kigezi Hospital, to which Kisiizi would be the successor. As Doreen wrote, 'the sound of the roaring waterfall as we stood was an apt reminder of the Water of Life which we prayed would flow continuously into the hearts of needy men and women coming to the hospital.'

The work of transforming a flax factory into a hospital began immediately but it was not until March 1960 that two wards, with a total of 24 beds, were open to receive patients. Experienced workers who joined the staff were Eriya Kabarira with his wife Irene, who had worked at Kigeme, and Mary Sherratt, an experienced nursing sister from Burundi. And as Dr John Sharp noted, 'My father, although retired, has nevertheless given invaluable help and advice to the "raw recruits", and mother's green fingers have been busy among the vegetables. As we are thirty miles away from Kabale we would be rather cut off were it not for their frequent visits.' Doreen got to know her mother-in-law well at this time and admired her organizing and practical abilities. She found that Esther, by nature an outspoken person who could, at times, be misunderstood, had a motherly, caring heart for those around her. She gave herself as a wife and mother and was fully behind Len's pioneering work, often at great cost to herself in the lack of physical comforts and in sometimes dangerous situations. It was she who laid out the gardens at Kisiizi.

Dr and Mrs Len continued to live on Sharp's island. As Doreen remembered, 'For those who went to spend a few days there it was a real haven of peace and tranquility. Arriving from the mainland to this idyllic island by motorboat or canoe was like entering another world. For one thing, watches had to be put back an hour, providing for the workers arriving on the islands early in the morning to come in the light. If you were staying in the small guest house you would be right near the water's edge with views of the lake at all times of day from the mists of early dawn to the glorious sunsets. There was always a welcome and hospitality in the spacious home of Len and Esther, and the garden, so carefully laid out and tended by Esther and her helpers — you could hear her giving directions for the day to her gardeners as you had a leisurely breakfast — was just the right place to find renewal for the jaded missionary.' However, Esther's health deteriorated and with high blood pressure and attacks of angina, it was necessary for them to move urgently to sea level, which they did early in 1961. They rejoiced to know that Nora and Dick Lyth would be working at Kabale and John and Doreen Sharp at Kisiizi, 'helping our dear Bakiga in these difficult and changing days'. After a farewell from his much loved leprosy patients, and a Church farewell tea party in Kabale, they left by car for Kanamai, a few miles north of Mombasa. Their daughter Joy met them in Kampala and went with them to the coast to help them settle in.

There followed two happy years for Dr and Mrs Len: new surroundings, new friends, a Kenya Church Centre next door with fellowship and activities taking place at times, a new garden to develop and a small sailing dinghy for Dr Len, not one he had made himself this time, and for Mrs Len, the convenience of all 'mod cons' for the first time in their own home, except of course when on leave in UK. Their cottage near the beach within the lagoon gave them safe bathing, and Ruanda friends and family loved to come for holidays. Their happiness was increased when their daughter Joy married Leon Gower, headmaster of Butobere senior boys school, near Kabale, on 3rd March 1962, in Mombasa Cathedral.

During the last few months of her life, Mrs Len's thoughts were often filled with the Second Coming of Christ. While a Ruanda missionary was visiting them, she suffered a severe heart attack. Joy and John joined their parents the following day, but in the early morning of 5th November, after a prayer to God for Len, Christ came to take her to himself.

Following Mrs Len's death, Dr Len's health deteriorated seriously, but much though he missed Esther, he kept himself busy and involved with life around him. His daughter Mary joined him in December, making her home there with him in his cottage by the shore for 14 years. Mary has said, 'We had a very simple life. We were very close to the sea. He had a boat so we would sail in the lagoon or go out to explore the reef, returning with the next tide: it was enjoyable and good for us both, but he was lonely without Esther.'

At the end of 1963, Dr Len and Mary spent a few weeks in Kigezi. Most of this time Len spent helping his son John at Kisiizi after visiting his African friends in Kabale. He stayed at Kisiizi during January, while Mary started her first journey under CMS as Travelling Secretary for the Kenya Hospital Christian Fellowship. Her work involved travelling throughout Kenya to encourage staff of all professions in their Christian lives, service and witness. Some distant visits took her away from home for two or three weeks at a time. Meanwhile Dr Len supported her with prayer and was often involved with conferences held at the church centre next door, preaching and leading Bible studies. Ken Jones remembered of this time, 'On a visit when Mary was amusing our children, my wife Valerie said, "Mary is good with children", and Dr Len replied, "She's good with old men too!"'

All the time Dr Len followed world events and kept himself widely informed. The atrocities in Ruanda and Uganda after independence were subjects of his concern and earnest prayer. He was a member of the Ruanda Council all his life.    It was with mixed feelings that he saw Joy and Leon leave Africa for UK in 1964, but it was all in God's plan, for it provided a home for him on three visits to England that he was to take in the following years.   In 1965 he went to England for medical reasons, after which he was advised to avoid all physical exertion.   His two devoted helpers coped faithfully with every task and learnt skills for everything needed, and were always on call for him if Mary was away.

Royal Navy ships would come into Mombasa from time to time on goodwill visits, and the ratings were employed in useful activities in the community. Once when Ark Royal was in port, a request was made for men to clear an area for a football pitch at the Kenya Churches' youth centre next door to Dr Len's home. A simple task, the officer said, but after the ratings had failed to dig out a large palm tree, they decided to blow it up. A charge was laid at the foot of the tree. Everyone stood well back. Bang, a cloud of sand, but the tree was still there. A stronger charge was laid. Bang, more dust. Frustrated, a third much larger charge was laid. A bigger Bang, but the tree was still unmoved, so the officer ordered a massive charge. There was a huge explosion and the palm disappeared over the tops of the other trees, falling in pieces over a wide area. Unfortunately large chunks came straight through Dr Len's roof and into the room where he was sitting. He went round to see the triumphant sailors whose faces soon turned to dismay when they heard what had happened. There were many apologies and they then had the extra task of repairing the damage.

For John and Doreen, there followed years of great progress but also testing. In 1965, they experienced a fresh outpouring of the Spirit in the hospital and among the staff, and as Doreen described, 'the Lord worked so that there were those who were filled with the Spirit and others were awakened to understand what he could do for them. It was during this rewarding time spiritually that John began to have the first symptoms of illness and for a few weeks he was in Kampala having tests but there was no definite diagnosis.'

In March 1966, Dr John and Doreen returned to the UK prematurely, on medical advice. On arrival in England, John was diagnosed as suffering from a tumour in the area of the brain affecting the visual field. The letter telling Dr Len and Mary in Mombasa of this diagnosis reached them on the evening of a day in which Mary had escaped almost certain serious injury or death when a cement water tank exploded near where she had been standing moments before. This miraculous escape gave them encouragement as they praised God for Mary's preservation and committed John, his treatment and his and Doreen's future into God's hands. John had an operation in which part of the tumour was removed and this was followed by radiotherapy. Sadly there was no improvement and he was 'finally released from all his weakness and translated into the presence of the Lord' on October 16th 1966. Through the kindness of a relative, Dr Len had been able to return to England to be with his son during the last few months of his life. There was grief in the Sharp family and great sadness in the Church in Kigezi. God had taken their first son from Dr Len and Esther while still a baby, and now John, to whom they were devoted. In the words of Dr Algie, he 'had already proved himself in every way as a doctor of outstanding ability, a preacher of the Gospel of great power in the vernacular, and in his life a radiant witness to the love of Jesus; then taken in the prime of life.'

There were many other tributes, such as that of E. Bisamunyu: 'His early leave to join the company of saints as his mother did was felt very acutely by the Bakiga, who had come to count on his kindness as much as his wisdom in medical services in the district. He was mourned by the Bakiga as one of their own.' He had strong bonds of friendship with local people, and understood their way of thinking, having lived there since childhood. He had started the hospital and established its work over eight years.

Doreen Sharp returned to Kabale in 1967 to help at the Kabale Prep. School, and then to work seconded to Scripture Union in training Sunday School teachers in village churches, working as a team with two Ugandan women. On returning to UK three years later, she worked in the Ruanda Office and was a member of the Ruanda Council.

In 1971 Dr Len and Dr Algie went to the UK for the Golden Jubilee of the Ruanda Mission (CMS) taking part and speaking at celebratory meetings in London and other cities. During that time a private family reunion was arranged for Len and Zöe's brothers and sisters. Back in Mombasa, Dr Len continued to follow Christ's example in preaching and healing, as he had all his missionary life, ministering to the hearts and bodies of neighbours living along the coast, bringing faith to a lonely white settler and treating all who came to his door: children from local villages and casualties from among the beach dwellers. He gave treatment and pain relief to people who came to him with numerous mishaps and injuries. Some of those he treated suffered from serious accidents or other emergencies, which meant he had to take patients in his car in the middle of the night to hospital some miles away.

The Kenya coast with its heat and humidity was a bad area for poisonous snakes. Many were killed over the years in Dr Len's garden, and on three different occasions his dogs were attacked or killed by them. One day the gardener reported that he had seen the tracks of a large snake coming towards the house, but none leaving it. A search was made but nothing was found. The next day Dr Len noticed that the books in a bookcase were protruding. So he pushed them back into place, only for the books to move out again towards him, so he put his hand behind a book to find the obstruction — to touch the coils of a snake! Helpers approached the bookcase armed with long sticks and wearing glasses. The books were hooked out one by one, to reveal a large snake, which was quickly dispatched. The common snakes were puff adders, green mambas, spitting cobras and pythons.

Dr Len kept in careful and interested touch with family members to the end of his life, and air-letters he sent to Doreen in increasingly wobbly writing show his loving concern for her and her three children, praying 'that you may be granted a double spirit of wisdom to make up for that which John's presence would have provided'.

Archbishop Erica Sabiti, of Uganda, Ruanda and Urundi visited his old friend near Mombasa and asked Dr Len to revise and enlarge his little booklet, *Great Truths from God's Word*, for the modern needs of the Christians. Erica gave Dr Len a number of additional subjects to be included in a new edition. This was a great encouragement to Dr Len who worked on it with Mary's help, just completing it before his final illness. (Mary was not able to take this further until after her own retirement and the new edition was printed in 2004).' [1]

As Dr Algie wrote, ' There in his little bungalow on the shores of the Indian Ocean, tenderly and cheerfully cared for by his elder daughter Mary, he showed to all who visited him the life of a Christian in suffering and the all sufficiency of Jesus to meet his need. Never a word of complaint! Never a trace of self-pity! His thoughts were fully occupied with the needs and interests of others, with the progress of the work he had done so much to begin and, above all, as he fed his soul on the living bread in Christ and in the word of God, he dwelt in a growing intimacy with his Saviour and Lord.' His life was frugal. He did not have access to the health and social services available in England, and since he had retired overseas, his pension was fixed (except when he visited the UK, when to his delight it jumped to the current amount). When he fractured a hip, he was unable to afford to hire a Kenya Red Cross wheel chair, so Mary fixed ropes to his chair and pulled him from room to room. He never asked the Rwanda Mission for help, not wanting money to be diverted from its work.

After a final period of almost continual sickness, God took him to his reward on 2nd March 1976.   Dr Milton Thompson who attended him wrote to Dr Algie, 'In those last days his spirit never faltered; he was serenely waiting for his Lord. On Sunday I took his hand. "David, I'm going Home, I'm nearing the end," he said, looking straight at me. He smiled and his face lit up with the joy of the Lord, full of peace, the peace of Jesus that passes all understanding. So, quietly he went to heaven.'

Kosiya Shalita, Len's friend, was one of many who were present at the funeral of Dr Sharp in the Cathedral on 6th March 1976.   David Milton Thompson gave the address, 'We are here today to lay to rest...all that is mortal of Leonard Sharp: doctor, missionary, teacher, preacher, servant and saint of God. Leonard had two guiding lights. Firstly, he and his fellow-labourers stood uncompromisingly for the complete inspiration of the whole Bible as being, and not merely containing, the word of God. He believed absolutely in the infallibility and trustworthiness of Holy Scripture. Secondly his aim was, in his own words: "the calling out of a living Church; men and women and children who have come to know the Lord Jesus Christ as their own Saviour from the guilt and stain of past sin and from its power day by day; men and women growing in grace, fruitful in service and in likeness to Christ". He was such a man himself and he longed for others to be the same.

'God honours men who honour his word. And so it was that there came to Ruanda a remarkable out-pouring of the Holy Spirit, which brought literally thousands to a personal knowledge of Christ, as they were broken and repented. This would hardly have been possible without the Biblical foundation so well laid, and insisted upon by Leonard and his friends. This work of the Holy Spirit spread to all East Africa and beyond, and its influence is still with us to this day in bringing men and women to the Saviour. The finest memorial that we can raise to this noble life is to renew our dedication to Dr. Len's Saviour and Master. To continue with the unfinished task until our Lord Jesus Christ comes again in his glory.'

A memorial service took place in London in May 1976. The sermon was given by Dr G Hindley, based on the farewell address Dr Len himself had given to Ruanda supporters and friends in London, on his retirement 1955.

Dr Len had placed the following epitaph on Esther's grave and left instructions for the same wording on his own grave:

**Jesus sent them forth two and two**
**And they went preaching the Gospel and healing everywhere,**
**The Lord working with them.**

In 1956, on their retirement, Dr and Mrs Algie moved into temporary housing at the Church Centre in Mbarara, in the Ankole district of Uganda. There they concentrated on translation work and also on outreach to refugees. When violence broke out in Rwanda in 1959, many Tutsi refugees crossed the border into Uganda and settled in a refugee camp in the Orukinga Valley, not far from the border. When Ruanda became an independent country in 1962, (changing the name to Rwanda), the Hutu government again attacked its Tutsi population and many of them had to flee for their lives and crossed the border into neighbouring countries. Many settled in Ankole, Uganda. It was a terrible precursor to the events of the genocide 30 years later. Despite the ethnic violence Dr and Mrs Algie visited Rwanda. 'Our car approaches a barrier on the road in Ruanda', Dr Algie described a frequent occurrence: 'the troops on duty come out to inspect papers and permits to travel through this land, once so peaceful, now so full of fear and hate. Some of the men are nice lads, others so brutalized and savage. "Would you like something to read?" we ask. And as they crowd round eagerly, we give out John's Gospel and *The Way of Salvation*, the healing word.'

Among the refugees were a number of Dr and Mrs Algie's friends whom they visited frequently and were often able to help, especially over their children's education and medical needs. Africans from Rwanda and Burundi would call in to see them for they were assured of a welcome, and Dr Algie often wrote letters of introduction to help them to find work. Expatriate teachers working in the local government school were also invited to their home for tea and fellowship. Dr Algie was sometimes invited to preach at Ntare Government Senior Secondary School and there he met Leon Gower, one of the masters, who married Joy Sharp a few years later. On many afternoons, Dr and Mrs Algie would combine their after-tea walk with visiting and encouraging families, Christian and non-Christian, who lived within walking distance of their home. Mbarara was a convenient half way stop from many church centres in Rwanda and Burundi, and missionary families, on the way to or from schools in Kenya with their children, would call in to see their honoured senior missionaries, often quite unexpectedly. Accompanying the missionaries would often be Africans from Rwanda and Burundi, who simply wanted to greet them and chat over their fellowship in past years. Back in the 1940s severe shingles with persistent pain had affected Mrs Algie's good arm. In 1967 she experienced complete healing from the pain, as well as final relief from lifelong migraine, for which she praised God.

Dr Geoffrey Stanley Smith records from his parents' Mbarara years, 'I remember some of Dad's letters some of which were largely to do with medical questions, as I was trying to keep him supplied with medicines he could not get in Uganda. Dad and Mum were delighted to have frequent visitors at Mbarara, and many remember the joyous welcome they received, with tea and cakes. In addition to Dad's translation work on the Bible, he had a regular commitment translating Scripture Union notes for schools and churches in the diocese. These involved the 180 miles' journey from Mbarara to Kampala for the printing. I suppose Dad felt personally responsible, having done the translation, for sorting it out with the printer. One other big area of activity was their involvement in the local refugee camp where 12,000 Gahini people and those from near the Uganda border had settled. When I visited Gahini and other centres in March 2005, I met families whom he helped over matters to do with children's education and other pressing problems. This was remembered with great joy 50 years later, when I met up with them.'

Zöe wrote: 'My chief interest is, and always has been, the Sunday School work here. Our faithful leader and superintendent, Mr Phinehas Butukaine, has left us to take a course of training in youth and Sunday school work at Selly Oak, Birmingham. He is a younger brother of the Rev Amos Betungura, now at the London College of Divinity. I hope some of you will meet them both. ... In our Sunday school we have a few faithful teachers left and recently the church has realized the need of appointing one of its evangelists as superintendent. This is a very hopeful move, and another encouragement is that some of the senior secondary school boys have started coming to teach. We would value your prayers for them.'

In the same way that Dr Len had managed to combine building houses, hospitals and churches with his medical work, so Dr Algie, being linguistically gifted, combined medical and translation work. In retirement, he did more of the latter, his major task being to co-ordinate and work with the teams translating the Bible into Rukiga and Runyankole. The Rukiga team was headed by Petero Kalebya and the Runyankole team by Eliezer

Mugimba. It brought Dr Algie great joy when the translation of
the Bible in the combined languages was completed, fifty years
after he and Dr Len started work in these parts of East Africa.
His letters record progress.

1956: 'On the 16th July, we shall have completed our first
six months since starting on the translation of the Bible into the
Ankole-Kigezi language.' A year later: 'Our team of translators is now four. I had long been asking for an English-speaking
African who would enable me to get into really close thought-
contact with my colleagues, and in a wonderful way the Lord has
given us just the man we needed. He is Mr Eliezer Mugimba. He
joined us in January and we finished Revelation together. So the
first draft of the New Testament was finished in about one year.'

Also in 1957: 'In preparation for the Uganda Diocesan mission
we had the Epistle to the Romans printed in Uganda, and it is
now being distributed far and wide. I was greatly cheered by
hearing one of the leading Africans in Ankole say of it: "It flows
beautifully in good Lunyankole, and at last I find I can understand Romans".... We have had an added task, the translation
of the Consecration Service for our friend and brother, Kosiya
Shalita. It seems wonderfully timed that, just as the new diocese
is founded, it will be having for the first time the word of God
in its own language.'

In 1958: 'Those of you who have been praying for the translation of the Bible into the Ankole-Rukiga union language will
rejoice with us that the manuscripts of the New Testament arrived
safely at Bible House on 19th August. There are still a few points
unsolved, but any small changes needed will be incorporated in
the proofs. We then began on the Psalms, and we have now come
to Psalm 59. So I hope that, by the end of October, they too will
be sent in. The Bible Society have promised to do their best to
let us have the New Testament and Psalms in 1959.'

16th July 1960: 'I am sure you will be glad to know and
praise with us that today the Bible (translated for the people of
Ankole and Kigezi) has been finished. Malachi was started this
morning and finished at 4.30 p.m. Of course, there is still much

to do as regards typing, revision and corrections, but the initial translation is done. It has taken four and a half years as it was begun on 16th January, 1956.'

1961-62 Review: 'The Bible we have been translating for five years is finished. The New Testament will soon be in circulation. The Old Testament will soon be in proof form. The Prayer Book is finished and 300 hymns are nearing completion, and the SPCK are prepared to print it. The healing word is on its way to a people more than ever torn by conflict: political, racial and religious. Pray that it may be used in the power of the Holy Spirit.'

Dr and Mrs Algie then went on leave. On returning they moved from house to house until their own house in Mbarara was completed. Zöe commented, 'How thankful we are to have a roof over our heads, when so many of our dear people in Ruanda have lost everything and are homeless. Algie has been busy reading and correcting the *Light of Life Studies in John* for Ruanda. He has also been running a language school at Kabale in Lunyankole-Lukiga and changing into that language the English names for places in the maps of the New Testament which are due out this summer.' They enjoyed 'a great family re-union at which Geoff and Jim with their families met for the first time since their weddings seven years ago; Nora and her family were with us, too.'

As Algie reported, 'The year 1964 was a vintage year for our translation team for so much of the effort of the past eight years seemed to come to fruition. The finished Bible is now in this country and a great Thanksgiving Day was held on 28th March this year at Kabale and Mbarara. When the prayer-book and hymns arrive, the worship of the whole Church in this area will be in their own language.' Having completed in 1956 the translation of the Bible begun by Harold Guillebaud for Ruanda, Dr. Algie and his team had now completed a similar task for the Ankole and Kigezi area of Uganda. But this was by no means all he was doing in these 'retirement' years. He and his team were writing Scripture Union notes to help people with reading the new Bibles, they were organizing systematic language teaching for new missionaries, they were sometimes asked to translate 'unexpected manuscripts such as the Constitution of the new Diocese of Kigezi', and they were cooperating in joint translation work with the Roman Catholics, now that, as Algie put it, 'The Bible is no longer a closed book to them...Who can tell what the Holy Spirit will do in these days of unparalleled ferment and change?' Now in his late seventies, Dr Algie was still keeping in step with the Spirit, and responding energetically to new situations.

On the 1st January 1968, a very special honour was conferred on Dr Algie, Constance Hornby and five others. At a meeting of the Kigezi District Council on a hillside with crowds of onlookers, the Secretary General of the Council asked the assembled members and the crowds, 'Is there any reason why this man should not be admitted to our blood-brotherhood?' 'No!' responded the crowds on the hillside. The Secretary-General, wearing the traditional robe, climbed on to the platform and sat down on a stool. Dr Algie followed, and sat on another stool facing him. The two men joined hands for all to see, as the solemn oaths of the ceremony were read. The Master of Ceremonies draped Dr. Algie with the traditional robe as he stood to receive the emblems of Kigezi, the spear and the billhook. He said 'Simiisi, we now give you a new name, Rugangura (Overcomer), because of your victorious struggle against sickness and Satan, which when you came here, you found robbing us of our peace'. Dr Algie made the most of the occasion. In his expression of thanks he reminded the people of the ancient blood-brotherhood custom by which the partaking of the blood ended the enmity between man and man and between clan and clan. 'Surely', he said, 'this is a God-given parable of the precious blood of Christ, the only means by which we can be reconciled to God and thereby admitted into that blood-brotherhood in our Lord, which is now uniting people of every tribe and culture in the world'.

In the last lap of Algie and Zöe's service at Mbarara, Zöe could no longer read, but her peripheral vision enabled her to see on-coming cars. Algie's diminishing visual fields did not stop him reading and driving. He commented 'Between us we had a workable and safe pair of eyes!' He had always been concerned for the thousands of ageing men and women who needed reading-glasses and had checked vision and supplied glasses whenever he could to people who rejoiced to read again the words of life. At Matana alone, in a few weeks, 760 men and women were checked and spectacles supplied.

In 1971, in the UK for the Golden Jubilee of the Ruanda Mission, with Dr Len present, Dr Algie was asked to comment on the changes in missionary activity as he had witnessed them: 'In those far-off days we left Britain as missionaries, woefully inexperienced, and landed in Africa, expecting to be leaders and teachers with authority to do as we thought best. Now we fly from UK and touch down in Africa to become fellow-members of the Church in this country with no authority whatever, and only acceptable to the Government of the country in proportion to the usefulness we can be to the Church and the nation, until such time as the jobs we are doing can be taken over by Africans — then our work permits will be withdrawn. Yet the doors are still open and the people are very welcoming to all who come to them as brothers and sisters in Christ.

'The whole pattern of missionary work may have to be changed; the Church itself may go through a process of major re-shuffling. But here in our perplexity, before us stands a Man with his drawn sword in his hand and he says: "As Commander of the army of the Lord I have now come." He has his plan of campaign perfectly worked out; our part is not to hang on to worn out tactics, or cling to organizations which have outlived their usefulness, but to trust him, to obey him and to love him with heart and mind and strength.'

One day in the mid-1970s, when Dr Algie was completing the Rukiga-Runyankole Bible with his two-tribe team, he confided sadly to Bishop Kivengeri, 'Festo, I don't know of anyone whom I have led to the Lord.' Festo replied, 'Algie, can you possibly tell the number of people who have been born again through reading the Bible you have translated?' The Bishop's words were a big encouragement for Dr Algie towards the end of his many years of dedicated work in Africa. A similar story is told by Dr Allen Bapty who was working at Kigeme in 1956 and was visited by Dr and Mrs Algie who had started the work there, against much opposition, in 1935. Allen was telling Dr Algie how, after six months at Kigeme he was feeling a failure and unsuited to the work. Dr Algie completely understood, saying that he too, often felt unfit for the work. 'I don't know of a single person who has come to trust in Jesus Christ through me,' he said, 'but we felt sure we were called here and we've had no clear guidance to go away. So we've stayed...We don't see success, we're not called to see success, we're called to be obedient, and to be witnesses to Jesus, and the love of the Father.' The constant stream of elderly people, many leaning on long thin sticks, who had walked for three or four days to see the Stanley Smiths, bore witness to the gratitude and affection of the people. And when, some weeks later, Dr Bapty mentioned to a group of fellow hospital workers what Dr Algie had said, they were aghast: 'What! There are many, many churches in the hills round about which have started because of him. He has been more effective than all you other missionaries put together!'

In 1975 Dr Algie had his first heart attack. While in hospital he wrote of a fresh encounter with his Lord, setting him free for the final lap of his earthly journey with inexpressible joy and praise. Later, as Dr Algie wrote, 'In 1977, our last year in Uganda, came an unforgettable June week-end at Kabale when we were invited by the Diocese of Kigezi to the Diocesan Centenary Celebrations (of the first Christian mission in Uganda in 1877). As Zöe and I stood there, our thoughts went back 56 years to the time when first Len and Esther, and then we with our little Nora just one year old came to Kabale for the first time, and we saw as on a wide panorama the ups and downs of those eventful years. And there we were again, facing now a vast rejoicing crowd of 15,000 people, praising God that there were many there, from those tiny beginnings, to testify to all his faithfulness "in bringing many sons (and daughters) unto glory" to this triumphant and joyful day. Those happy people were just a small part of the harvest which the Great Harvester, the Holy Spirit, had gathered into the granaries of the Kingdom of Heaven.

'Then came our decision to return to England, the packing up and the final journey to Kampala. Nora was able to come and help us pack up our belongings; our task was much simplified by being able to dispose of most of the heavy furniture to Kisiizi Hospital. This was a miracle of God's provision for them; a new doctor was expected in September, the money had come to build a second doctor's house, which would be completed in August, without any furniture available; and there close at hand was all our stuff! We set off for our final departure to Kampala on July 21st. Our Bishop had thoughtfully arranged for a driver to take most of our luggage in our little old VW, and gave us the use of his new Peugeot 504 with a splendid African driver — real VIP treatment! The VW had gone ahead, so you can imagine our consternation when about 50 miles out of Kampala we saw it in trouble at the side of the road. All our efforts to get it moving again were in vain; and then — miracle of miracles! Up came a huge transporter for carrying new cars to Zaire or Rwanda returning to Kampala empty. It took only a few minutes for our friends to persuade the driver to take our VW to Kampala. Down went the ramp, up went our car up the ramp, and off they went to Namirembe Guest House, for only Shs 720 — instead of Shs 5,000 for a lorry.'

'There was to be one more farewell party, but perhaps for us the most moving of all. It was organized by Mr John Bikangaga, Chairman of the Makerere University Council. He had invited about 200 of our personal friends from Kigezi and Ankole to a tea-party in the International Hotel. Here the panorama stretched before our minds was the widest of all; its span stretched from 1915, when first Dr. Len and then I (9 months later) arrived in Mengo, sixty-two years before our final departure from Africa. This party was a moving expression of the love they had for us from the earliest days, when we were working there among them. This heart-warming time was made all the richer by the presence of Nora, who with her husband Dick Lyth had served in Uganda for 12 years. Dick was Headmaster of Kigezi High School; on the next tour he was the creator and pioneer of the Christian Rural Service; and finally he was chosen to be the first Bishop of the new Diocese of Kigezi. The next day we flew for the last time with hearts full of thankfulness to God for all his mercies to us and to our family; as well as gratitude to a host of our African friends for their love to us, and for their fellowship, often challenging and always so helpful, fellowship in the grace of our Lord Jesus.'

Dr Algie's final year in England was based in Chorleywood, where Dick was on the staff of St. Andrew's Church. They were able to stay for most of that time with Nora and Dick. Nora writes of this time: 'They stayed with us in our little bungalow with an attic and we had lovely times together. ... We had a caravan in the garden for all the visitors and family to stay, as a spare room. They enjoyed so much the church fellowship of St Andrew's, and folk loved them too. How thankful we are that we were given this happy year together, when all the children and grandchildren and great-grandchildren were able to come and visit them'. Of her father Nora wrote, 'We watched him accepting his increasing weakness with faith and hope and courage of a very high order — uncomplaining for himself and thoughtful only of others. He was only seriously ill for a few days and his mind remained astonishingly clear, so that he was able to send his farewell messages to a great many, both black and white; on his final day he was even heard working on some translation point.' Dr Algernon Stanley Smith died on Sunday 28th July 1978. His death coincided with the Lambeth Conference and so six African Bishops were able to be present at the funeral service; it was a time of joy and triumph (ending with the Hallelujah Chorus), as he would have wished.

Zöe continued to live with Nora and Dick. She was truly looking forward to heaven, but she confessed that the process of dying filled her with some alarm. Just a week before she died, Dick and Nora went on a planned holiday, and Nora arranged for her to stay the week in a local residential home, where the manager was an old friend of Zöe's. She was in good health, but after a day or two a very gradual and gentle stroke took away her awareness, and she slipped away peacefully to her beloved Lord. Throughout their 56 years together in Africa, Zöe's little book of daily Bible verses, given by her mother, was packed from 1919-1978 with births, weddings and bereavements of countless friends and family in Africa and the UK. This demonstrated her touching care and love towards young and old who got to know and love Dr and Mrs Algie, very much to their enrichment and joy. Mrs Zöe Stanley Smith died on 21st April 1980 at the age of 88.

Dr and Mrs Algie had faced their hardest trial, comparable to John Bunyan's Slough of Despond, in the 1940s, when he was trying to draw together and heal the 'revival' group and those who had reservations, a difference which threatened to divide the Church. As a result, Dr Algie would experience 'the dark night of the soul' for days or even weeks, his wife always at his side, sharing his suffering. Indeed, she suffered doubly, because her special brother Len, together with Esther, were going through it too. However there was light at the end of each tunnel, and they triumphed gloriously, finishing their courses with joy, in a Church bound together in love.

Looking back over his long association with Dr Len, as friend from student days, colleague and brother-in-law, Dr Algie wrote, 'I hope it is not sentimental to say that Len's friendship was for me of the kind of Jonathan and David, and how true that was of our partnership. We were labelled 'co-founders' of the Mission, but Len was always the senior partner, for God endowed him with outstanding gifts. Perhaps the first was the gift of leadership. Personally I thank God for all I learnt from him and for his wise guidance as we sought God's will for the policy of the Mission. With this gift he combined an inflexible determination to carry through what God called him to do; and in keeping with that, unshakeable faith in the word of God and his gracious promises. Then too, he was a man of vision.'

Vivid memories of Dr Algie were recorded by Dr Joe Church: 'He was a superman indeed, a brother, closer than a brother! How I praise God for that CICCU missionary breakfast on 22nd November 1925 when we listened to Algie appealing for Ruanda, and for the call of God that changed the whole course of my life.

'We saw him years ago, climbing those hills and valleys of Kigezi, planting and shepherding the many village churches. We saw him listening — he was a wonderful listener to endless 'words', as they are called in Africa, in cases and problems that had to be talked out, slowly and carefully. The teachers and the evangelists loved him for that. "We must wait till Algie comes", became the frequent remark when a problem cropped up on our stations, as they were always doing. He was not an encyclopaedia, but he had wisdom — the Wisdom that has a capital 'W'. And I never, I think, saw him ruffled.

'He steeled himself to stand pain. He once had to extract one of his own teeth that had become infected; Dr Len told me this. One day on safari, one of the six cylinders of our Gahini hospital car began giving trouble, and we could not tell which it was. Algie calmly said, 'I'll show you the quickest way, Joe'. He rolled up his sleeve, and with the engine idling, he gripped each plug in turn with his thumb and finger. This sent his whole body into spasms, as each sparked, until he found the dead one.' (He once used this 'E.C.T.' technique on a deranged patient who, having been grunting like a pig, was cured instantly.)

'I remember his furious tennis at Kabale…His car driving.' (Algie had determined that when he was 80 he must drive his little car at 80mph along a stretch of the long straight British-built tarmac road connecting Kampala to Kabale. This he did.) 'I think he was one of the bravest men I have ever known. He wore that coveted blue and white MC ribbon for bravery, but we never quite knew how he won it.

'"Ask Algie" was not just a lazy man's way out! He was gifted at everything. He would quite quickly find the mistake in the hospital accounts, that had stopped them balancing. He would scrub up and help with that difficult operation which we had been keeping till he came. He would get down to architectural plans on the drawing-board, with ruler and squared paper, for some new building, yet he always encouraged our own ideas. At night we would lay them before the Lord in prayer and in fellowship with African leaders, especially Yosiya and others.

'We were often trying new ideas especially after the Holy Spirit began to move in our midst. As we often said you can never have revival without some problems. We knew the answers spiritually but we needed Algie all the same! God seemed to be trying to get through with us on new lines of worship that are becoming common-place today in some churches in England.

'Problems of revival and church order and inter-mission co-operation did weigh heavily on Algie and for a time were too much for him. But we all rallied round, and as a Mission came to a deeper place of repentance and brokenness. Bishop Jim Brazier once wrote that Gal. 2.20 formed the basis of our message where we see the bent 'I' bowing at the foot of the Cross. In closing there seem to be three 'C's' that epitomise the life of Algie: Caring, Courage and Christlikeness. We praise for every memory of our leader and say with our African brethren "Till we meet"'.

In going out together, Dr Len and Dr Algie followed the same pattern that Jesus used, and the same instructions that Jesus gave the disciples when he sent them out in pairs (Luke 10). He sent them out, ordinary people, to the villages where he was about to go. It's the same pattern that God uses today, to go out into his world, wherever we are, and make disciples or followers of Jesus from all nations.

Dr Algie described his friendship with Dr Len as like that of David and Jonathan. Their loyalty, respect and commitment to each other, and above all their love for the Lord Jesus, bound them together to spend their lives in his service. And at the end of the journey looking back, they were amazed at how God had led and helped them every step of the way. How he opened doors for them at the right time, getting them into Rwanda and then Burundi; how he arranged unexpected meetings with key people as they looked for important sites for future mission stations; how he helped them through difficulties, hardship and suffering to praise God for it all.

Dr Len did not want any memorial, saying that the churches he had built were his memorial, and when Dr Algie was asked the same question he replied. 'No memorial', and then as he thought of those magnificent churches, St. Peter's church at Kabale, Christ Church Matana and Emmanuel church on Bwama, he said 'They are Len's memorial; they will do for me as well!'

The doctors wanted no credit for themselves, but they paid tribute to the many parishes, Friends of Ruanda, the Ruanda Council Office, staff, family and friends and very many others who had given them their prayerful and generous support, and not least their own wives, 'Missionary work would have all come to a stop if there were no brave women, and we men wouldn't have been able to do half the work God gave us to do if we had not got these wonderful wives to help us.'

Above all they gave praise to God. It was his work, he knew what he planned to do and brought it to pass.

' Hallowed be Thy Name. Thy Kingdom come. THY WILL BE DONE ON EARTH AS IT IS IN HEAVEN'

---

1 *Since the publication of 'Great Truths from God's Word' in 2004, this book has been translated into Kirundi and Punjabi with other translations in progress.*

# Chapter 14

# Old friends revisited
## 2004 - 2005

In 2004 Mary Sharp, Joy and Leon Gower and John Sharp's grandson, also named John Sharp, visited Kigezi (after a 40 year gap for Joy and Leon). They were given a great welcome. Many people who remembered Dr and Mrs Len came to greet them and talk about their memories. They included doctors, clergy, teachers and academics from many professions, bricklayers, carpenters and hospital workers. Some who were too frail to come sent representatives, others brought photos, treasured since 1960. Many people who had known Dr and Mrs Len spoke of their happy relations with them, especially the teaching of Dr Len and his compassion and sympathy for all who were sick or in any kind of trouble. Then in 2005 Geoffrey Stanley Smith visited Rwanda and Burundi, and met many people who remembered his parents.

Joy Gower describes how, after a visit to the government senior secondary school near Kabale where her husband Leon had been Headmaster, 'the Kabale diocesan office arranged an itinerary for us. We stayed at a pleasant little diocesan guest-house, and many Africans came to talk to us and recordings were made. We also went to the new St Peter's Cathedral for a thanksgiving service and were introduced, and each of us spoke. St Peter's Church (later Cathedral) has been succeeded by a larger cathedral behind it, and my father's fine building is now the library of the University.

'Another day we went to Bwama island. My father's old boat-men who used to ferry lepers to Bwama when they arrived at the lakeshore were waiting to greet us before we got into a boat to take us across the lake. We were welcomed at Bwama with a feast in the old hospital central entrance hall, now staff office for the secondary school, which has taken over the buildings. Many old people had come from their homes to see us. We spent the night on another island where Dr and Mrs Parry had built their house. A visitors' centre with accommodation for guests has been built there.

'The following day we were taken to Sharp's Island where a very large crowd had gathered. Singing and shouts came across the water as we approached. We were helped ashore by many hands, flowers and garlands given to us, and we were swept up to our old home with much celebration. It was very moving and a great tribute to our parents. On the outside our house looked much the same, just shabbier, but inside it had been gutted with a view to making it into one large conference hall.' (A young doctor visiting from UK in 1968 had noted the English feel, the smooth lawn, the photograph of the Trinity College Cambridge 2nd XI hockey team still on the wall of the deserted and unfurnished rooms). Joy continues, 'They had prepared a feast for us, and afterwards we sat outside for speeches and a display of dancing, much of it very vigorous. We then separated so that as many of the people as possible had the chance to talk to one or other of us. We wrote down some of the testimonies. I took photos and sent a copy to every one who had come and had known Len and Esther.

There was a service of Thanksgiving in Emmanuel Church, Bwama, where Mary preached. The church was as beautiful as when it was built, lovely proportions and roofing beams, and the aluminium lettering for texts on its walls, that we had helped to cut out, were still in place. Outside, the church retained its tower but sadly had lost its tall steeple in one of the ferocious storms that would sweep down on the lake. That steeple had been raised to its place without a crane by a wonderful piece of engineering, and stood through many years. After a meal with the Archdeacon on Bwama island, we returned to Kabale.

'Sharp's Island is still beautiful but all the lawns are long grass. Many of the trees had died or were dying and the flowerbeds long since gone. Tall reeds that grew round the shoreline except on Bwama and Sharp's Island had grown back round these too. In my father's day, no reeds were allowed round these two islands, so that they were not breeding places for the flies and mosquitoes which would threaten the health of residents. There were still purple water lilies and beautiful birds. The people living on the hills round the lake seem very poor. No industries are possible, only growing crops and bee-keeping. There is the beginning of a tourist industry on the lake, which employs a few. School fees are difficult to find, and the Bwama school tries to keep fees as low as possible and so has little to spend on maintenance and equipment.

'There were changes in Kabale too. There were more buildings on the hill, but the old ones were still standing, even our house built in 1921, though it had been altered and partially rebuilt. The lawns and grounds laid out by my mother for a prep school were still there unaltered, but whereas houses and gardens used to be laid out with lawns and flowers, now the buildings were surrounded by high fences and padlocked gates, probably a result of the Amin years of terror and other change.'

These are some of the memories and testimonies we recorded:

**Canon John Bikangaga BA (London)** former Constitutional Head of Kigezi District, Lutakirwa Ngabo.

When Len arrived in 1921, the people were bothered by major diseases: typhus, yaws, leprosy, sleeping sickness and dysentery. First typhus, which was because the people were dressed in skins which had lice. He fought against that and influenced the government to arrange the smoking of the skins which the people wore, then he fought the yaws and finally established the leprosy work at Bwama. He spearheaded the medical work in this area, and at one time appeared to be doing it single handedly.

**Eli Nathan Bisamunyu BA (London)**

The vision of Dr Sharp and Dr Stanley Smith to plant the germ of education in Kigezi and guide it towards academic standards of British institutions were well ahead of the Colonial Government. The doctors with supporting labour from the Bakiga built Kigezi High School and other schools. Many of the buildings are still serviceable. The results of the pioneer work of Dr Sharp and Dr Stanley Smith have been self-evident through the large number of academic, medical, artistic, and religious professionals this small district has contributed to every facet of Ugandan life. Every child educated in Kigezi today will owe them and their families a vote of thanks. The faith and courage that brought them will remain a remarkable source of inspiration for the children of these hills and a critical part of their history.

**Jolly Baburukamu** Member of Anglican Consultative Council and member of joint standing committee (executive) and focal person for international Anglican womens' network at A.C.C. Former Provincial Mothers Union President, Kigezi.

My mother, Barbara Tibangagwa, married in 1949 and died in 1995. She worked as a nurse with Dr Sharp at Kabale and at Bwama. She said Dr Sharp had a heart for Africa and Kigezi in particular. She had a very good relationship with Dr Sharp but a special one with Mrs Sharp whom we called 'Kirungi'. Dr Sharp was always preaching the Gospel and teaching the Bible.

He went out of his way to go out to people, treating them in their homes rather than always making them come into the hospital. The most interesting time for my mother was going to Bwama island to take care of the lepers. You know that there were no motorboats then and it was sometimes dangerous for canoes to be on the lake. People discouraged her from nursing lepers but she loved the Lord and she did it for him.

### Kabale Diocesan Centre

We remember Dr Sharp for the history he made here. At the beginning he was a teacher. Most African children at first feared to go to school because they were told that white people would eat children and they ran away from them. Dr Sharp wisely managed to convince the chiefs to start a school and he started with the sons of chiefs so that after learning to read and write, they could spread the Gospel in their own language. Dr Sharp also helped Constance Hornby to begin a girls' school so that the sons of chiefs would have wives who could also read and write, and so education could go on to the next generation. If a girl became pregnant before marriage she would be taken to Kisiizi and thrown over the falls. That would be the end of her life, so girls feared to leave their homes.

### A clergyman son of the late Samweri Butaara

My father used to work with your father. Your family was very instrumental to mine because of the introduction of the Christian life to our family, beginning with my father who became saved during the time of your parents. My grandfather was a man who had nine wives having their own gods. But my father, for a long time up to his death lived a Christian life, which was not the case with the others. So when I meet you I really feel I have met people who prepared to help my family. My father died in 1973, but we always heard him make comments about your family. My father used to talk to us about education, going to school.... My mother was a village woman but she also enjoyed a Christian life because of my father. They were wedded in the church, they were all saved, she lived a happy life in the whole village, just because of Christianity. At first they would be abused by other members of the village, but they persuaded these people and she died a saved lady. And we have maintained that spirit in our family. We are all Christians, and I think that is one of the reasons why I am working in the Bishop's Office, otherwise without that background I don't think it would have been possible for my grandfather's family.

**Rev Canon John Kimote.** Retired Teacher and Pastor (In charge of Bwama island after the settlement closed).

I would like to tell you about what happened at the island when I was there. I was still young when I was there in 1948 as a teacher from college at Kako, Masaka. I was posted to the Primary School that was led by Sister Grace Mash. She was still young then. We worked together for a long time, 31 years, just teaching in the school.   I met Dr and Mrs Sharp who were just working wonderfully. They were not old. Oh it was very wonderful, especially in 1935 when revival came. He was a doctor, a farmer, a hunter and I remember he preached the Gospel round the villages, before the churches were there. He just went on preaching the Lord, and he used to send some teachers to help him round the lake. And he built so many churches round the lake. He was a teacher really, a very good teacher, and also a doctor, so if you combine all these things that he did... I came to know the Lord when I was a teacher and a young man. After 17 years I left teaching and I joined the Church at the Theological College Mukono. Then I went back to Bwama. Dr Parry was there and he was ordained as a pastor. For some years he worked in the church, then he left, and I took over as a pastor. After a short time you know, I took over an archdeaconry of 14 parishes. Then I decided to go home as I was 65 years old. So now I am at home with my family and I praise God, and especially for the life of our beloved father in the Lord, Dr Sharp, and his family. Now I am talking with my sister, Mary, praising God that she understands what happened in their time.

My names are **Aggrey Turyamubona**, Turyamubona is the surname and it means 'We shall see God'. We shall see Jesus, I think I was called that name during the time of the revival. My parents had just seen Jesus and they felt they should call me that so that everybody who comes to this world could be able to see Jesus. I was called to work at Kisiizi Hospital after my course at Matawa in 1963. I was called to work as a hospital secretary, and I worked there for 7 years. I left immediately after Dr John Sharp had died. But his father used to visit our hospital to advise us on different issues. I personally was privileged to meet him because I learnt a number of things. I learnt how to make bricks and to make plans for the buildings and I was blessed too, to start a project of planting trees round Kisiizi Hospital . If you visit Kisiizi Hospital today you will see a very big plantation where they are cutting timber. I started with that project by being inspired by your father Dr L Sharp. So later on our electricity broke down, and Leonard Sharp taught me, I had never known anything about physics, but he was able to teach me how to connect water to the water shoots and mend the electric generator so I learnt everything and so I was able to help when he left, I used to help with the power at Kisiizi Hospital. He was the one who taught me how to do it. And secondly he used to give us some lectures about faithfulness, about hard working. I was a young man and I inherited that being faithful and trustworthy was important in whatever had to be done. I worked with Dr John Sharp. I was a teacher in Sunday Schools with Dr Sharp, with Smith, with many others, so I came to know Jesus Christ as my Lord and Saviour. I would like to add that I am happy to meet Mary because we met at one time at Kisiizi Hospital in 1966, and she preached to us the Gospel of Jesus Christ together with her friend from Kenya, Patrick Osuka.

**My name is Rev Canon Ezra Mahega.**

I came to know Dr Sharp and his family in the 1940s when I was here in Kigezi High School as a young boy… I came to know him better, because the head master used to take us to Bwama, and especially to Nzuyera (Sharp's Island). When we met him and his wife, they welcomed us very warmly and prepared lunch and cups of tea for all the school children. After that it became a special place for Kigezi High School boys to have a picnic there. And that is how I got to know his son, John Sharp who worked at Kisiizi Hospital. Dr L Sharp was very kind and very serious in his work, he used his leisure time to work on patients. So we praise God for his work here especially to preach the Gospel, to heal the sick and the lepers. Many lepers accepted Jesus Christ as their personal saviour through Dr Sharp and his wife. And John Sharp, when he came to Kisiizi, he took steps to preach the Gospel. At that time I used to go to Kisiizi, and he was a very kind boy, hard working and then unfortunately he died.

**My name is Canon Shem Kasigazi.**
    I knew Dr Sharp. He helped us by giving us books and taught us how to preach the Gospel in Kigezi. I remember that he preached the Gospel at Kisoro, for it very definitely killed that goddess (Nyabingi). We had very many people and we are very thankful for that gospel. So Dr Sharp gave that word 'Jesus came to conquer the devil', that really helped us to know Jesus.
    When we visited him he prepared tea and every thing we needed and his wife used to give us books and converse with us. When the time came and God called me to work at Bwama, Dr Sharp was no longer there, but he prepared the work we did. I was working as a government servant, but I used to co-operate with brother Kimote, so that the work the doctor did could continue. To look after the houses, the education, and even the canoes and some people were still there, blind people, just to look after them, so we did our best with that work till the day we left the place for other duties…. We thank God that Dr Sharp gave us the foundation of where to start to build the Church up to now. Now the Church is a diocese, through the work of Dr Sharp.

**Rev Canon W Komunda**
    I was born in 1920, at Bukinda. Later, I knew Dr Sharp and

his friend Dr Smith, They came to Bukinda to see the Christians. I heard them preaching the gospel to us about the love of God. I knew really that they were the people of God. I heard at that time of the revival. They visited every church, building new churches up. By 1939 so many churches were built in Kigezi. In 1949, I, and my brother Shem, were students at the Normal School and Rev Ezekiri Balaba took us to visit Bwama island, and the home of Dr Sharp. We were like their children... so the house became ours, because we became their children at that time. We had things to eat. We sang hymns. Later John Sharp came to Kisiizi, I knew him very well because I came here and my wife was working in KPS (Kabale Preparatory School) and was a friend of John Sharp. We worked together, we preached the gospel together, it was one fellowship, until your parents left.

When Dr Sharp went to heaven I was here as a pastor. We thank God really for the work your parents did, through his hard work but also led by the Holy Spirit, and your sister and John. Now we praise God for when I received Jesus as my personal saviour and the power of the Spirit in 1935 when I was 15 years old. And up till now God has led me in the steps of these two people, Dr Sharp and Dr John Sharp, through the Gospel they preached. Now I am 84 years old, and they still call me out to preach the gospel. I need your prayers.

### An old man at Kihihi, Kinkizi.

My father was a patient at Bwama. He took me there to stay with him because my mother died when I was two years old. My father became an assistant in the hospital. Everything was good and shared. Once, when my father was out on the lake in a canoe, there was a storm and my father sunk in the lake in his boat. Dr Sharp came in his motorboat and saved him from death. I went to Bethany School with Miss Mash. After school I decided to work in the hospital and I was given work there. Dr Sharp was a very great help to me to speak English and it was arranged for me to go to Mengo hospital for further training. Dr Sharp was a very good doctor and when he went to Kinkizi to see people and those who were infected with leprosy, he took me with him as a dispenser.

I am **Fasi (Faith) Rwamytwe.**
I saw Dr Sharp when I was young. When he used to come to the hospital people would say, 'Ah, this is Dr Sharp'. They used to bring people to the hospital suffering from yaws, and he healed them and every kind of disease. Later he was the first person to preach the gospel in our villages. He used to tell parents to send their children to school, but some parents were ignorant and did not believe that if they sent their children to school, it would help them in the future. Dr Sharp built the church, before that we had a very small one near the school. It was a very big church. I remember when he moved to Bwama island, but being young I did not understand all that they were doing. There was a time when we had meetings, we understood and welcomed our Lord Jesus Christ.

**François Mbirigi** , one of Dr Sharp's carpenters at Matana.
I remember Kosiya Shalita coming and he went everywhere trying to make friends with people. At first, he was ignored but gradually he broke down their fears with his love. Eventually he was joined by Dr Sharp who taught him carpentry, and on Sundays I heard the good news of Jesus which entered my heart until this day.

Travelling with Mary, Joy and Leon in the summer of 2004 was a young medical student, also named John Sharp, the grandson of Dr John and his wife Doreen. He spent six weeks in southern Uganda, and was very aware how different his experience was to that of his great-grandfather and Doctor Algie, the pioneers. Unlike them, 'I flew there at 600mph, travelled on (fairly) well built up roads, and lived in guest houses and lodges.' One question in his mind was that of the relative merits of long and short-term mission, of which the lifelong commitment of the pioneers and the modern gap years are extreme examples.

(Something in between, a commitment of perhaps three to ten years, is often practised nowadays.) He commented, 'I was, in most part, convinced that long-term mission is more effective and genuine. I met people whose lives had been affected by the efforts of those first missionaries, and this, I assume, came about partly because of their lifetime commitment to the work. Presumably the presence of a living Church in the area is also partly a result of their work, and I saw that in Kabale. Having said this, I also see that nowadays it is not necessarily a requirement to stay in a country for life. For one thing, travel is so much easier now, that one can travel fairly frequently. For example, I have been to Albania with a Christian Medical Fellowship team three times in the past two years, helping to support and encourage Albanian Christian medics. Although we go there for only a week, we can use that time to build them up as Christians, and then we can keep in touch with them by e-mail.' John realized too that the doctors at that time needed to commit themselves to the leprosy and other medical work for a long stretch of time, whereas on the medical side of things nowadays it is more appropriate for western-trained doctors to provide periodic training but not to stay at a hospital long-term.

While John was studying at Cambridge, he found that 'my non-Christian friends were quite militant in their dislike of the idea of mission. However, talking to Christians in Uganda, I realized that none of them would regret that their forefathers had been told the Gospel. This experience allowed me to return to university with ammunition to answer those who think that cross-cultural mission is condescending. It is a message of good news that far outweighs the difficulties that go along with people from one culture interacting with those of another.

'The joy of meeting other Christians was particularly evident for me at Kagando, where I was able to mix with other young Christians, and at an international conference in Kampala. It was so good being able to share our lives. I was particularly impressed by the fellowship at Kagando, where the Christian students meet up every lunch for prayer and praise. If only that could occur at my medical school! Travelling with Keith Waddell, an opthalmologist and a Christian, let me see the value of discarding those parts of British culture that cut us off from cross-cultural work, but also made me aware of the need to remain friendly, loving and humble towards others.'

Dr Geoffrey Stanley Smith visited Rwanda and Burundi in 2005, and was concerned to learn of the multitude of splinter sects — over four hundred currently in Rwanda alone. He was reminded of his own experience when working at Buhiga many years before, of the 'pot and pan man', a patient who felt that his role in life was to start a new religion, with Geoff as a co-leader. At church services he would create an orchestra by banging pots and pans of different sizes in the hope of gaining new converts to his faith. Alarmed on this visit by the burgeoning of such sects since Independence, Geoff realized afresh the need for sound scripture teaching in the theological colleges of Africa, and for the revival to continue to bind all God's people together in love. He also rejoiced to meet many people who had fond memories of his parents:

### Margaret Rose Serubibi

I remember my mother, Eseri, telling me how she first met the Smith family. They used to walk and one day they came to my mother's home, where she was playing with other children, but because she was so bright, joking and laughing, she went to meet them. Mrs Stanley Smith asked if she would come and stay with her children so that they could learn how to speak Rukiga. Her brother Adoniya, became a house boy for them and my mother stayed there without fear, playing with Nora, Eve, Geoffrey, and other children. She stayed with them many years. She was loved and she called Nora her sister. They picked up the first words of greeting and how to say 'Wabale,' (thank you) and so on. She wondered at the love shown to her and started to learn good habits. I remember one thing I was told by my mother. She used to say 'Margaret, always speak the truth, and never tell lies'. She told us to have the motive to work, to be grateful for what some one has done, to say thank you and to say yes please. These words helped me so much in my growing up. I remember in school our teachers would tell us things and we would say 'Thank you'. Then the other children would say 'Why do you say thank you?' But I learnt this good behaviour that my mother had learnt from the Smith family. So we grew up nicely because of my mother.

The Stanley Smiths and the Guillebauds arranged a marriage for Eseri with Robert Serubibi in 1929, here in Kabale. The Guillebauds loved my father, they put him into primary school, then he went to Kings College, Budo, and he became a clergyman. My mother had her own house now. I was born in 1931, in August. Mrs Stanley Smith said I should have the name Margaret Rose after our princess who was born in 1930. This pleased Eseri very much. One day my mother found my sister climbing on the table. We were fighting over a bowl of porridge, and she said, 'Ah, you have reminded me of when Nora and Eva broke a dish, they were fighting over it because they wanted to lick it!' When Mrs Stanley Smith came in they both dropped it! My mother said to us, 'I am not going to beat you, Nora and Eva did the same, as it seems that all children behave like this'. So she did not punish us.

### Bishop Adoniya Sebununguri

Because they came to Africa not only do we have the Bible in our own language but also the way of salvation ... Nobody ever saw them angry.

### Bishop Venuste Mutiganda

When Dr Smith was at the Groupe Scolaire, Butare, looking after the Protestant boys and translating the Bible, he was also busy planting 20 churches around Butare. He also arranged for the church at Butare to be changed for a very much better one nearer the centre of the town. ...Now there is a cathedral there with young and old praising the Lord

## Rev Timoteyo Ngendanzi (Matana)

I remember Dr. Smith on one of his visits. I think he was preaching and he said, 'It is more blessed to give than to receive and to feed people than to be fed.' I shall never forget that message.

## Rev Yohana Nizeyimana

I lived at Gisanze where Dr Algie measured the site for the church where there is now the Stanley Smith Health Centre. I remember Dr Smith had time to talk to all the chiefs nearby, so that the site was agreed on. But his chief aim was to reach their hearts for the Lord. He had a little book for us called *The Way of Salvation* which we love, and so the Gospel spread.

## Pastor Anastasie (Kigeme)

I remember Doctor Smith by the way he loved to talk to the poor, humble and despised people. He loved to greet and comfort any who were in distress. His greatest gift was the love with which he treated our illnesses.

## Eliphasie Munyankiko (Kigeme)

I remember very well Dr Smith used to read to us from *Pilgrim's Progress* and teach us to sing. He loved playing the harmonium. I shall never forget those times at the end of the day. He brought to us the knowledge of God and we became Christians. He and Mrs Stanley Smith built us a house and the blessings he prayed for us and our children are with us now. The heritage of his work and prayers has had a powerful effect on our whole family.

## Foibe Munyankiko (Kigeme)

As a girl, I remember Mrs Smith giving me one of Eve's dresses. She taught me to read in the dust. She taught me to learn by heart John 14 and this helped me in the fiery trial of the war when my brothers were killed and God helped me to get the victory in my heart.

**Eseri**, daughter of Enoch Kanyetambi (no longer alive)
When Dr Smith saw my father as a young boy he asked him if he would like to work in hospital. He seemed to be already prepared for that and he was soon working in the hospital, preaching the Gospel and testifying for the Lord Jesus.

**Dolatiya Rutwe** (Buzumbura)
I remember Dr and Mrs Smith. Dr. Smith loved singing to us. He would meet with us schoolchildren and they would talk to us about happy marriage and that love was the most important thing in marriage. Mrs Smith showed us her weak left arm and told us how Dr Smith had said to her many years ago 'I'll be your left arm for you'. Once when I was ill with malaria, I could not swallow the quinine. He laid his hand on my head and I felt better straight away! He had such love in his hands. He said, 'I will pray for you'. He loved preaching the Gospel of the love of the Lord Jesus and peace through forgiveness bringing true unity.

Semugeshe (Chief at Kigeme) was a special friend, but he had many wives. When he was in prison Dr Smith visited him as often as he could and he helped him to repent and accept Jesus. There were many other chiefs who came from the Roman Catholics and they were drawn by his love for them and he always urged them to repent of their sins and some were saved. We praise God for the seed he sowed so faithfully.

At the height of the revival Dr Smith had a very difficult time trying to draw people together who were splitting up. He prayed patiently, listening and humbly trying to help everyone to hear what the Holy Spirit was saying to us.

**From the Church at Shyira** (Translation of a farewell letter to Dr Stanley Smith.)
Sir, We, the members of the Church at Shyira, want to choose out some of the thoughts in our hearts and set them down briefly in saying Good-bye to you to-day.

We thank God for the love you had in your heart long ago while you were still in England to come to the rescue of this land

and to open it up by means of the Gospel. And we thank you that you heard the call and came.

Though we don't know in what condition you found Ruanda, yet we know we were in a deep pit and a very evil one, while Satan was on the throne in Ruanda doing according to his will. As we think of how you entered Ruanda and how you found it, we would liken you to people entering a thick forest, being torn by thorns and by the weariness of the way, and tried by the conflicts provoked by many things and by the people who were there in their blindness.

But now we praise God in a way no words can describe for the fire of the Gospel which you brought. This fire has now caught on, and we are saying good-bye under conditions far better than when we welcomed you. For that which you came preaching has now entered our hearts; now we are under the sway of the blood of Jesus which he shed. God be praised for having saved us by the death of his Son (see John 4. 42). He has loosed us from the bonds which held us captive. Praise be to Jesus! (see Psalm 107. 13-16, and Rev. 1. 5).

Take these words back to Europe. You have not laboured in vain for we have been shown Jesus Christ, and most especially the power of his blood. And now you must salute our brothers in Europe, those who prayed for us before ever we knew these things. We have had a door opened to us to enter into eternal life and many of us have entered in. Tell them to go on praying for us very much, and for those who are not yet saved. Thank them before God for our brethren whom they have sent to us. We still need more who are willing to surrender themselves and come, having a real burden. Tell them for us that we pray for them. Good-bye. We will go on praying for you that you may come back with an abundant blessing (Romans 15. 29).

**Name not recorded**

I thank God very much for those first messengers who came to Kigezi in 1921, when we were in such darkness and I now know him through the Gospel which those men preached to me. They sometimes shook my hand and so I knew they had love. This attracted me to what they taught and I began to love their God and also I began to feel in my heart that I wanted to know the words of their God, so I continued under instruction till I was baptized in 1927. After this, I was trained as an evangelist but I had little peace in my heart until 1933, when there were special meetings in Kigezi led by Dr Stanley Smith and the Rev Kosiya Shalita. Then I was convicted that I was guilty before God and that the Son of God died for me to take away my guilt, which I still had because I would not believe in him. Thereafter I sought for that faith but could not find it but I continued to long for it and also to know what salvation really meant. Then in 1935 there was a convention, led by Dr Joe Church and the Rev Blasio Kigozi and Canon Barham, when I again heard God's voice. I put my faith in Jesus and was saved. What helped me was the hymn, 'What can wash away my sin?' I believed and repented of all my sins and the Son of God forgave me then and has done ever since.

In 1944, I attended a course of training to be a Lay Reader at Ibuye in Urundi. It was on my return to Kigezi that I became very ill. This greatly discouraged me and weakened my faith and zeal. However God in his love sent Dr Sharp and his wife to me and I felt I must talk with him. He examined me and said I must come into hospital for medicine but he said that what I needed most was to trust in Jesus more to help me to get well. From that time I began praying more to Jesus and I recovered. If anyone says to you, 'Trust in Jesus', then do it.

## Other tributes
### Bishop Festo Kivengere

Len's life was devoted to spreading God's kingdom, and it is only those associated with him who realize to the full all that he has done in Rwanda, yet all of us in East Africa thank God for the life and ministry of a true man of God.

**The Most Reverend Erica Sabiti, former Archbishop of Uganda, Rwanda and Burundi.**

I used to see Dr Algie when I was a boy at Mbarara High School, where he often called with Dr Len Sharp to see the Rev Canon Grace, our Headmaster, who was like a father to me. From that time, about 1915, I was attracted to Dr Algie. God in his eternal purposes and plans for his children brings certain people into our lives. We meet thousands and get to know them but they don't all permanently affect our lives. Some do, even when we are separated by events and distances. Dr Algie is one of those who came to hold a special place in our hearts. I was drawn to him because of his love, care for people and humble attitude to all. Many Africans would bear witness to this, and he drew many to his Saviour, through his healing ministry and through the preaching of the Gospel.

He loved and knew the word of God. I still remember the Bible readings given over fifty years ago at Kigezi Hospital when I was there for over a month, and what he taught us about the Jewish Tabernacle, its hangings and colours and how it was a picture of Jesus Christ. I do praise the Lord: it was through him that I accepted the Bible as the word of God, and in simple faith have by the grace of God adhered to it as the word of God, in spite of other teachings I have come across. It was through him that I understood what an evangelical Christian stands for.

From 1939, after I had come to know both Len Sharp and Algie and had been ordained as a minister in the Church, we were posted to Kinoni Parish, just on the side of the road from Kabale to Kampala. The Sharps and the Stanley Smiths often stopped to see us, and we would have fellowship and pray      together. Most of the missionaries of those days from Rwanda, Burundi and Kabale made our home a stopping place, so Geraldine and I felt and still feel we are part of the Rwanda Mission through the founders of the Mission.

We praise God and thank him for the vision he gave to Len Sharp and Algie Stanley Smith, and to their dear wives and to their children, some of whom were called to follow in the footsteps of their parents and come to Africa, and other missionaries too. There are no words which can express our appreciation of these who have gone ahead to be with the Lord. They have received their welcome home and their joy will be complete when they meet with their African brothers and sisters whom they brought to the Lord through their ministries.

Dr Len and Dr Algie both served God in Africa for 62 years. Their story is one of triumph from tiny beginnings, to the salvation of thousands in Kigezi, Rwanda and Burundi; from the challenge to finance the work, through the remarkable way that (unknown to them) God used Government decisions to make the first foothold in Ruanda possible, to the overcoming of opposition both to the establishment of mission sites in Ruanda-Urundi and to starting the leprosy work, and later to the setting up of Kisiizi Hospital. The hope is that it will be a challenge and encouragement to faith for Christians today and will enable them to learn more of the faithfulness of God and the trustworthiness of his word, which shows that although true discipleship will bring opposition, God brings his followers, through perseverance, to maturity and blessing.

# Appendix

## Genealogical background of Leonard Sharp

Leonard Ernest Steigenberger Sharp was born on the 29th June 1890, the third child in a family of eight, to John Emilius Ernest Steigenberger Sharp, known by his third name Ernest, and Mary Elizabeth (née Ballance). Ernest and Mary were both of Huguenot ancestry, and through the marriage of their grandparents in 1806, John Ballance and Elizabeth Heudebough, these two family lines were joined. John and Elizabeth had ten children and of these Eliza Ballance married William Sharp, father of Ernest, and Charles Ballance married Caroline Heudebough Pollard, the mother of Mary, so Ernest and Mary were also first cousins.

## Answers to Mary Sharp (Dr Len's mother)'s prayers for her children

Four of Mary and Ernest's children served as missionaries: May, Leonard, Zöe and Norman; also Ruth for a short while in West Africa. Five joined the professions: Guy chose a naval career and went to Dartmouth College; Leonard, Olive and Ruth went into medicine and Norman was ordained and went to Persia.

## Dr Len's Testimony

Dr Len's article 'A Pioneer Mission' is quoted in part in chapters 2 [1] and 10 [2] and the final section is given here:

'First count the cost. There will be loneliness and disappointments. There may be illness and pain. There may be bereavement, or an early grave. Face it. Is it worth it? And I would like to add my testimony, that not one good thing has ever failed which the Lord spoke. He has been faithful to his promises. He has never failed me, nor left me alone. So friend, you can trust him absolutely.

'There is one thing to remember when you make your decision, How will it look from the end of your life looking back, when it will be too late to choose again? Do you want to regret a life spent in second best things? Would it not be best, like Paul, to be able to say, "I have finished my course. I have kept the faith. Henceforth is laid up for me a crown of righteousness."'

'Let me remind you of the reward:

"If any man serve me, him will my Father honour."

"Come ye blessed of my Father, inherit the kingdom."

"Where I am there shall also my servant be."

"He shall sit with me in my throne."

"They that be wise shall shine as the brightness of the firmament and they that turn many to righteousness as the stars for ever and ever."

"If thou will be perfect, go sell that thou hast and come and follow me."'

## The Aims and Basis of the Ruanda Mission

(Published in every issue of *Ruanda Notes* while that publication existed: 1921-1971).

This basis was expressed in the Constitution of the Ruanda Council, established in 1926.

In short, it asserted:

1. Belief in the complete inspiration of the Bible.

2. Determination to preach full and free salvation through simple faith in Christ's atoning death on the Cross.

3. The guarantees received from CMS safeguarding the future on Bible, Protestant and Keswick lines of doctrine regarding sin and repentance, salvation and assurance, temptation and victory, consecration and testimony.

4. The aims of growing into the likeness of Christ and holiness of life in daily living in the world, dependent on daily feeding on the Scriptures, prayer and fellowship.

## Historical background and cultural change.

The 19th and 20th centuries were times of colonial expansion. In 1916, the area of Ruanda and Urundi was conquered by forces from the Belgian Congo. At the end of the war, the Treaty of Versailles divided German East Africa, with the vast majority known as Tanganyika going to Great Britain but the westernmost portion to Belgium. This area was formally referred to as the Belgian Occupied East African Territories. In 1924 this became Ruanda-Urundi when the League of Nations issued a formal mandate that granted Belgium full control over the area.

Despite the mandate rules, that the Belgians should develop the territories and prepare them for independence, the people were exploited using the indigenous power structure, with a largely Tutsi ruling class controlling a mostly Hutu population. The anger which grew from this oppression was largely focused on the ruling elite rather than on the colonial power, and the resulting divisions were to play a disastrous role in the decades after independence.

In the early 1960s the countries of East Africa gained their independence. Rwanda and Burundi became separates states, with their names changed. Names of towns were also changed, such as Bujumbura for Usumbira, and Buye for Ibuye.

Over time the usage of some words changed, so 'heathen' which had meant those who worshipped other gods now means primitive or uneducated; 'houseboy' or 'hospital boy' meant male servant or hospital assistant; using these terms did not imply any sense of inferiority. The word 'leper' has been changed to 'leprosy sufferer', just as the names for other diseases and handicaps have also changed.

There have also been changes in views on hunting since the time when hunting was a normal sport in the early 20th century. Several missionaries carried guns for protection for themselves and also for villagers who called them for help against attacks from dangerous animals, to provide meat on long safaris, and for occasional sport. African men usually carried spears.

Following indiscriminate shooting of animals at the turn of the 20th century in Kenya, the British administrations in the East African territories introduced very strict conditions for hunting game. Huge herds of animals roamed the plains near the great lakes, many of them very dangerous so some form of control was required. It was long before the concept of game parks. Annual gun licences permitted and limited the numbers of animals that could be hunted according to their type and numbers, and others were protected. A separate expensive elephant licence was required, limited to two elephants, provided the elephant's tusks were definitely over a certain weight, not easy to estimate; no females and no young. The licence expired at the end of the year and a new one was required. Any infringement meant a heavy fine, the confiscation of the ivory and revoking of the licence, which was not reissued. An injured animal was always followed up and destroyed.

Uganda was a British protectorate, and development was achieved by working with the chiefs to set up administration, health centres, telegraph communications and reasonable roads. But Dr Len and Dr Algie went further in their care for the ordinary African people, setting high Christian standards. This was welcomed by many such as Eli Nathan Bisamunyu who wrote, 'they improved every aspect of life for the Bakiga in Kigezi, getting rid of harmful beliefs and practices and setting up a good hospital and schools and churches.'

**The legacies of their lives and work:**
This account of their lives ends by looking at the long-term results of the two doctors' work. These speak to us of their faith in God and obedience to his will through the Holy Spirit, as they followed in the steps of Jesus Christ.

**Medical**
The doctors started their medical work near the Rwanda border at Kabale in 1921. It began in a small two-roomed dispensary, and before long the first hospital was built on the next hill, which became their first mission station. As they went through into Rwanda and Burundi, mission stations were established and hospitals built to cater for the huge numbers of patients who came for treatment. These hospitals are now run by Governments. Once Kigezi hospital was established, Dr Len set up the leprosy settlement and hospital on Bwama island where about 30 to 40 patients were able to be discharged each year. In 1948 Len introduced new leprosy drugs which were so successful that he foresaw the closure of the settlement and hospital. When that happened, clinics were set up in village areas where patients were monitored as out-patients. The island buildings were used for other purposes. The scourge of leprosy was eliminated in Kigezi. What happened to the Bwama leprosy settlement and when did it close? In November 1966 Miss Pat Gilmer SRN SCM went to help. New drugs were added to the treatment and in 1968 Bishop Dick Lyth and the Diocesan Council voted for the closure of the settlement and the dispersal of patients to their own homes, where they could be treated as outpatients, at the district dispensaries. The scheme was under the supervision of Pat Gilmer. Only the few who had no homes stayed on Bwama Island under the care of the Church. A small unit for sick leprosy patients was built at the new Kisiizi Hospital and Pat lived near them. Pat visited Dr Len, by then retired in Mombasa, and he rejoiced that the work so near to his heart was nearing completion. Unfortunately the change was not understood in Kigezi and there was a period of wide-spread leprophobia. It took time for the staff at dispensaries

to be willing to treat the patients and Pat had to visit each dispensary in turn each month, personally giving them their tablets for the following four weeks. Once again, it was an archbishop who showed the example of Jesus in accepting these sufferers. On a visit to Kisiizi, Archbishop Janani Luwum insisted on seeing the Leprosy Unit. He stopped, shook hands with every patient and spoke to each in their own African language. In time attitudes changed and dispensary staff were eager to show Pat the improvement they saw in the patients under their care. New and more effective drugs became available, which were added to the treatment, and in 1970, the 'wonder drug' Rifampin became available which rendered a patient non-infectious in a week and in milder cases, cured in a matter of months. With multi-drug treatment leprosy was eliminated in the district.

But the other medical needs of the people remained acute and Dr Len worked to meet them, and in due course was able to obtain Kisiizi as the site of a new hospital. After retirement he helped his son John to get the new hospital running effectively. After John's tragic death, others carried on the work. Now 50 years later, Kisiizi is a large Church of Uganda hospital, with new buildings and a nurses' training school. Major surgery is carried out and medical students are able to spend their 'medical electives' at the hospital. There are plans for further expansion. Kisiizi is a wonderful legacy to Dr Len's choice of the site and the prayers of the Kigezi church and of many others.

### Education

When Dr Len and Dr Algie started at Kabale in 1921, every village church needed to have a literacy class, so that everyone could read the Bible when it became available. A central school, Kigezi High School, was started to train evangelists. Would the doctors have guessed that 80 years later Kabale would have the Bishop Barham University College with 700 students training for degrees, including theology? The doctors would want no credit for that, and their comment would be that God is interested in the whole man, wanting everyone to reach their full potential.

Eli Nathan Bisamunyu was one of the first Kigezi High School boys to graduate, in 1953, with a degree from Makerere University, which had become part of University College, London. His words show how, under God and from small beginnings: 'The results of the pioneer work of Drs Sharp and Stanley Smith have been self-evident through the large numbers of academic, medical, artistic, religious, scientific, and engineering professionals this small district has contributed to the life of Uganda and to organisations abroad. The faith and courage that brought them to Kigezi in 1921 will remain a source of inspiration for the children of these hills, and a critical part of their history'.

Schools were also started at each mission station in Rwanda and Burundi for the many children who would become future leaders.

**Translation**

When Harold Guillebaud joined the Mission, straight away he started to learn the language of Ruanda and to translate the New Testament, parts of the Old Testament and numerous hymns. The Bakiga could understand reasonably well the language of the neighbouring people of Ankole in which a translation of the Bible already existed.

As the years passed the need for a new Bible translation for the Bakiga and Ankole people became clear. Although their languages were so similar, actually the tribes were very different: the plains of Ankole being good for cattle, while the steep hills of Kigezi were better suited for cultivation. Also, unlike the Bakiga, the Ankole had a similar ethnic divide to that in Ruanda. Such differences did not make it easy to agree on a common translation.

By 1964, Dr Algie had finished translating the Bible into a version acceptable to both the Bakiga and the Ankole people. Petero Kalebiya of Kigezi and Eliezer Mugimba of Ankole formed his team and together they suceeding in prodiucing a translation which was welcomed by both Bakiga and Banyankole. Scripture Union notes and other booklets were also translated. Dr Algie was thrilled to think of the Bible bridging the tribal boundaries within God's family.

## Church

The doctors' guidelines had always been to preach the gospel to everyone so that people could be transformed into living Christ-like communities. For both of them it was the living Church which counted most. They had seen so much of this in the early days, with evangelists out in the hills, faithfully passing on what they had learnt. People responded with joy to the message of the creator God, far more powerful than the evil spirits who kept them in the bondage of fear. This true God loved them and cared for his people and forgave their sins through Jesus' death on the cross. The evangelists would come to the mission centres for further teaching; and the large church buildings were invaluable for the many occasions when huge crowds would come.

About 15 years after the doctors had begun their work, the first enthusiasm began to wane and some people's faith and membership of the church became nominal. But by now Ruanda had the New Testament and parts of the Old Testament in their own language and it is the word of God that brings light, understanding, and convicts of sin. With this and the prayers of supporters at home, missionaries and African Christians, God sent revival in 1935. Starting at Gahini and Kabale many men and women were convicted of sin and confessed their sins publicly and with great emotion and distress. There was renewed zeal to witness to God's love and forgiveness, and a desire for fellowship and holiness and being open with each other. Missionaries as well as Africans were revived, and Dr Algie and Dr Len rejoiced in answered prayer. In great movements of the Spirit of God, counter attacks come from the devil, causing disunity and division, and the Ruanda revival was no exception. There was criticism and hardness of heart towards others, who did not share exactly the same experiences. This was a very hard time for the doctors, who were thought mistakenly by some, to be anti-revival and compromising. Dr Len was deeply concerned at some of the physical manifestations and lack of love among some of the revivalists; and he kept guiding people back to the teachings of the Bible. Dr Algie, with his graciousness and love, together with Dr Len, longed for unity among Christians, and was dismayed that revived Christians could be so opposed to each other. As they had recognized, God could break down barriers and gradually attitudes changed and the excesses began to die away.

The Anglican Churches of Uganda, Rwanda and Burundi became separate self-governing provinces with their own archbishops. They have had to face grievous trials: evil dictatorships, tribal hatred, civil war and genocide. In spite of many discouragements and difficulties, they are working to heal the wounds with courage and firm faith in Jesus Christ and his word. In this they have the example of the founders in their faithfulness to the Scriptures, dependence on the Holy Spirit and persistence in prayer.

1   *See pp 21,22*
2   *See pp 163,164*

# Bibliography

*CMS Journal, The Gleaner*   1920

*Ruanda Notes*   1920 onwards

*Uganda 1919*   Bishop Willis   1919

*Ruanda's Redemption*   A C Stanley Smith & L.E.Sharp
                Three editions in the 1930s

*Great Truths from God's Word*   L.E.Sharp
             Booklet 1939   Book 2004

*Road to Revival*   A C Stanley Smith   1946

*An African Nebuchadnezzar*   A.C.Stanley Smith   1946

*Island of Miracles*   L.E.Sharp & Janet Metcalf   1950

*Grain of Mustard Seed*   Lindsay Guillebaud   1959

*Breath of Life*   Patricia St. John   1971

*The Problem of Success*   Gordon Hewitt   1971

*Faith under fire*   Antoine Rutayisire   1998

# Index